Instructor's Manual to accompany

Sound
and
Sense

*An Introduction
to Poetry*

SIXTH EDITION

Laurence Perrine
and
Thomas R. Arp

SOUTHERN METHODIST UNIVERSITY

HARCOURT BRACE JOVANOVICH, INC.

NEW YORK   SAN DIEGO   CHICAGO   SAN FRANCISCO   ATLANTA
LONDON   SYDNEY   TORONTO

This manual is dedicated to the memory of William A. Pullin, loyal friend, inspired editor, friend to education, who pushed for its expansion.

LP

FOREWORD

In response to considerable demand, this Instructor's Manual for the Sixth Edition of *Sound and Sense* has been expanded to include some commentary on every poem. With some discussions we have included bibliographical references to other discussions, but we have not done this uniformly or systematically. Instructors wishing to locate other discussions should consult critical books on the poet in question (especially those that have indices) and Joseph M. Kuntz and Nancy C. Martinez, *Poetry Explication: A Checklist of Interpretation Since 1925 of British and American Poems Past and Present* (Boston: G. K. Hall, 1980), which lists explications through 1977. The annual bibliographical issues of *The Explicator* and *PMLA* may be checked for explications from 1977 to the present.

With the interpretations and judgments offered here, we should be foolish to expect universal agreement; indeed, we have not always agreed with each other, and for that reason, though we have checked and criticized each other's work throughout, we have appended after each discussion the initials of its main author. These discussions will serve their purpose if they provoke a more careful scrutiny of the poems and an intelligent dissent. Certainly, the approach we take to any poem is only one of various possible approaches. Jupiter does not speak in any of these comments. Jupiter speaks in the poems. The oracles that report him here are neither priests nor prophets, but fallible human beings like yourselves.

Laurence Perrine and Thomas R. Arp

CONTENTS

PART ONE   THE ELEMENTS OF POETRY

1. What is Poetry?

Alfred, Lord Tennyson   **THE EAGLE** (page 5)

The first stanza presents what one sees looking at the eagle, perhaps looking up at him, with the sun above him and the blue sky around him. The second stanza is more concerned with looking down from the eagle's vantage point; it presents what *he* sees. The first stanza is more static (with "clasps," "close," "stands"), the second stanza more dynamic (with "crawls," "watches," "falls"). These are small points, but they help to organize the poem. The expressions mentioned in the first study question are all figurative.   LP

William Shakespeare   **WINTER** (page 6)

The words "merry" and "sings" are used *ironically* (see page 98).*   LP

Wilfred Owen   **DULCE ET DECORUM EST** (page 7)

The poem makes its bitter protest against the idea that dying for one's country is "sweet and becoming" by describing the agonizing death of one soldier caught in a gas attack during World War I. (We infer from the last two lines that the soldier is dead; what we witness in the poem is the anguish and horror of his dying.)

The speaker is a fellow-soldier, a member of the same patrol, and a witness of the dying. His account is given some time after the event (as measured by weeks or months), for he has re-experienced it in recurrent nightmares ever since (15–16). From our knowledge of World War I and of the poet's own experience, we may infer that the speaker is English, that the gas shells were German, and that the action occurred in France or Belgium. The speaker has probably been furloughed back to England at the time of his account, for the person he ironically addresses as "My friend" would seem to be an older man who is patriotically recruiting teen-aged boys into the service of their country, or into readiness for it (the word "children" is undoubtedly an overstatement of their youth.)

*Unless otherwise specified, all page references in this manual are to the text of *Sound and Sense*, Sixth Edition.

The simile in line 1 compares the soldiers' packs to sacks carried by beggars. The word "softly" (8) is particularly sinister, for it connotes something gentle but here denotes something deadly. The phrase "sick of sin" (20) means "sick from sin." The most remarkable image in the poem is the simile in lines 13-14. The mustard gas used in World War I was greenish in color, hence the man caught in it seems "as under a green sea . . . drowning." The under-ocean effect is enhanced by the fact that he is viewed by the other soldiers through the misty panes of their gas masks, which were like the goggles in the helmets used by deep-sea divers at the time. Finally, the man is literally drowning (being suffocated) in that his lungs are being deprived of oxygen; but the mustard gas also corrodes the lungs, thus leading to the uglier imagery in lines 21-24.

The theme of the poem is obvious: It is NOT sweet and becoming to die for one's country in modern warfare.   LP

William Shakespeare   **SPRING** (page 10)

Though a light, semihumorous poem, "Spring" beautifully displays Shakespeare's poetic skill. It pivots about a contrast which divides each stanza exactly in the middle. Spring is the time of flowers and birds and delight, and to this traditional aspect of spring Shakespeare yields the first four lines of each stanza. It is also the time of love; but in treating this aspect Shakespeare gives the traditional treatment of spring a wry twist. The cuckoo's note reminds the married man not only (as Tennyson points out) that "In the spring a young man's fancy lightly turns to thoughts of love," but also, less pleasing thought, that in the spring young wives are most likely to prove unfaithful. "Cuckold, cuckold!" the cuckoo seems to say to the husband by way of warning. The poem thus throws into contrast the innocent and delightful with the unpleasing or painful.

The poem twice makes skillful use of *metonymy* (see page 62). The wild flowers, Shakespeare says, "paint the meadows with delight" (4). The metaphor in the verb "paint" prepares for the metonymy in the word "delight." What the flowers actually paint the meadows with, is color, but Shakespeare, by substituting the effect for which the color is the cause, makes the line doubly meaningful, for it suggests both cause *and* effect. In line 8, by using "word" instead of *notes* for the cuckoo's call, Shakespeare leads us to read a pun into "cuckoo"—for it is indeed the word "cuckold" which the married man fears, not the bird-notes which suggest it. And thus the poet prepares us for the second metonymy—"ear." It is the married *man*, of course, who hears the cuckoo, but Shakespeare, by using the part for the whole, reduces the man imaginatively to the one quivering, sensitive organ which will receive the insult when he is cuckolded.

For flowers to represent the spring, Shakespeare might have chosen from a whole seed catalogue. His daisies and violets are traditional enough, and we are not surprised to find them. But why has Shakespeare chosen lady-smocks and cuckoo-buds? Because they serve double duty. The lady-smocks throw a connecting loop into the second stanza, to line 13, and this loop ties the two stanzas together. The cuckoo-buds prepare us for the cuckoobird and the implied *cuckold* which are the central subjects of the poem.

The word "tread" (12) deserves special attention. "Turtles" are turtledoves, and the traditional poet, writing of the innocent pleasures of spring, would have said, "When turtles *mate* . . . ." But Shakespeare used the technical or barnyard term for the copulation of birds, and thus introduces a more earthy note. He continues: "When turtles tread, *and* rooks, *and* daws . . . ." The repeated "and's" are not there simply to fill out the meter. They have the effect of enormously magnifying the activity. The line is not at all the same as "When rooks, daws, and turtles tread." With all this activity going on, no wonder the married man is apprehensive.

Pattern also works effectively in "Spring." The iambic tetrameter pattern with alternating rimes that Shakespeare uses in the first four lines of each stanza is generally a tripping measure, appropriate to light and cheerful and songlike matters. It is highly appropriate for spring flowers and merry larks and meadows painted with delight. But in the last four lines, the pattern changes, and so does the mood. The change is signaled in the phrase "Mocks married men," where the jammed meter and the heavy alliteration inform us that the subject matter is shifting to something more solemn. The rime pattern also alters, shifting from alternating rimes to riming couplets. The iambic tetrameter continues; but the lines now, instead of tripping along merrily, are broken up. They are broken first by the extra-metrical trochaic "Cuckoo," placed on a line by itself, thus interrupting the iambics and tetrameters and receiving a heavy emphasis appropriate to its importance. Second, the pattern is broken in the following line by the ending of the sentence in the middle of the line, thus separating it into two sharply divided parts, the first half trochaic, the second half iambic. We simply *cannot read* these last four lines with the same blithe abandon with which we read the first four lines. The cuckoo's call breaks into the stanza with the same violence with which it breaks in on the married man's peace.

[This commentary is adapted from Laurence Perrine, *The Art of Total Relevance: Papers on Poetry* (Rowley, Mass.: Newbury House, 1976), pp. 7–10.]

Emily Dickinson **A BIRD CAME DOWN THE WALK** (page 11)

Besides its marvelously exact observation of a bird's behavior*, the poem shows the immense distance between the natural world of the bird and the human world of the speaker, as Charles R. Anderson points out in his excellent discussion [*Emily Dickinson's Poetry: Stairway of Surprise* (New York: Holt, 1960), pp. 117–19]. As long as it is unaware of the human presence, the bird goes naturally about its affairs.

*Though never named, the bird is surely a robin. It eats worms; it has beady eyes and a velvet head; it is the right size; it is not one of a flock (like sparrows); and it allows the human presence nearer before taking fright than any other nontame, nonflocking bird. Robins were plentiful in Amherst (Dickinson's village) in spring and summer and are a favorite subject in her nature poems.

3

It eats an angle-worm, raw, as a human being would never do, and hops aside for a beetle, something normally beneath human notice. Then it drinks "*a* dew" from "*a* grass" (from the human perspective, dew and grass are collective entities: we speak of "the dew" and "the grass" and must specify "a drop of dew" or "a blade of grass" to see them as the bird habitually does. Notice how similarity of sound here suggests an unstated metaphor: the blade of "grass" is the bird's "glass" from which he drinks). In stanza 3 the bird intuits an alien presence, glances nervously all around, and stirs his head "like one in danger." When the human observer tries to bridge the gap between their two worlds, cautiously offering a friendly crumb, the bird's instinctive impulses take command, and it flies off swiftly, literally putting a distance between itself and the human observer.

In sound the first fourteen lines of the poem are unremarkable. There are a few mildly harsh words: "walk," "angle," "drank," "hopped," "beads," "crumb"; and there is an appropriately awkward juxtaposition of two stressed syllables in "hopped sideways." When the bird takes flight, however, moving into its natural element (line 15), the language turns magically euphonious: a succession of long *o*'s, "unrolled," "rowed," "home," "oars," "ocean") is combined with liquid *r*'s, *l*'s, *m*'s, and *n*'s, and with soft *v*'s and *f*'s, to create a beautiful flow of sound. The one slight interruption of this euphony comes in the last two lines with the alliterating *b*'s of "butterflies" and "banks" and the repeated *p*'s of "leap" and "plashless." The metaphorical image suggested is of a swimming hole in which butterflies leap off the banks of a pool into water; but since the "banks" and the pools are both really air, they make no splash and what we hear in the alliterative *b*'s and repeated *p*'s is those imaginary, nonexistent splashes. LP

Lawrence Ferlinghetti **CONSTANTLY RISKING ABSURDITY** (page 12)

The poem compares the poet to a circus performer and entertainer—high-wire artist, acrobat, and clown ("a little charleychaplin man") who, apparently, will try to catch the leaping form of Beauty while balanced on the high wire of truth—an almost impossible feat. The extended simile (which includes metaphor and personification) emphasizes that the poet must be constantly entertaining (poetry must give pleasure), but that he is also concerned with such higher realities as truth and beauty. It also emphasizes that the poet's task demands the utmost skill and precision and involves constant risk: a false step by the high-wire artist can cause death; a slip by the poet in published work involves public exposure of ineptitude. The sublime and the ridiculous are often narrowly separated, but in their reviews critics are quick to flay the poet who strives for the first and falls into the second. Ferlinghetti shows his own agility as a performer with a constant flow of double meanings and "sleight-of-foot" tricks (the play upon "sleight-of-foot" is appropriate both for the high-wire artist who performs magic with his feet and for the poet who does it with metrical feet). Serious? Yes. Solemn? No.

4

The arrangement of words on the page mimics the succession of short hurried steps that the acrobat takes across the wire before pausing to balance himself anew. LP

Robert Frost **THE PASTURE** (page 13)

The speaker is the poet himself, whom we know to have been a farmer during much of his early writing career. He is going out to perform a few farm chores, and he is inviting the "You" of the poem to accompany him. The "You" may be a visitor to the farm, or it may be the young wife addressed in so many of Frost's early poems. By the mere act of placing it first in the volume, however, Frost gives the poem an additional (symbolic) meaning it would not otherwise have had. The invitation is being issued, not just by farmer to guest or husband to wife, but by poet to reader, and at this level it is an invitation to read the rest of the poems. The nature of the chores symbolically suggests the subject matter of his poems, which is mostly New England rural, seldom urban. LP

A. E. Housman **TERENCE, THIS IS STUPID STUFF** (page 14)

Housman's poem compares the efficacy of three things for helping one lead a satisfactory life: cheerful poetry, liquor, and pessimistic poetry. The first two, by making one "see the world as the world's not," arouse expectations that life can rarely fulfill. The result is disappointment and disillusionment. Pessimistic poetry, by truly picturing a world containing "much less good than ill," prepares one for the troubles that are sure to come. Thus fortified, one can withstand their shock and lead a satisfying life.

In the first verse-paragraph a friend playfully criticizes Terence (Housman) for the kind of poetry he writes and gives a delightful parody of it in the two lines about the cow. Reading his poetry, the friend claims in a humorous overstatement, is driving Terence's friends mad and causing them to die before their time. He pleads with Terence to write cheerful poetry instead.

Terence replies that if his friend wants gaiety and cheer, liquor is more efficacious than poetry. It makes the world seem a "lovely" place and oneself a "sterling" lad. The only trouble is that this picture is "all a lie." By implication cheerful poetry likewise misrepresents the world. Liquor and optimistic poetry are for "fellows whom it hurts to think." Their effect is temporary and ultimately enfeebling. They offer escape, not a solution.

In the first six lines of the third section Terence sums up his philosophy. To train for ill is to prepare oneself for the world as it is. One can do this by reading the kind of poetry Terence writes. It will strengthen "heart and head" and prepare one's soul for adversity. Many students misread the poem at this point. They fail to see that "the stuff I bring for sale" is Terence's poetry, metaphorically compared to a bitter brew that is "not so brisk" (so intoxicating) as the literal ale of the second-verse paragraph. Its "smack is sour" because it was wrung out of bitter experience.

In the final section Terence clinches his point by telling a parable. Mithridates immunized himself to poison by first taking a little and then gradually increasing the dosage. As a result Mithridates lived a long and satisfactory life. Similarly, Terence implies, one can immunize oneself against the troubles of life by reading the kind of poetry Terence writes.   LP

From *The Book of Job*   **HAST THOU GIVEN THE HORSE STRENGTH** (page 16)

The vivid images and metaphors, the personification, the rhetorical questions, the use of grammatical parallelism, and the rhythm of these lines all contribute to making them a powerful evocation of experience.   LP

2. Reading the Poem

Thomas Hardy **THE MAN HE KILLED** (page 19)

The hesitations and repetitions of stanza 3 beautifully reflect the thought processes of the speaker. The pause after "because" (9) occurs because he is groping for an explanation. When he finds one, he must repeat the "because." He then has to convince himself that this answer is correct and sufficient. He does this (or tries to do it) by telling himself three times emphatically that it is: (1) "Just so"; (2) "my foe of course he was"; (3) "That's clear enough." But despite this triple emphatic effort at self-assurance, we know that the attempt is unsuccessful, as it trails off into "although . . ." LP

A. E. Housman **IS MY TEAM PLOUGHING** (page 21)

The word "bed" signifies literally the bed that the living man sleeps in, metaphorically the grave that the dead man lies in, and symbolically a lot in life, or condition of existence. The word "sleep" has corresponding meanings: of sleeping, of being dead, and of having a certain lot. In addition, it gathers up from the last stanza the meaning of sleeping with a woman, that is, of making love.

The poem at first seems cynical, suggesting, as it does, the transience of human loyalties. On reflection, however, few people expect a man not to remarry after a first wife has died. (Housman's poem probably doesn't refer to marriage, but the principle is the same.) In general, Housman's poetry is pessimistic about man's chances for happiness, but Housman is not cynical about human courage or human virtue. Compare "On moonlit heath and lonesome bank" (page 50). LP

Robert Frost **HYLA BROOK** (page 24)

The speaker begins by regarding the brook as it is at the end of May or the first of June: a mere trickle. He reflects that in a week or two it will have no water at all, and in a parenthesis contrasts it as it will be then with what it was in April. In lines 10–12 he speaks again of the brook as it will be in mid-June and July, but uses the present tense. By sacrificing logical consistency, he gains for the reader a greater sense of immediacy, and for the poem a greater concision. The brief return to the future tense in line 13 reminds us that it is the future appearance he is talking about, not its earlier or its present appearance.

By omitting the phrase "If sought for" (line 2), the paraphrase loses the implication that the brook, instead of advertising its presence as it did in April with its burbling and its chorus of tree toads, its moving water and its mist, will have to be actively searched for; and by omitting the phrase "it will be found" it loses the play of paradox implied by the countermeaning: it will *not* be found. That is, it will be found to have disappeared. The paraphrase sacrifices complexity and richness for clarity.

The paradox just referred to springs from the central paradox of the poem (line 12): the idea of a brook that is not a brook. Should a brook be defined in terms of the water that flows through a channel or of the channel that carries the water? The paraphrase (not altogether satisfactorily) tries to resolve the problem by distinguishing between the water, which disappears, and the brook bed, which doesn't. But the attempt demolishes the poetry and isn't too successful even as logical elucidation. With complex poems, paraphrase is difficult.

The brook in the poem is named after a type of tree toads (also called "peepers") which in the spring, alongside brooks, make a loud trilling sound, noisy but not displeasing. The poem captures this half-musical, half-unmusical nuance by balancing the verb "shouted" against the simile, "like . . . sleigh bells." But since sleigh bells belong to the winter season, which is even further in the past, the poet compares them to the "ghost of sleigh bells," leading him on to a comparison of mist to the ghost of snow. Not only are the similes auditorily and visually accurate, but both involve the return in ghostly form of something that has vanished. They also enhance the poem by making possible the presentation of Hyla Brook through the full cycle of the year: winter, spring, early and midsummer, and fall (represented by last year's fall of leaves matting the brook's bed in summer).

"As it will be seen" (13) means also "as will be seen if one looks through other books for poems about brooks." The phrase "taken otherwhere in song" may also have a shadowy second meaning: "written about when they were in full flow and making a pleasant sound." But primarily "song" here (as opposed to line 1) refers to poetry rather than to a pleasant water sound.

The most richly ambiguous line in the poem is the last. Though made up of the simplest words, its meanings elude paraphrase. We love the things we truly love for their unique and individual character, not for their unchanging perfection? We love the things we love for reasons that cannot be rationally explained? Love is of the heart, not the mind? Perhaps, though in a less assertive tone, Frost's final line says much the same thing as lines 2–3 of Shakespeare's sonnet 116 (page 304): "Love is not love / Which alters when it alteration finds." All this, and more.   LP

Thomas Campion **THINK'ST THOU TO SEDUCE ME THEN** (page 26)

Though written by a male poet, the poem has a female speaker. Students may be deceived by the word "Ruth" (10) into thinking otherwise. "Ruth" is here a common noun meaning pity or compassion. It is capitalized because it begins a line and because it is a personification. Though more familiar to us in its negative adjectival form *ruthless*, the noun is used by Milton in *Lycidas* (line 163: "Look homeward Angel now, and melt with ruth") and by Housman (*A Shropshire Lad*, XLIV).

Proof that the speaker is a woman (addressing a man) rests on four points of evidence:

1. The words "seduce" (1), "woo" (4), and "courts" (5) normally refer to male activities. The *OED* defines *seduce* as "To induce (a woman) to surrender her chastity." It defines *woo* as "To solicit or sue a woman in love; to court, make love." It defines *court* as "To pay amorous attention to, seek to gain the affections of, make love to (with a view to marriage), pay address to, woo," listing eight historical examples (from 1580 to 1870) in all of which a male is courting a woman.

2. In lines 5–6 the speaker uses four masculine pronouns. A male speaker would have to say, "*She* that courts us, wanting art, soon falters when *she* feigneth, / Looks asquint on *her* discourse, and smiles when *she* complaineth." In these lines, the speaker is generalizing. The pronoun "us" refers to the female sex in general. So we do not have here a unique case of a woman trying to seduce a man.

3. In the seventeenth century, angling or fishing was chiefly a male activity (stanza 3).

4. If "Ruth" were a nominative of direct address, it would have to be followed by a comma. (Compare the difference between "God, forgive me" and "God forgive me." The first is a petition addressed to God; the second is an exclamation addressed to whomever the speaker is talking to.) In this line "erred" means *wandered* and "from" means *away from* (NOT *because of*).

The speaker is a sophisticated, self-confident, undoubtedly upper-class woman. She is not offended by the man's object but by his manner of trying to obtain it. (We can't be sure whether the man is proposing marriage or trying to seduce her, but her reaction would probably be much the same in either case.) She wants an accomplished lover—one who is articulate, graceful, fluent, able to flatter subtly. In line 7, "fit" is a verb. In reading line 8, one should emphasize "pins" rather than "crooked." Her objection is to his using a naked bent pin rather than a concealed hook. Only "gudgeons" (a. small freshwater fish; b. dupes, gullible persons) can be caught by such "poor tricks of treason." She wants finesse and artful flattery in a lover. She will not wed or bed with a fool.

The man addressed is a bumbler—a Sir Andrew Aguecheek (see Shakespeare's *Twelfth Night*)—unable to speak the proper words, and unable to fit to them the proper gestures. He "smiles" when he complains of his yearning, his lovesickness, his suffering. He "falters" when he feigns. (In Shakespeare's *As You Like It*, Touchstone tells Audrey that "the truest poetry is the most feigning, and lovers are given to poetry." *This* lover has no poetry in him.)   LP

Emily Dickinson   **THERE'S BEEN A DEATH IN THE OPPOSITE HOUSE** (page 26)

The speaker in this poem has not been informed of the death across the way and apparently does not know who has died. He is not one of the neighbors who "rustle in and out." Probably he is a visitor in the house from which he watches. But he is no stranger to the ways of country towns: he knows by the signs immediately and intuitively that a death has occurred. He is a sensitive observer, able to report and to interpret precisely and imaginatively what he sees and to enter empathetically into the thoughts and feelings of the children who hurry past.

What he focuses on is the *difference* that the death makes in the ordinary life of a house. The house itself seems to have a "numb" look, as if stunned by the unusual occurrence. Neighbors—mostly women, for their skirts "rustle"—come and go, offering help and sympathy. The sick room is ventilated, a mattress hung to air across the window sill. The children hurry by, scared, for death to them is mysterious and vaguely terrifying: they can think of the corpse only as "it," not as a person, and they wonder if "it" died on the mattress they see. The minister enters "stiffly," not relaxed: this is a solemn occasion, and he will be the most important person in the funeral ritual. He immediately takes command. The milliner and the undertaker arrive to measure—between them—the corpse for the coffin, the mourners for black veils and other mourning apparel, and the house itself for getting the coffin in and out and perhaps for hanging with crepe bunting. (The word "house" is used, throughout the poem, as a metonymy to indicate, not just the house itself, but the activity and the people around and within it, including the corpse. It is not the house itself that is "numb" but the people within it; but the house itself seems to reflect this numbness in the way its window opens. Even the minister reflects it in his stiffness.) The speaker concludes with an account, not of what he sees, but of what he knows will soon be seen—the funeral procession of black coaches hung with tassels that will take the body and the mourners to the cemetery. He then generalizes his opening observation—how easy it is to tell when a death has occurred in a country town.

Some students will have difficulty with the tone of this poem, seeing it or the people in it as regarding death callously, impersonally, or coldly. The mistake may result from misinterpreting the role of the speaker (who is an observer, not a participant) or from misconceiving the "numb" look (which signifies, not lack of emotion, but the stunned state following or accompanying too much emotion) or from identifying the attitude of the children toward the corpse with that of the adults or the observer. The poem focuses on the outside of the house, not on the dead person, because that is what the observer sees; but all of the activity he sees results from the presence of the dead person within. The tone of the poem reflects the awesomeness of death and its solemnity. Part of the speaker's attitude is revealed in his reference to the undertaker as the man of the "appalling" trade (in the double sense of "horrifying" and "putting a pall on" a coffin) and to the funeral procession as a "dark" parade (dark literally because of the black badges of mourning but with the additional connotations of mystery and awesomeness).

Though written by a woman, this poem has a male speaker. Campion's "Think'st thou to seduce me then," though written by a man, has a female speaker. An instructive point can be made from this juxtaposition. LP

10

Mari Evans **WHEN IN ROME** (page 27)

The first speaker is a white woman, the second her black maid. We are given only the unspoken thoughts of the second speaker, hence the inclusion of her words in parentheses. (The poet's use of her own name for the second speaker suggests that the poem grows out of personal experience.)

Though the white employer's words take the outward form of affection and solicitude ("Marrie dear . . . take / whatever you like"), their tone, without her realizing it, is subtly patronizing. The invitation to take "whatever you like" is qualified by "don't / get my anchovies / they cost / too much!" And her utter ignorance of what the black servant likes to eat betrays the essential emptiness of her solicitude. The phrase "take / whatever you like / to eat" functions on two levels: *take whatever you wish to take*, and *take whatever you* like *to eat*. There is almost nothing in the icebox that the black woman really *likes*.)

The black woman's attitude is one of repressed antagonism. Consciously or unconsciously, she knows she is being patronized, and though she is accustomed to speaking outwardly in terms of respect ("yes'm"), her resentment expresses itself through the use of irony: "what she think, she got— / a bird to feed?" and "yes'm. just the / sight's / enough!" The last phrase can be read in two ways.

The title and the conclusion are an allusion to the familiar saying "When in Rome, do as the Romans do." Rome in the poem serves as a metaphor for the white world, and the speaker is tired of having to eat what whites like to eat rather than what blacks like to eat. LP

W. H. Auden **O WHAT IS THAT SOUND** (page 28)

Some readers may assume that, because of their hysterical tone, lines 1–2 of each stanza (except the last) are spoken by the woman. This assumption, however, makes it difficult to explain why the first speaker kneels in stanza 4, and why the second speaker remains so calm throughout. If we reverse this assumption, these difficulties are resolved in what can be seen as a tale of treason and betrayal.

The man (who speaks in lines 1–2 of each stanza except the last, which is spoken by the poet) is a traitor or rebel who is hiding out with his mistress in a house on a mountainside; he is the "quarry" wanted by the soldiers. Knowing himself wanted, he is alarmed at the sound of troops in the distance, and his terror mounts as they approach. When they leave the road (stanza 4), he kneels so as not to be visible above the sill of the window. (In stanzas 2–4 his questions concern what *he* sees through the window; in subsequent stanzas he is dependent on the woman to report what *she* sees.) Having no reason to think his hiding place known, the man tries to convince himself that the troops are headed elsewhere—the doctor's, the parson's, or the farmer's—but they are coming for him. Moreover, they come directly; they do not have to search or make inquiries; obviously, they have been tipped off. Who has tipped them off? Clearly the woman, whose vows have indeed been "deceiving,"

11

and who *may* be a secret agent. Her knowledge of the situation accounts for her coolness, so markedly in contrast to the hysteria of the man, and her purpose has been, by minimizing the import of the situation, to hold the man in the house until the soldiers can get there. (The drumming sound, she tells him, is "only" the soldiers, and they are "only" performing their "usual" manoeuvres—in light of subsequent developments, an obvious lie.) When it is too late for him to make a break, she leaves, so as not to witness any violence.

Auden's ballad concerns terror, menace, and betrayal in a world where politics rule, not love. The initial obscurity of the situation increases the terror, and is appropriate to a world in which real purposes and motivations are kept concealed.

[This commentary is adapted from an item in *The Explicator*, 30 (Jan. 1972), 41, by Laurence Perrine and Jane Johnston.]

Sylvia Plath **MIRROR** (page 30)

Although the speaker is the personified mirror, who in the second stanza goes on to personify itself as a lake, the subject of the poem is the woman who looks into the mirror and learns the truth of the changes in her appearance that time brings. Like a person, the mirror looks outward, observing—and meditating about—the objects that come into view. But unlike a person, the mirror has no preconceptions, does not distort its vision with emotional responses. It is godlike in its detached truthfulness, even if it is a little god with a limited area of observation.

As a lake (and perhaps like a pool into which Narcissus plunged in adoration of his own beauty), the mirror still will give only the truth about the surface of reflections, no matter how the woman might want to find a deeper truth. Candlelight and moonlight, which cast flattering dim gleams of romantic imagination, are by comparison with the mirror's faithful images "liars."

What the searching woman finds in the truthful reflection is the sad fact of aging: the little girl that she was is now dead, and the old woman that she will become lurks in the depths of time, waiting to appear and terrify her.   TRA

Philip Larkin   **A STUDY OF READING HABITS** (page 30)

Even the slow student should see that neither the language nor the attitudes of the speaker in this poem could possibly be those of a poet. To clinch the case, one can point out that Philip Larkin is by profession a librarian as well as a poet.

The speaker is a weak person, unable to face reality, who escapes reality as boy and adolescent by reading "escape" fiction, either in pulp magazines or in paperbacks. As a boy (stanza 1) he identifies himself with the virtuous hero, the man who overcomes villainy by physical force. As an adolescent (stanza 2) he vicariously engages in sex escapades by identifying with the bold villain (Dracula type) or the picaresque hero (James Bond type). As a young man he reaches a stage at which reading no longer conceals from him his own failures—he now recognizes himself in the weak secondary characters—and he must find escape in alcohol.

Even better than Hardy's "The Man He Killed" (page 19), this poem demonstrates that poetry need not be made out of lofty, dignified, exquisite, or even original language. The language here is vulgar, slangy, and trite; yet it is perfectly chosen to express the intellectual poverty of its speaker. The good poet chooses his words, not for their beauty or elegance, but for their expressiveness—that is to say, their maximum appropriateness to subject, situation, and speaker. Trite language need not make a trite poem, as this piece effectively demonstrates. And even working within the limitations of deliberately trite language, Larkin achieves striking effects. The word "ripping" (10), for instance, has not only its slang meaning of "exciting" or "great" but also its literal meaning (here) of "ripping the clothes off of"—a doubleness of which the poet was probably aware, the speaker unaware. The student might be asked to paraphrase this poem in genteel or "correct" literal English, to see what it loses by such treatment.

In "Terence, this is stupid stuff," Housman agrees with the speaker that "ale's the stuff to drink" for "fellows whom it hurts to think" and that one should "Look into the pewter pot / To see the world as the world's not"; but for wiser fellows, Housman recommends reading. However, Housman is recommending quite a different kind of reading from that engaged in by Larkin's speaker; he is recommending a kind in which one can "see the world" as the world *is*. Thus, Housman is in diametrical disagreement with Larkin's speaker, and probably in perfect agreement with Larkin himself.   LP

Robert Herrick   **HOW ROSES CAME RED** (page 31)

Herrick uses a fanciful creation-myth to pay tribute to the beauty (fair complexion) of his lady. A charming and playful bit of flattery.   LP

3. Denotation and Connotation

Emily Dickinson **THERE IS NO FRIGATE LIKE A BOOK** (page 33)

Miles suggests a measurable and therefore a lesser distance than "lands"; also, it suggests distance only. "Lands" suggests not only distance but difference—not only far lands, but foreign lands, perhaps even fairylands. The connotations of *cheap* are unfavorable; of "frugal," favorable. "Prancing," besides participating in the alliterative sequence of "a page / Of prancing poetry," brings to mind the metrical effects of poetry and the winged horse Pegasus, symbol of poetry in Greek mythology. LP

William Shakespeare **WHEN MY LOVE SWEARS THAT SHE IS MADE OF TRUTH (SONNET 138)** (page 34)

Because of the pun on *lie*, students frequently misconceive the tone of this sonnet as light. It might better be called dark. The pun is grim, not merry. Trapped in a love affair that he knows to be unworthy of him, too weak to break loose, the speaker cynically resigns himself to continuing it, though he knows his mistress is unfaithful. He cannot leave the honey-pot; it has become a "habit."

The attraction of the affair is sensual, as shown by the two meanings of "lie"—conjunction at the physical level, separateness at the spiritual. Not only do the two lovers lie to each other, the speaker lies to himself, and *knows* that he lies to himself. He *pretends* to believe the woman's lies (2) in the hope that she will think him young and naive (3-4), and he makes himself think in one part of his mind that the deception works (5) though he knows in another part that it does not (6). A no-longer young man—one who is fully learned in "the world's false subtleties," including his own—he has ambivalent feelings toward his mistress and toward himself. Line 11 is not mature wisdom but rationalization. Love's *best* habit is trust, not *seeming* trust. Mature lovers can accept each other's faults without needing to lie to each other about them, and the speaker would not feel insecure about his age if he were confident of his mistress' love for him.

The speaker is a number of years older than the woman and is uneasy about the discrepancy. He cannot be really *old*, else he would have no chance even in his own mind of making her think him young.

"Simply" (7) carries its older meaning of "foolishly" (cf. the nursery rhyme "Simple Simon met a pieman") while "simple" (8) means "plain" or "unadorned." "Vainly" (5) primarily means "futilely" (cf. "in vain") but with overtones of "in such a way as to please one's vanity." "Habit" (11) is a garment or clothing and also a customary practice. "Told" (12) means both "spoken" and "counted." LP

In "The Naked and the Nude" Graves is concerned with both semantic and human values. Though seemingly he uses differences in human behavior only to illustrate differences in the connotations of two words often regarded as synonyms, actually he is as much concerned with moral as with lexical values. This ambiguity begins in the first stanza. If Graves were talking only about words, his proper beginning would be "For me, *naked* and *nude* . . . ." or "For me, the words 'naked' and 'nude' . . . ." By introducing two definite articles and omitting italicization or quotation marks, Graves forces us to take "the naked and the nude" as people. At the same time, by having them "construed / As synonyms," he forces us to consider them as words. This duality of interest persists throughout the poem.

The moral qualities characteristic of the opposed kinds of people connoted by the two words are in part named in the last line of stanza 1 and in part suggested by the kinds of behavior shown in stanzas 2 and 3. In general, the naked are natural, honest, unashamed, unselfconscious, undesigning; they are swayed by some passion (love, truth, or justice) which carries them beyond mere self-concern. The nude, in contrast, are deceptive sly, and designing; by artifice and trickery they seek to attract attention to themselves and arouse prurient desire for their own pleasure or profit.

But ambiguities and paradoxes abound. In stanza 2 Graves' three examples are lovers, doctors, and a Goddess. The lovers are deeply consumed by physical desire, but reciprocally and unashamedly so; their passion is a natural part of their love. The physicians, on the other hand, in their passion for diagnostic knowledge, are completely beyond physical desire. Notice, however, that, though the physicians illustrate the moral quality concerned, it is their patients who are "naked." Finally, the Goddess, nonhuman and immortal, will not be among those sent to the underworld by death in the final stanza. The shifts of category in the second and third examples are explainable by Graves' dual interest in lexical and moral values.

In stanza 3 the nude both boldly flaunt and slyly conceal their charms, like a dancer with fans or veils, to entice and hold the gaze of onlookers. "Draping by a showman's trick / Their dishabille in rhetoric," they are paradoxically both clothed and unclothed, nude but not naked. Thus arrayed in illusory attire, the nude assume a holier-than-thou attitude and pretend to be more modest than the plainly naked, while actually more seductive. The reference to "rhetoric" keeps the interest focused on semantic as well as moral values; the word "rhetoric" suggests verbal embellishment of the plain and unvarnished, just as "nude" suggests embellishment of the "naked."

Though, in stanza 4, both the naked and the nude tread the "briary pastures of the dead," it is clear that the nude, who in this world defeat the naked in terms of material reward, in the underworld will get their comeuppance. At this point, Graves is clearly talking about people, not about words. But, in this stanza, the poet keeps his interest in words alive by giving the word "naked" a brilliant new twist in connotation: in the last line of the poem it means, not just "unclothed," but "unpro-

15

tected"—cruelly exposed to the lashes of the Gorgons' whips. Though both the naked and the nude may be pursued by the Gorgons (whose "long whips" suggest serpents torn from their hair), it is the nude who will suffer cruelly from their exposure.

[This commentary is adapted and abridged from an item in *The Explicator*, 39 (Fall 1980), 36–38, by Laurence Perrine and Margaret Morton Blum.]

Exercises (page 37)

2. (a) steed, (b) king, (c) Cathay, (d) nightingale, (e) kiss, (f) Samarkand, (g) secret agent.
3. (a) slender, (b) old-fashioned, (c) elfin, (d) loving, (e) petite, (f) prosperous, (g) revelation, (h) dog, (i) write, (j) intelligent, (k) famous.
4. (a) children, (b) brother.
5. *double entendre.*
6. having acted foolishly.
7. a. *Taper* means candle and also, as a verb, to diminish, to become gradually less. ("The Deserted Village")
   b. *Phantom* has pleasanter connotations than the other alternatives; unlike them, it does not suggest something from the grave. ("She was a phantom of delight")
   c. *Solid* has both its original literal meaning (the watch is solid) and a derived metaphorical meaning (it affords substantial joy). It thus completes the irony of the comparison of the watch-case to a good conscience (which is also "concealed" and also a provider of joy). (*Love of Fame*: Satire II)
   d. *Casements* and *perilous* have the romantic connotations demanded by the context. *Perilous* suggests knightly adventure (the Siege Perilous, a perilous quest); *danger* suggests something more like a road sign ("Danger—Men Working") or a label on a medicine bottle. ("Ode to a Nightingale")
   e. *Still* means both "yet" and "silent." ("Ode on a Grecian Urn")
   f. *Lug* implies the same kind of brutal contempt implied by *guts*. (*Hamlet*, III, iv)
   g. *Told* means both "said" and "counted" and is also a pun on *tolled*; it is thus appropriate both to a "tongue" and to the iron clapper of a bell counting the midnight hours. (*Midsummer Night's Dream*, V, i)
   h. The *lyre* is the instrument associated with the muse and with ancient poets.
   i. *Precious*, though derived from the same Latin root as *price*, is most frequently applied to emotionally or spiritually valuable things (children, freedom, wisdom) (*As You Like It*, II, i)
   j. *Tire* (attire) combines the meanings of *to clothe* and *to fatigue* or *to wear down*. ("A Time to Dance")

Edwin Arlington Robinson **RICHARD CORY** (page 39)

Despite the popularity and apparent simplicity of this poem, it is often badly misread by students, who reduce it to the platitude that "great wealth does not guarantee happiness." Such a reading ignores nine-tenths of the poem. What the poem actually says is much more terrifying: that good birth, good looks, good breeding, good taste, humanity, *and* wealth do not guarantee happiness. The poem establishes all these qualities as being Cory's, and the "people on the pavement" thought that Cory "*was* everything' (not "*had* everything") to make them wish that they were in his place. This larger meaning must be insisted on. "Richard Cory" may not be as great a poem as, say, Robinson's "Mr. Flood's Party," but it is a genuine poem, neither superficial nor cheap.

The word "gentleman" is used both in its modern sense of one who is well behaved and considerate of others and in its older sense of one who is well born. The first meaning is established by Cory's courteous and uncondescending "good morning" to the "people on the pavement" and by his being "admirably schooled in every grace." The second meaning is established by a constellation of words that, by their primary or secondary meanings, suggest aristocratic or royal privilege: "crown," "favored," "imperially," "arrayed," "glittered," "king," "grace," "fine" ("crown" here means "top of the head," but it is also a symbol of royalty; "clean favored" means "clean-featured," but "favored" is also "privileged"; "grace" means a "social nicety," but it is also the term used for addressing a duke; "in fine" means "in sum," but "fine" implies also a quality of character and dress. Notice how the adjective "quietly" before "arrayed" imbues Cory with good taste: he dresses finely but unostentatiously).

Cory's first name has as its first syllable the word *rich* and is the name of several English kings, including the gallant Richard *Coeur de Lion*. His last name has a sonorous sound and is a good English name such as might belong to the New England landed gentry. It is in addition suggestive of such French words as *cor*, hunting horn; *coeur*, heart; and *cour*, royal court.

It is not just that "pavement" alliterates with "people." A pavement is lower than a sidewalk: it establishes the commonness of the "people" in contrast with the higher status of Cory; it has the "people" looking up at him.

The surprise ending is not there for its own sake. By setting up an ironic contrast, it suggests a number of truths about life: that we cannot tell from outside appearance what may be going on inside a person; that often the people we envy have as many troubles as we, or more; that, as has been said above, birth, wealth, breeding, taste, and humanity do not ensure a happy life.

There is an excellent discussion of this poem in Norman C. Stageberg and Wallace L. Anderson, *Poetry as Experience* (New York: American Book Company, 1952), pp. 188-92. I expand slightly on the present discussion in *The Art of Total Relevance: Papers on Poetry* (Rowley, Mass.: Newbury House, 1976), pp. 97-99. LP

Henry Reed **NAMING OF PARTS** (page 40)

The poem presents a corporal or sergeant giving instruction to a group of army trainees. There are two "voices" in the poem, but their dialogue is conducted within the mind of one person, probably that of a recruit. The first three-and-a-fraction lines of all but the last stanza are the spoken words of the sergeant as heard by the recruit. The last two-and-a-fraction lines of these stanzas, and the whole of the final stanza, are the unspoken thoughts of the recruit. This interpretation can be disputed, for there is some ambiguity about the "speaker" in the poem. Exact determination, however, is unimportant. Whoever the "speaker" is, he is a sensitive person. His unspoken thoughts furnish a comment on the instruction he receives or is compelled to give. (Compare the ensuing discussion of "Judging Distances.")

The instruction takes place out-of-doors. It is spring. Not far off are gardens in blossom, with bees flying back and forth, cross-pollinating the flowers. The time apparently is just before or just after the outbreak of a war, during a period of rapid mobilization, for the equipment of the recruits is incomplete. Their rifles have no slings and no piling swivels.

The meaning of the poem grows out of the ironic contrast between the trainees and the gardens, both of which have symbolical value.

Besides lacking slings and piling swivels, the trainees have not got a "point of balance," in one sense the point on the rifle at which it balances on the finger, in another sense a psychological point of balance in their lives. Living in barracks, apart from wives and sweethearts, they are living an unnatural kind of life. Their lives are incomplete, like their equipment. By learning the parts of the rifle, they are preparing to kill and be killed. They are living a regimented life. Being raw recruits, they are awkward. Their lives are tedious, as expressed by the repetition of dull phrases. The rifle is a mechanical instrument, and their lives are likewise mechanical.

The gardens represent the natural, the free, the graceful, the beautiful, the joyous—everything that is missing from the lives of the trainees. The bees, by fertilizing the flowers, are helping to bring about new life. The trainees and the gardens thus symbolically represent a series of opposites: death versus life, incompleteness versus completeness, the mechanical versus the natural, regimentation versus freedom, awkwardness versus grace, drabness versus beauty, tedium versus joy—the list can be extended. Through this ironic juxtaposition, the poet indirectly makes a statement about the kind of life imposed on man by war and preparation for war.

The poem is heavy with sexual implications, and, if handled with tact, discussion of these will open up a further dimension of meaning. If handled clumsily, such discussion will give this aspect of the poem a false emphasis and send students away thinking it a "dirty" poem. Men segregated from women tend to become obsessed with sex and to think of women as sexual objects rather than as persons. The absence of normal contacts between the sexes is one reason for the lack of a "point of balance" in the recruits' lives. Many words and phrases in the poem symbolically or connotatively suggest sexual "parts" or actions: "thumb," "bolt," "breech," "rapidly backwards and forwards," "assaulting and fumbling," "cocking-piece." The instructor must rely on his own discretion as to how explicit to be about these matters, remembering that they are properly overtones and undertones, not the burden of the poem.

The language and rhythm of the poem beautifully support its central contrast. The words of the sergeant are prosy, and their rhythm is a prose rhythm, frequently faltering and clumsy. In the lines about the gardens, the words are beautiful, and the rhythm flows. The transition from smooth to halt is especially striking in the middle of line 17.

The poem is discussed by Richard A. Condon in *The Explicator* 12 (June 1954): 54. LP

Henry Reed **JUDGING DISTANCES** (page 41)

In 1962, I wrote to Mr. Reed as follows:

There are apparently two speakers in this poem. The second speaker begins with "There to the west" in the fourth stanza and speaks through the fifth stanza; he speaks also the seventh stanza. Is there any reason for your not putting quotation marks around these two passages to indicate the change of speaker? Would you object to their being introduced? Your reading of the poem on the Library of Congress recording makes the change of speaker quite clear for the listener. . . .

Mr. Reed replied:

Even though there are (in a sense) two voices involved in the poem, and even though in recording it, I may have seemed to distinguish between them, the poem was written for the printed page (nearly twenty years ago, before poetry-recording was much thought of) and I must beg that any re-punctuation of it be done after my death rather than before it. It is difficult to explain why I think it is better that it should not include the "shock" of quotation marks: but I really like to think of it as an *interior* dialogue, and quotation marks would externalize it too much for my liking. After all, the same thing applies to "Naming of Parts."

This situation is similar to that in "Naming of Parts" (see the preceding discussion), and the meaning grows out of a similar contrast. A group of trainees is receiving instruction in judging distances and in reporting the direction and distance of artillery targets. The "interior dialogue" takes place in the mind of one of the recruits and presents the voice of the instructing officer and the recruit's replies, spoken and unspoken.

The contrast is between the situation of the recruits and a pair of lovers, and it may be expressed in a series of paired opposites—destruction versus procreation, intellection versus feeling, the abstract and general versus the concrete and specific, death versus life—with the juxtaposition generating a similar meaning about the life imposed on man by war.

19

The contrast is effectively carried out in the language used: the stripped, artificial, almost unreal language used in reporting directions and distances opposed to the rich, poetic language used by the recruit in lines 22–27. The army "officialese" conveys a sense of unreality, the language of poetry a full-bodied reality: "what appear to be animals" versus "sheep may be safely grazing" (reminiscent of the title of a well-known organ composition by Bach); "a pair of what appears to be humans" versus "under the swaying elms a man and a woman lie gently together."

"Maps are of time, not place" in the army, in that one reports the direction of a target by reference to the positions of figures on a clock dial. "Dead ground" in the second-to-last stanza means unoccupied ground—that is, plain flat ground without landmarks; but, since "maps are of time, not place," the phrase takes on an additional meaning for the trainee in the last stanza. He has been in the army for approximately a year and a half. This period, for him, has been "dead ground"—a period of meaningless existence separating him from life, love, joy, everything represented by the lovers—a life that he knew before entering the army. LP

David Wagoner **BEING HERDED PAST THE PRISON'S HONOR FARM** (page 43)

There are three sets of "prisoners" in the poem. First, there is the poet himself, temporarily confined by a large herd of cattle which stare at him as "another prisoner." He is in his car, which, we know without needing to be told, has numbered license plates on it. Second, there are the cows, who "All wear numbers clipped to their ears" and are being driven to pasture to feed "behind barbed wire like a work-gang" and will later be confined for milking in concrete stalls. Third, there are the inmates of the state's prison system, who are also "numbered" (17)—as we know so well from prisoners' photographs.

The poet has chosen Holsteins not only because they are the most common breed of milk cattle in the United States, but more particularly because of their black-and-white coloring. Black and white imagery is important throughout the poem. The poet is white. The cows are black-and-white. Eightballs are black (with white numbers). Milk is white. The cowpoke is black. Traditional prison garb is black-and-white.

The poet has clearly chosen both diction and imagery to connect the three kinds of "prisoners" with each other. Thus the poet is "herded" past the honor farm. He is "cowed" by the enormous size of the cows' udders. Though *his* hands are on the steering wheel, it is the prison cowpoke who in the last line is "steering" him out of the herd (and a *steer*, incidentally, is a castrated male bovine, or ox). The cows "like solitaries" (prisoners in solitary confinement) are "stalled in concrete" (Is the poet's car "stalled" on a "concrete" highway?). The cowpoke splats his boots down "like cowflops." While telling the poet "exactly where" he "can go" ("to hell"?), he is "cutting" him "out of the herd." (In cowboy lingo, separating a specific animal from a herd is called "cutting" it out.) There are contrasts, of course, as well as comparisons. The cowpoke is tall and the cows seem gigantic, but the poet feels "dwarfed" in his car. The cowpoke is a "trusty" (a convict granted special privileges for good behavior); the poet's hands on the steering wheel squeeze much too tight to be "trusted."

Though the poem relates a simple incident, it raises complex moral questions. Are we not making black-and-white moral distinctions when we divide the world into two classes, one of which is put in prison, the other of which is not? Are we not all "prisoners" of a system which does this? Can the system possibly be just when most of those outside are white and a disproportionate number of those inside are black? Perhaps the questions come to a focus in Wagoner's brilliant allusion to Shakespeare's phrase "the milk of human kindness" (*Macbeth*, I, v, 17). By putting it in a context where both the literal and metaphorical meanings of "milk" are operative, and by adding a negative prefix to "human," the poet asks whether it is human or inhuman, kind or unkind, to keep cattle or people in prisons, and to identify individuals by numbers rather than names.

Some additional comments: "Closer" (1) is better than *nearer* because of its nearness to *enclosure*. The poet compares the cows' eyes to "eightballs" (black) rather than to *cueballs* (white) because he wants to suggest the familiar phrase "behind the eightball" (derived from the game of Kelly pool) meaning "In a disadvantageous position from which it is impossible to escape." The cows are in such a position. Wagoner gets a double meaning from "insurmountable" by dividing it between two lines. In line 17 he again makes additional meanings possible by omitting the commas which would normally separate a series of adjectives preceding a noun. We can read "black" and "numbered" as two words or as one (*black-numbered*); we can read "trusty" as a simple adjective (*trustworthy*) or as a noun used adjectivally (a prison "trusty"). LP

Langston Hughes   CROSS (page 44)

The speaker is a "cross" (literal) between black and white, and this is the "cross" (metaphorical) that he has to bear. There is also an overtone of the adjectival meaning "angry" in the title. LP

Siegfried Sassoon   BASE DETAILS (page 44)

The poem expresses the resentment of a front-line soldier in the First World War, exposed to the constant dangers, discomforts, and deprivations of trench warfare, toward the frequently casual attitudes and soft lives of officers assigned to staff duty at the base, safely located miles behind the front. Although we can't know his rank, the speaker is almost certainly an officer and is perhaps, like the poem's author, a captain. Company commanders (captains) and platoon commanders (subalterns) suffered the highest mortality rate during World War I because they had to lead their men "over the top" on charges across "No Man's Land" against withering enemy fire. The speaker expresses his bitterness through irony; he is really strongly averse to being the kind of person and living the kind of life he describes so deprecatingly.

The title expanded to manifest both its meanings might read "Ignoble Particulars about Officers Detailed for Duty at the Base."

"Fierce" is used ironically (fierce manner, inward timidity). "Scarlet" suggests the red face of someone who is choleric, acts fiercely, is short of breath, and drinks too much, as well as implying the red lapel tabs and cap bands worn by staff officers in the British army. "Puffy" means both short-winded and fat. "Guzzling and gulping" connotes gluttony. "Scrap" minimizes the seriousness and horror of battle by reducing it in importance to a street-corner altercation between kids. "Youth stone dead" has ambiguous reference: it may refer either to the utterly vanished youthfulness of the returning majors or to the young men left literally dead on the battlefields. "Toddle" suggests second childhood and senility.   LP

Robert Louis Stevenson **THE CAREFUL ANGLER** (page 45)

After the pastoral and idyllic connotations of words like "angler," "nook," "morning," "lilied," "brook," "noon," "romantic," "riverside," "evening," "tranquility," "dine," and "breathing" in the first seven lines, the coarse connotations of "cram" and "belly" in the final line take the reader by surprise, explode the tone of the poem, and turn the angler into a figure of fun.   LP

4. Imagery

Robert Browning **MEETING AT NIGHT** (page 47)

Robert Browning **PARTING AT MORNING** (page 48)

The auditory imagery of "Meeting at Night" is strongly reinforced by onomato-poetic effects. In lines 5–6 the sound of the boat's hull grating against the wet sand of the beach seems echoed by the series of *sh*, *ch*, and *s* sounds in "pu*sh*ing . . . quen*ch* . . . *s*peed . . . slu*sh*y *s*and." In line 9 the sharp *p* of the onomatopoetic "ta*p*" is repeated in "*p*ane," and the *-tch* of the onomatopoetic "scra*tch*" is par-tially anticipated in "*sh*arp" as well as repeated in the rime.

Both meanings suggested for the last line of "Parting at Morning" are applicable. The "world of men" does need the contributions of the male speaker to its daily labors; and the speaker himself—as Browning's answer implies—needs the companion-ship of men as well as the love of a woman. LP

Richard Wilbur **A LATE AUBADE** (page 49)

An *aubade* (from a word meaning dawn) is a sunrise love song, a morning sere-nade, a lyric addressed at dawn to one's sweetheart. The word is used whimsically here, for, though the lovers have recently awakened, the time is almost noon. It is a very late aubade indeed. The woman has apparently made some gesture toward rising. ("It's almost noon," she has said. Implication: it's time to get up and go about one's business.) The man is pleading with her to stay in bed with him a while longer, and then to cap their lovemaking with some delicious snacks from the ice-box.

Are these lovers unmarried? The question is irrelevant to the theme of the poem, and ought not to be raised. If students insist on bringing in a moral issue, however, (and some will), one should be prepared to point out that the poem does not answer the question one way or the other. The lovers might be a recently married couple with no children as yet. They are in a house with two stories, not in a bachelor apartment, and the woman knows her way to the refrigerator.

The poem is a celebration of the delights of the senses. Both the woman, who would rather "lie in bed and kiss / Than anything," and the man, who orders up a connoisseur's menu from the kitchen, know how to savor these delights. The images chosen appeal to touch (kisses, chilled wine), to taste (wine, cheese, crackers, pears), and to sight. (Though white wine and blue cheese refer more to kinds than to colors, they suggest, when combined with "ruddy-skinned pears," a visual as well as a gustatory treat. The arrangement of items indeed suggests the eye of a painter, a

Cézanne or Renoir, as well as the palate of an epicure.) All the images suggest a keen appreciation of such delights by the lovers, not coarse sensuality or gross over-indulgence.

The poem belongs to the *carpe diem* tradition, famously exemplified by Herrick's "To the Virgins, to Make Much of Time," with its opening line "Gather ye rosebuds while ye may." The theme of such poems is "Time flies; therefore enjoy to the full-est each moment as it passes."

The speaker in the poem is a cultivated person, familiar with "centuries of verse," with Schoenberg's music, with the appearance of old books ("liver-spotted pages"), and with the manner of library research ("sitting . . . in a carrel"). It is clear that he is thoroughly acquainted with the life of the intellect, but has not allowed intellec-tual interests to dull or dry up his delight in the senses. In listing the activities that the woman might otherwise be engaged in, he manifests a wry wit and describes each in a manner that makes it seem unattractive ("liver-spotted," "cage," "raucous," "screed," "unhappy," "bleak") beside the pleasure he proposes. The woman, we may infer, has qualities of mind and imagination similar to his own. He does not need to explain to her the "rosebuds-theme of centuries of verse"; he knows she will understand his references to "Schoenberg's serial technique" and to carrels and old books. He can apparently count on her for an appreciative response to his quiet humor. There is between them a mutuality of mind and taste. LP

A. E. Housman **ON MOONLIT HEATH AND LONESOME BANK** (page 50)

The speaker is a Shropshire lad, watching his sheep by moonlight, close to a crossways. He is thinking about his friend, who is to be hanged next morning in Shrewsbury jail at 8 A.M. (the traditional hour for English hangings). The time is roughly contemporaneous with the composition of the poem—that is, the closing years of the nineteenth century. We know that it is after the industrial revolution by the reference to railroad trains. We know also that a century before, criminals were hanged in the country, by the crossways, and their bodies left hanging as a warning to passers-by. At the time of the poem, they are hanged in urban jails. (In our own time, England has abolished capital punishment.)

The attitude of the speaker toward his friend is expressed first in the word *careless* (5). Since the speaker does not know the offense committed by the "careless shepherd" long ago, it is significant that he calls him "careless" rather than "criminal." The implication is that he just "got into trouble," not that he did evil. He was the victim of bad luck—he did not act out of evil intention or because of original sin. This attitude is confirmed when the speaker calls his own friend "a better lad, if things went right,/Than most that sleep outside." It was "things" that went wrong for the lad, not *he* that went wrong. He, indeed, was "as straight a chap" as "treads upon the land." But his bad luck was not unique. The double time-reference shows that lads with good hearts and good intentions have been getting into trouble since time began. The speaker's universe is one in which luck or chance is the governing force, not one that is run by a beneficent deity. That this attitude is Housman's as well as the speaker's is indicated by the minimal characterization of the speaker, the absence of dramatic irony, and its consonance with attitudes expressed in the rest of Housman's work. Line 9 is particularly significant: "They hang us now in Shrewsbury jail," *not* "We hang them now in Shrewsbury jail." The speaker identifies himself with lads who get into trouble, not with a righteous society punishing criminals. The lot of his friend is representative for him of the lot of mankind.

The visual imagery of the poem, dominated by moonlight, softens the emotional focus, contributes pathos, casts a delicate melancholy over the situation appropriate to the tone. The auditory imagery—chains clanking, whistles blowing, trains groaning, clocks ringing—is most effective in the third stanza—first, because the sound of a train at night is one of the loneliest sounds in the world; second, because it tells us that the lad in Shrewsbury jail is awake all night before his hanging—hears every train that passes, every whistle that blows; third, because it brings before us the fact of change—industrialization, technological progress, urbanization. This imagery tells us that the externals of life change—but the fate of man remains the same.

The kinesthetic imagery—the sensations of the throat strangling, the neck snapping—involves some of Housman's most brilliant use of language. The triumphant pun on "ring" and *wring* (many students miss this) telescopes the grammatical process and takes us immediately from the initial signal, the ringing, to its final result, the hanging, making an imaginative leap across all intervening action. The heavy alliteration and consonance in the phrase "strangling in a string" let us hear the rasp of the victim's throat (in each word a single vowel is surrounded by five consonants, as if choking the life out of it), and the use of the word "string" (instead of *rope*) emphasizes the indignity of the victim's end. The verb "snap" (21) brings out a double meaning in the phrase "link of life," which is metaphorically the bond that binds body and spirit together but is literally the neck.

[This commentary is abridged from a fuller analysis in the essay "How to Read a Poem" in Laurence Perrine, *The Art of Total Relevance* (Rowley, Mass.: Newbury House, 1976), pp. 78–88.]

Emily Dickinson   **A NARROW FELLOW IN THE GRASS** (page 51)

The subject of the poem is snakes and the (male) speaker's fear of them, and it is vividly rendered through Dickinson's effective use of visual, tactile, and visceral imagery and through her consistently surprising but precise word-choices.

The word "fellow" (twice used for the snake), when contrasted with nature's "people" (17), suggests someone of inferior class and breeding. The adjective "narrow" is exactly right for a snake, but who ever used it of one before? "Rides" suggests effortless motion, without legs. But the characteristic of the snake principally emphasized in the first two stanzas is the suddenness of its appearance. (The departure from normal word order in line 4 not only provides an oblique rime for line 2 but gives unusual emphasis to "sudden.") One is not aware of the snake's presence until the grass parts unexpectedly at one's feet and one catches a fleeting glance of "a spotted shaft"; then the grass closes again and opens further on, this time without revealing the snake. (The grass is not that of a mown lawn, but the ankle- or calf-deep grass of a field.)

Stanzas 3–4 indicate how alien to man is the snake's habitat and emphasize the suddenness of the snake's *dis*appearance. Though "occasionally" snakes come out to forage in a field or enjoy the sun, their preferred habitat is the swamp, land too wet and cool for man to use even for agricultural purposes. Yet the speaker "more than once" when "a boy, and barefoot" (thus vulnerable to snakebite) had come across one basking in the sun and, mistaking it for a discarded whip-lash, has stooped to pick it up, when it suddenly "wrinkled" and vanished.

The first two pairs of stanzas indirectly suggest the power of the snake to startle the speaker, whether by sudden appearance or disappearance. The last two stanzas, partly through effective contrast with each other, reveal the snake's power to inspire deep fear in him. With several of "nature's people" (e.g., squirrels, birds) he has struck up an acquaintance, and he feels for them "a transport / Of cordiality." But he has never met "this fellow" (the snake), either by himself or in the company of friends, "Without a tighter breathing / And zero at the bone." The images in the final two lines strike home with the shock of pure terror. "Tighter breathing," with its unexpected adjective, is precisely accurate for that feeling of constriction in the chest which makes it difficult to breathe. And to contrast with "cordiality" (warmth of heart) in stanza 5, we are given—not just a chill, or cold, or even freezing —but "zero" (the lowest point on the centigrade scale), and not at the heart but at the "bone" (cold piled upon cold).

Many students will have difficulty with the image of the "whip-lash / Unbraiding in the sun," the participle suggesting motion to them. But the basking snake is motionless. A whip-lash of braided leather left out in the sun too long will begin to dry out and disintegrate, its thongs loosening and cracking. The snake, with its mottled leather back, has a similar appearance. When the boy stoops to pick up what he thinks is a whip-lash, it suddenly comes to life and hurries off.   LP

Adrienne Rich   **LIVING IN SIN** (page 52)

The central contrast of the poem is between glamorous expectation and realistic fulfillment. The central emotion is disillusionment. The woman had thought that "living in sin" with an artist in his studio would be romantic and picturesque. The phrase "living in sin" suggests (here) the free, unconventional Bohemian life. The word "studio" connotes something appealing, not just a top-story room in a walk-up flat. The sentence in lines 4–8 gives the picture that had arisen in the woman's mind when he had urged her to come live with him. She had not foreseen that the apartment might be dirty, creaky, and bug-infested, with noises in the plumbing—that furniture would have to be dusted, windows cleaned, beds made, and dishes washed—

and that her lover would not be romantic all the time. The irony of the situation is that "living in sin" with an artist in his studio proves not much different from marriage to a workingman in a run-down apartment. LP

Robert Hayden **THOSE WINTER SUNDAYS** (page 53)

The central images evoke coldness and heat, and are extended into the emotions reported and experienced by the speaker: his sense of cold indifference to his father in contrast to the emotional warmth expressed in the father's loving care, and in contrast to the warmth the speaker feels for his father now.

The father's actions all imply love: even on Sundays, when he need not rise early to work for his family's sustenance, he is the one who undertakes the task of driving coldness from the house. And he goes beyond the necessity of providing warmth, adding the care of his son's appearance (the "good shoes" that need to be polished for church).

The coldness is made especially vivid in the sensory images which describe it— "blueblack" in the pre-dawn darkness, and so solid and brittle that its retreat from the heat causes it to splinter and break. But the physical warmth of the house cannot dispel the emotional chill: the speaker flatly asserts that "no one ever thanked him," and the household continues to suffer from "chronic angers."

The poem moves from past to present tense, and from memory to self-castigation, with the repeated lament "What did I know, what did I know." Thoughtless and indifferent childhood gives way before the mature knowledge "of love's austere and lonely offices," and the poem ends in regret and remorse. TRA

Gerard Manley Hopkins **SPRING** (page 54)

Hopkins's poem is an Italian sonnet. The octave is descriptive, the sestet makes a religious application. The abstract statement of the first line is made concrete with rich particularized imagery in the rest of the octave, and this richness of imagery is supported throughout the poem by richness of sound—alliteration, assonance, consonance, interior rime, end rime.

In the sestet Spring is compared to the Garden of Eden, and this in turn to childhood. The three things thus compared have at least three things in common: (1) they are characterized by abundant beauty, sweetness, and joy; (2) they each occur at the beginning of something—the year, human existence, individual life; (3) they are innocent, free of sin. But the mention of Eden reminds the poet that human beings were thrust out of paradise through the sin of Adam and Eve. He therefore exhorts Christ, the innocent "maid's child," to capture the minds of girls and boys before they too spoil their lives by sinning. The poem is—or ends in—a prayer.

The poem is as rich in associational connections as it is in imagery and sound.

For example, blue, the color of thrush's eggs, is the color of the sky, thus of "heaven," and is also the Virgin Mary's color, symbolic of purity. White, the color of lambs and pear blossoms, symbolizes innocence, as do lambs themselves, which in additional have symbolic association with Christ. Thus religious connotations are already implicit in the octave, ready to be activated by the explicit references in the sestet. LP

John Keats **TO AUTUMN** (page 54)

Opulently rich in imagery, "To Autumn" is also carefully structured. The first stanza deals with the ripening process, the second with harvesting activities, the third with natural sounds. Although each stanza blends various kinds of imagery, each gives prevalence to one kind. The first stanza is dominated by images of fullness and tension, a kinesthetic-organic imagery apparent in such words as "load," "bend," "fill," "swell," "plump," "budding," and "o'er-brimmed." The second stanza places greatest emphasis on visual imagery. The third stanza stresses auditory images, some of them onomatopoetic ("wailful," "bleat," "whistles," "twitter").

The poem is also structured in time, the three stanzas presenting a progression both in the season and in the day. The first stanza presents early autumn: fruit and nuts are coming to ripeness. The second stanza presents mid-autumn: everyone is engaged in harvest activity. The third stanza presents late autumn: the harvest over, stubble-plains remain, and the swallows gather for their migration southward. In parallel movement, the first stanza presents morning: mists are on the fields and the sun is "maturing" (perhaps in the triple sense of climbing the sky, moving toward the winter solstice, and bringing the fruits to maturity). The second stanza presents midday and afternoon: the reaper, overcome by lassitude and the fume of poppies, sleeps on a "half-reaped" furrow, and the worker at the cider press watches "the last oozings hours by hours." The third stanza presents evening: sunset streaks the clouds and touches the stubble-plains "with rosy hue," crickets and birds resume their songs.

This double movement in time toward endings, plus the question asked at the beginning of stanza three, points to the theme of the poem—Keats's most persistent theme—that of transience. In this poem, however, Keats does not regard transience with the anguish manifested in "Ode on a Grecian Urn" and "Ode to a Nightingale." Autumn (symbolic of the latter part of life) has its beauty (its "music") as well as Spring (symbolic of youth); and the images of the third stanza, though touched with melancholy (the day is "soft-dying," the small gnats "mourn," the light wind "lives or dies," the swallows gather to depart) are as lovely as those in the first (when one thinks "warm days will never cease"). The mildness and beauty of the images throughout the poem, the peacefulness especially of those in the third stanza, and the assurance that Autumn has its music too, all reveal a serene acceptance of passing life.

The poem is a sustained apostrophe, addressed to a personified Autumn. Though this personification is most explicit in the second stanza, where Autumn is pictured in various roles as a harvest worker, it is manifested also in the first stanza (where Autumn is "bosom-friend" of the sun, conspires with him, and blesses the vines) and in the third (where it is exhorted not to "think" of the songs of Spring). The sun is also personified, and the fecundity of nature in stanza 1 results apparently from the union of female Autumn and male sun.   LP

5. Figurative Language 1: Metaphor, Personification, Metonymy

Frances Cornford **THE GUITARIST TUNES UP** (page 57)

The guitarist is compared negatively with a "lordly conqueror" and positively to a lover or husband; but, since all three are men, the figurative element in this simile is slight. It is strong, however, in the other half of the comparison—that of a guitar with "a loved woman." Here there is no question of the essential unlikeliness of the things compared. (The similarities exist in the curved shape, in the capacity to utter sweet sounds, in responsiveness to the man's touch, and, most of all, in the way they are approached by the man—with "attentive courtesy.")

The literal and figurative terms of the simile come together in the pun on the word "play"—meaning (a) to perform music, and (b) to engage in sexual play. LP

Robert Francis **THE HOUND** (page 57)

The dual possibilities of the "hound's intent" are underscored by the poet's craftsmanship each of the three times they are mentioned. (1) The four-syllable word "equivocal" occupies a whole line of the poem. (2) The opposed possibilities in lines 4–5 are given in a riming couplet (the only one in the poem) and by the exact duplication of the meter in the two lines (the only adjacent lines in the poem that match each other exactly). (3) In line 10 the two possibilities are designated by two alliterating monosyllabic nouns ("teeth," "tongue") naming parts of the dog which serve as metonymies respectively for a hostile or friendly intent.

The basic meter of the poem is iambic dimeter, though only lines 2, 7, and 10 are perfectly regular. All lines rime, but in an irregular pattern. LP

Robert Frost **BEREFT** (page 58)

Time: fall; evening. Place: an isolated house with a wooden front porch in disrepair on a hillside overlooking a lake. The speaker has opened the front door to inspect the weather. A storm is coming up. The door tugs at his hand. The wind swirls the leaves up against his knee like a striking snake. There are waves breaking in foam and spray against the shore of the usually placid lake.

There is "something sinister" in the tone of the poem as well as of the wind. The title, the imagery, the massed rimes all give the poem such ominousness and weight as to overbear any comfort the speaker may hope to give himself in the last two words.

30

The sounds of the poem reinforce the oppressive tone. Although the poem is sixteen lines long, it uses only five rime sounds, almost only three. Ten lines end in rimes containing long -o- sounds, reinforcing the onomatopoetic "roar" and the desolation of the twice-repeated "alone" (see discussion of phonetic intensives on page 187). Four lines end in rimes with prominent -s- sounds reinforcing the onomatopoetic "hissed." The two remaining lines end only in an approximate rime ("abroad"-"God"), further weakening the force of the last line to reassure the speaker or the reader. The onomatopoeia of "hissed" is supported not only by the rimes, but by the repeated -s- alliterations in the lines following; it is anticipated in the repeated -s- sounds of the lines preceding.

The wind in line 3 would seem to be compared to a wild beast The "restive" door is personified—as if it had a will of its own. The speaker's "life" (15) is like some habitation he lives in larger than his house—but no stronger. LP

Emily Dickinson **IT SIFTS FROM LEADEN SIEVES** (page 59)

The subject of "It sifts from leaden sieves" is snow, though nowhere is this subject named. Instead, it is developed through a series of metaphors in which the literal term is represented by the pronoun "it." Most of these are metaphors of the third form in which only the figurative term is named ("alabaster wool," "fleeces," "celestial veil"). In lines 1–2 and 18–19, however, not even the figurative term is named. In 1–2 it is flour; in 18–19 it is some kind of soft white cloth or lace. These are metaphors of the fourth form.

The "leaden sieves" refer to the darkened sky or clouds from which the snow is falling (a metaphor of the third form). But kitchen sieves were ordinarily (during Emily Dickinson's time) tinware; hence another metaphorical process is involved in the substitution of "leaden," with its connotations of heaviness and darkness in the weather, as opposed to the lighter, shinier connotations of tin. "Wool" as a figurative term for snow suggests softness and whiteness, but the introduction of "alabaster" as an adjective brings in an additional comparison, making the snow whiter and giving it a surface crustiness or hardness.

"Face" is an appropriate metaphor for a natural surface (even a dead metaphor in such phrases as "the face of a cliff"), but faces are seldom "even"—so this is a special face, a face compared to something having a smooth, flat surface. "Unbroken forehead" works in a similar way: this is an unwrinkled or unfurrowed forehead. The harvested field of "stump and stack and stem" is metaphorically compared to a room once inhabited (before the harvest) by a personified "summer" but now "empty" (no longer filled with growing grain). The "artisans" are snowflakes, the ghost-like weavers of the fleeces, veils, ruffles, and laces. At the end of the poem the snowflakes stop falling, but their creation—the variegated designs of snow on the ground—remains. LP

Science and religion are usually regarded as opposites, but Archibald MacLeish here emphasizes their similarities as well as their differences. The scientist, like the saint, lives a life of almost ascetic devotion to a disinterested activity. Like the nun in her holy cell, the scientist in his laboratory is given up to a life of pure contemplation, untainted by the selfish passions and materialistic motivations that drive most men. Both the scientist and the saint have a faith—the saint in the indubitable existence of a benign Creator, the scientist in the self-contained completeness of the physical world. It is the nature of their respective faiths and concerns that differentiates them: the faith of one is in the unseen, the faith of the other in the seen; the interest of one is in the metaphysical, the interest of the other in the physical; religion asks *why?* and *what for?*, science asks *what?* and *how many?* One asks for ultimate reasons and purposes; the other is content to be descriptive.

But the work of Sigmund Freud, suggests MacLeish, has posed questions which ought to disturb the complacency of science. Freud, of course, was a scientist, but his work on the functioning of the human mind has suggested that life is more mysterious, less rational, less easily explainable in purely physical terms than previous scientists had thought. Even more important, Freud's work focuses on the subjective world of thought and dream and emotion rather than on the external world of mass and number and extent. Thus Freud's work has raised problems insoluble by ordinary laboratory analysis and measurement. It deals with an unseen world—one that cannot be counted or weighed.

The material just summarized might have been developed in an extended prose essay, but this would have been an intellectual exercise. Poetry is an imaginative exercise. MacLeish, through metaphor and symbol, presents an account at once richer and more condensed. The principal metaphor is the brilliant extended personification of Science as a nun, sitting in her cell, counting her beads. Words traditionally associated with religion, here applied to science, chime through the poem to sustain this metaphor: "saint," "devotions," "contemplated," "religion," "rosary," "holy," "pure," "beads," "faith." (But notice that in the cell of science "There is no darkness ever." It is illuminated by the light of knowledge, never plunged into the darkness of doubt, self-questioning, or remorse—religion's "dark night of the soul," prerequisite to salvation.) The principal symbol is the sea shell held out in the hands of Freud. Curled and convoluted like the human brain, it suggests, when held to the ear, the existence of an unseen world, the murmuring of a distant sea, the mysterious ocean of the human mind, posing questions that the simple faith of science is incompetent to answer, containing depths that science cannot plumb.

MacLeish is poetically exact in his use of words. "Simple" (line 1) means plain and also foolish; "tell" (line 9) means both to count and to say; "perfect" (line 18) means not only unblemished but completed.

[Reprinted from Laurence Perrine and James M. Reid, *100 American Poems of the Twentieth Century* (New York: Harcourt Brace Jovanovich, 1966), pp. 161–62.]

Thomas Heywood **PACK, CLOUDS, AWAY** (page 62)

In this love poem—a joyous aubade—clouds, day (1), air, lark (3), bird, nightingale (7), robin (11), birds (12), black-bird, thrush (13), stare, linnet, cock-sparrow (16), and birds (20) are all apostrophized without other personification. By my count—I consider "elves" (17) grammatically an appositive and figuratively a metaphor—there are fourteen of them. By their brevity, terseness, and quick succession, they lend excitement to the poem. Line 20 ends the poem with an apostrophe, as line 1 had begun it with two, and thus forms a more fitting conclusion than would line 10.

The even-numbered lines of each stanza, plus the odd-numbered line of the refrain, all use the same feminine rime sound (perfect or approximate): *sorrow, morrow, borrow, morrow, morrow, borrow; furrow, morrow, sparrow, morrow, morrow, furrow.* The odd-numbered lines (except for the refrain line) all contain internal rime. This great profusion of rime, together with its repetitiveness, mimics the profusion of birdsong that the speaker calls for (and, like Indians who do a rain-dance before the rainy season, undoubtedly gets). The repetition of the phrase "good morrow" (three times in each stanza) keeps the occasion and nature of the song constantly before us.

There is no profundity of thought in this lyric, but there is a great deal of joy.

For other *aubades*, see Richard Wilbur, "A Late Aubade" (page 49); A. E. Housman, "Reveille" (page 85); Robert Browning, "Song" (page 129); Philip Larkin, "Aubade" (page 134); John Donne, "The Good-Morrow" and "The Sun Rising" (pages 274–75); and, like Larkin ironically stretching the definition, Jonathan Swift, "A Description of the Morning" (page 308). For a definition, see Glossary. LP

Emily Dickinson **A HUMMINGBIRD** (page 63)

"Route" and "rush" are metonymies, naming the direction and the motion of the bird as a substitution for the bird itself; "resonance" presents the metonymy "emerald," referring to part of the bird's coloration with an aural term; "revolving wheel" metaphorically represents the rapid motion of the bird's wings, comparing them to the disappearing spokes of a whirling wheel, for the speed of a hummingbird's wing-beats causes the optical illusion that they have disappeared.

While the first quatrain refers to the motions of the bird, it is itself static, a collection of nouns and prepositional phrases without predication. These phrases thus refer to two characteristics of a hummingbird in flight: its ability to hover motionlessly in the air and its sudden, almost magical disappearance from sight as it speeds away. These lines *name* motion, but do not have the completeness of sentences moving through grammatical correctness.

Lines 3–4 also contain examples of synesthesia, the substitution of one sense for another. "Resonance" is an auditory phenomenon that is here attributed to sight or color, while "rush" implies the sensation of motion and is applied to another visual phenomenon, the color "cochineal." These substitutions intensify the sensations,

33

and create the mystery that is solved in the concluding four lines, which answer the implied question "What *was* that?" The poem is in the form of a riddle (one of the poet's regular tactics) presenting first a series of vivid sense impressions, then a hypothetical solution—but never, in the body of the poem, identifying the hummingbird by name. The opening quatrain is also made compact by the four alliterated *r*'s and the two *e*'s.

These first four lines seem to exist all in a moment of stopped motion, and give way to the slower motion of the next image. The observer turns to look at "every blossom," and takes note of the time required for them to return to their normal positions. The "tumbled heads" of the flowers are childlike, and the speaker in the last two lines seems to offer them an explanation for the tumbling they have just gone through, an explanation drawn from Shakespeare's play of magic and reconciliation. The bird that has ruffled their hair is as swift—and as magical—as a postman who travels thousands of miles in a single morning.

For a full discussion of this poem, see Charles Anderson, *Emily Dickinson's Poetry: Stairway of Surprise* (New York: Holt, 1960), pp. 114-16. TRA

Exercise (page 65)

1. Personification and metaphor: day = a man; sky = a blue urn; sunlight = fire. ("Ode")
2. Simile: words = sunbeams.
3. Personification: Joy, Temperance, Repose = persons.
4. Metonymy: pen = literature or persuasive writing; sword = armed might or armies. (*Richelieu*, II, ii)
5. Metaphor: oaths = straw; human desire or impulse = fire in the blood. *(The Tempest*, IV, i)
6. Metaphor: conventional minds or souls = furnished rooms. (Nothing in a furnished room belongs to or is original with its occupant.) ("The Cambridge Ladies . . .")
7. Simile and personification: lizard, snake = flames; flame = a released prisoner. (*Adonais*, xviii)
8. Literal.
9. Metonymy: face = woman. After this substitution, however, the statement remains figurative. A literal translation would be "Is this the woman for whose sake (or for whose beauty) a thousand ships were launched?" The reference is to Helen of Troy. (*Doctor Faustus*)
10. Metaphor: the speaker = a worm (or some similar mean creature). In addition, *heaven* might be considered a metonymy for *sky*. (*Hamlet*, III, i)
11. Simile: feelings of lovers = the horns of snails. (*Love's Labours Lost*, IV, iii)
12. Metaphor: the desert = a lion. ("Sister Songs," II)
13. Literal. (*Richard II*, III, ii)

34

14. Metonymy: blood and tears = love and sorrow. ("When I survey the wondrous cross")
15. Metonymy: west = setting moon; east = rising sun; sun = day. (*Maud*, I, xxii)
16. Simile: present poems = pain dipped in honey. An additional metaphor resides in the comparison of pain to something, such as bread, that can be dipped in honey.
17. Metaphor and personification: clouds = sheep; wind = a shepherd.
18. and 19. When asked the difference between these two statements, students usually say that the first expresses certainty, the second possibility. The real difference is that the first is metaphorical, the second literal; that is, it is literally true that we *may* die tomorrow, but it is literally quite unlikely that we *shall* die tomorrow. *Tomorrow* (in 18.) = the day of death; the underlying metaphor is a *lifetime = one day*; and the meaning is "Life is very short; therefore we should enjoy it while we can." The imaginative force that shrinks the span of a lifetime to a single day is destroyed, and the statement rendered drab and prosaic, when this passage is misquoted, as it so often is. "Eat and drink," of course, is somewhat more than literal in both 18. and 19. The sense is "Let us be merry and enjoy ourselves" (we are being urged to drink wine, not water). Eating and drinking may be taken as a symbol, or a metonymy, for living the good life.

Robert Frost **THE SILKEN TENT** (page 66)

The poem consists of a single simile sustained through fourteen lines comparing a lovely and loving woman to a silken tent. It also consists of a single sentence winding easily and gracefully through the strict formal requirements (meter and rime scheme) of an English sonnet. It thus exemplifies in its form the paradox which is central to its content—the idea of freedom achieved within bondage.

Many students have preconceptions about tents that may interfere with their reading of the poem, and it may be well to start discussion by exploring what kind of tent the woman is being compared to. It is a tent made, not of coarse canvas, but of silk. Silk suggests beauty and fineness. The silken fabric of the tent is supported by a "central cedar pole." Cedar is a durable, aromatic wood, and its Biblical associations ("cedars of Lebanon") make it suggest worth and value. This upright pole ("pointing heavenward") is itself supported by silken guy-ropes that are staked to the ground around it. The tent is circular, for it is bound to earth "the compass round" (both words suggest circularity). When its guy-ropes are slack, the tent "gently sways at ease," and the tent-pole, though not "strictly held" by any single guy-rope, is yet "loosely bound" by all of them. It enjoys the freedom of a bondage that becomes apparent only when one of the ropes goes taut. (It may be helpful to take some pictures of such tents to class. There is a small one in *The American Heritage Dictionary*, p. 1327.)

What kind of woman is portrayed in this comparison to a tent? The first four lines suggest outward beauty, delicacy, gentleness, freedom, and composure. The

35

next three lines suggest strength and sweetness of soul, and a firm dedication to spiritual values. The second half of the poem develops the paradox that, though apparently free and independent, the woman is "bound / By countless silken ties of love and thought / To everything on earth . . ." "Countless" and "everything" are overstatements (at least as applied to the tent); literally she is attached by love and concern to many, many people—family, friends, neighbors, children, fellow human beings. Some students will be thrown off by the word "capriciousness," associating it with "feminine caprice." The capriciousness, however, is not in the tent (the woman) but in the "air" (her environment). Some change of circumstance, a sudden gust of wind, causes a tug or pull on her, to which she responds. In human terms, she is needed, and responds to the need.

Frost's poem is a lovely tribute to a lovely and loving woman who exemplifies Frost's belief that worthwhile freedom consists in bondage to what one deeply loves or cares about. Elaine Barry has an excellent discussion of this poem in her book *Robert Frost* (New York: Frederick Ungar, 1973), pp. 94–97. LP

Sylvia Plath **METAPHORS** (page 67)

The speaker is a pregnant woman. The "loaf" and the "fat purse" are her belly, swollen as if she had eaten a bag of green apples. The "red fruit" (like the "yeasty rising" and the "new-minted" money) is the unborn child; "ivory" refers to its skin, "fine timbers" to its delicate bones. The "train" is pregnancy; the "nine syllables" are the nine months of pregnancy. The poem has nine lines. Each line has nine syllables. LP

Philip Larkin **TOADS** (page 68)

Toads are squat, cold-blooded, warty creatures, and, though they can be handled quite harmlessly, their warts do contain a poisonous fluid that oozes out when they are attacked and makes the attacking animal sick. The speaker in this poem, no doubt the poet himself, lugubriously but humorously complains that he is encumbered with *two* toads. The first, specifically identified as work, squats *on* his life, binding him down to a repetitious six-day routine, all for the sake of the weekly or monthly paycheck and an old-age pension. The second toad, left unidentified, squats *in* him, and represents those internal qualities that prevent his throwing over his job and using his wits to live a day-by-day existence, choosing the risky free life over the safe unfree one.

Why is the second toad not identified? Because it represents no single nameable quality but a combination of qualities that the speaker himself might find it difficult to specify with any exactitude: timidity, prudence, middle-class morality, love of material comforts, perhaps even conscience (though the speaker would be slow to claim this last).

In the final stanza the speaker won't go so far as to say that the first toad embodies the second toad's spiritual truth, but neither does he deny it, and pretty clearly it at least comes close to doing so. That is why he will probably never rid himself of either toad. As so often in Larkin's poetry, the speaker finds himself in a dilemma, caught between alternative choices neither one of which is fully attractive to him.

The poem is remarkable for its use of an expressive colloquial diction that can modulate through the plain, the slangy, and the vulgar (*"Stuff your pension!"*) yet gracefully pun on that vulgarity with an allusion to one of Shakespeare's most exquisite passages—Prospero's speech in *The Tempest* that includes the lines ". . . We are such stuff / As dreams are made on, and our little life / Is rounded with a sleep."

The phrasing "Lots of folks . . . Lots of folks" (*not* "Lots of folks . . . These folks") seems to indicate that the people mentioned in stanza 3 are not quite the same as those mentioned in stanzas 4–5. Those in stanza 3 "live on their wits" and probably make a fair go of it, perhaps even blarneying their way to fame or the girl or the money, if not all three. "Lecturers" seldom "live up lanes." The people in stanzas 4–5 are paupers, still they don't actually starve, and the toad *work* doesn't squat on their lives. LP

John Donne **A VALEDICTION: FORBIDDING MOURNING** (page 69)

Izaak Walton, Donne's first biographer, tells us that Donne wrote this poem to his wife and gave it to her before leaving on an embassy to the French court, a project that would separate them for two months. His wife, who was with child at the time, had been reluctant to let him go, as she feared some ill during his absence.

Without this biographical information, however, we can know that the speaker in the poem is not dying. In the famous simile that concludes the poem, it is the traveling foot that "comes home" to the fixed foot, not the fixed foot that follows after the traveling foot to join it in some other place (such as heaven). Students often get the wrong notion of this poem, partly because of the title, partly because of the death-image in the first stanza. It should be pointed out to them that the dying "virtuous men" in this stanza belong to the figurative part of a simile, not to the literal referent. The sense is "Let us part from each other as silently and imperceptibly as a dying virtuous man parts from his soul."

The love of true lovers (members of the "priesthood") is a love of souls and minds rather than primarily of senses; therefore they can never be truly parted, and they do not "carry on" (like "lay" lovers) when they are physically separated. Donne has skillfully managed his meter so as to force an equal accent on both syllables of *absence* (15), thus bringing out the pun. Absence, for the "laity," is literally *ab* + *sense*: to be away from sense, to be separated from "eyes, lips and hands."

Three similes compare the parting of true lovers to the parting of virtuous men from life, to the expansion of gold beaten into gold leaf, and to the separation of the legs of a pair of compasses. A metaphor compares it to the almost imperceptible

37

"trepidation" (trembling) of the spheres (as contrasted to the gross movements of the earth—flood, tempest, and earthquake). LP

Andrew Marvell **TO HIS COY MISTRESS** (page 70)

Perhaps the greatest obstacle to student understanding of this poem is its title. The word "mistress" has none of its most common modern meanings: the "lady (2, 19) of the poem is, in fact, a virgin (28). Also, the word "coy" means no more than *modest* or *reluctant* without its usual modern connotations of teasing or playing-hard-to-get. The lady is reluctant to accede to her lover's pleas because of "honor" (29), which requires that she preserve her virginity until marriage. But the young man is not proposing marriage. In short, this is a seduction poem. It is also a *carpe diem* poem. The speaker belittles the lady's "honor" as of no importance in the face of the brevity of life and the imminence of death. Life being so short, they must enjoy their pleasures NOW! He puts his argument into syllogistic form: (1) *If* we had time enough, your coyness would not be a crime; (2) *but* time rushes on, death comes quickly, and nothing follows; (3) *therefore* we should make love *now*.

The poetic force of the poem derives, not from the cogency of the syllogism, but from the fancy, wit, and imaginative force with which it is presented. First, the speaker elaborates the temporal with a spatial dimension. If they had "world enough, and time" (he says), not only could they stretch out his courtship from "ten years before the Flood" (an immeasurably distant time in the past) till "the conversion of the Jews [to Christianity]" (an inconceivably remote time in the future), but they could pass their time separated by oceans and continents (she looking for rubies along the river Ganges in India; he complaining, in verse or song, of her coldness by the river Humber in England). He could allow his "vegetable love" to grow "Vaster than empires, and more slow." (The phrase "vegetable love," suggesting a love bloodless and unimpassioned, capable only of growth, subtly makes such a prospect seem undesirable.) He could also spend the amount of time praising her beauty that each of its features deserves, and would end up praising her heart (implying that his love for her is more than physical, and he would be glad to demonstrate if he had time). The tone of this first section is fanciful and playful; it is appropriately the longest of the poem's three sections for it depicts a state of nature in which there is no need to hurry.

At line 21 the tone changes dramatically. It becomes urgent. The speaker constantly feels "Time's wingèd chariot" about to overtake him. Time is at his back; and ahead (after death) he sees nothing but "Deserts of vast eternity" (eternity is a desert, a vast blank, a place without life). In the grave, she will lose her beauty; he will no longer be able to sing her love songs; she will lose her "long-preserved virginity" ("You're going to lose it anyway," the lover implies; "would you rather lose it to me—or the worms?"); her "quaint honor" will turn to dust (the word "quaint" has a slightly deprecatory connotation here, suggesting something without real importance; and a sexual pun buried beneath the word further trivializes the "honor" it is attached to); and, finally, his "lust" will turn to ashes (the speaker is quite frank here in confessing that his desires are physical). This section ends with a wry irony: the grave would seem a perfect place for making love—dark, quiet, private— but, strangely, no one makes love there.

Therefore, says the speaker, let us make love while we are young and eager, desiring and desirable. Let us love, not with a "vegetable love," but like "amorous birds of prey" (fiercely, like hawks or eagles). Let us devour time before time devours us. Rather than remaining as far apart as the Ganges and the Humber, "Let us roll all our strength and all / Our sweetness up into one ball" (a sphere is the most compact concentration of matter) "And tear our pleasures with rough strife / Thorough the iron gates of life." (There is considerable disagreement about the exact meaning of the "gates of life" image, but the tone and meaning of the lines are clear enough. The tone is resolute and determined; the meaning is, Let us love, not passively and delicately, but passionately and actively). Thus, though we cannot make time stand still (we cannot hold back death), we can make it seem to pass very quickly (excitingly, vitally, rather than dully or monotonously).

The poem concerns time more than love. It is perhaps the intensest, most urgent *carpe diem* poem in English. The poet has chosen love-making as a symbol for any activity which involves living intensely. As an argument for seduction, the poem is certainly specious. The lady, by waiting till she can fulfill her desires honorably, may save herself fifty years of misery. Conceived of, more generally, as an argument for spending one's hours in pleasurable, useful, or rewarding activities, the argument has greater force. The person who has to "kill time" out of boredom is a pitiful failure. The speaker is determined to master time rather than let it master him. LP

Anonymous **WEEP YOU NO MORE, SAD FOUNTAINS** (page 72)

The speaker is a lover who is exhorting himself to cease weeping. He does so in figurative language, apostrophizing his eyes and comparing them to fountains. (The metaphorical status of the "fountains" is indicated by the parallelism of line 1 with line 14, where the "sad fountains" become "sad eyes.") In urging himself to stop weeping, the speaker draws an example from nature. The snow on mountain tops melts slowly or "gently," he reminds himself, and his tears likewise should cease to "flow so fast." The word "sun," literal in line 4, becomes metaphorical in line 5, referring to the speaker's beloved. "Heaven" undergoes a parallel shift in meaning: in line 4 it refers to the sky; in line 5, transformed to an adjective, it means "divine." Since his beloved does not view his weeping, it cannot function as a sign to her of his love. The antecedent of "your" in line 6 is "sad fountains" or the speaker's eyes. The antecedent of "That" in line 7 is "sun" (line 5) or the speaker's beloved. (The first "lies," in line 7, was originally printed—in John Dowland's *Third and Last Book of Songs or Airs*, 1603—as "lie," and is often reprinted so, but this makes no sense and is clearly a printer's error.) The speaker concludes the stanza by giving himself another reason to moderate his sorrow. His lady is not so much dead as "sleeping"—and sleeping "softly"; he repeats the phrase twice, in reversed order, to emphasize the idea and soften the harsh fact of death.

In stanza 2 the lover enlarges on the reasons why he should not weep. Death ("sleep") is a "reconciling" (of the soul to God, perhaps, or to life's adversities): it begets peace. (Line 11 is syntactically ambiguous, as "peace" could be either subject or object of "begets," but it is best taken as object, for "rest" parallels "sleep" and "peace" is the "reconciling.") The speaker then turns again to nature for a lesson. In the fair setting and rising of the sun he sees a symbol of resurrection. Since he has already, in stanza 1, identified his beloved metaphorically with the sun, the inference is clear. She who died "fair" (beautiful, young, pure) is assured of immortality. There is no valid reason for extreme sorrow, the lover argues, and he again exhorts himself to rest from weeping (rest, for him too, can be a reconciling). The verb "melt" (line 15) relates his eyes to the mountain snow of line 3, which at its lofty height melts gently or not at all. The poem ends with the repeated insistence that the beloved is sleeping softly.

The chief reason for taking the lady to be dead is that her death explains the lover's weeping. If she is not dead, we can only hypothesize that the lover weeps because of unrequited love, but this assumption must be imported into the poem, and it suggests itself only because so many poems written about this time had unrequited love as their subject. The assumption is the more unlikely, however, because the speaker nowhere reproaches his beloved for her coldness, as was usual in such poems; in fact, he has nothing but tender thoughts for his "sun" whose "heavenly eyes" are now closed. In addition, the opening lines of stanza 2 seem without significant function if the lady is only asleep. They present no reason why the lover should cease weeping. She is not likely to love him in the morning any more than she loved him in the evening, and the suggestion that she set "fair" in the evening seems false from his point of view if she went to sleep not loving him. (These four lines *could*, perhaps, be taken as concerning the lover rather than the beloved—he is telling *himself* to get some sleep—but this involves a violent and unsignaled shift in focus between lines 9 and 10, and presents the additionally improbable suggestion that the lover thinks he might get over his deep disappointment with a good night's rest.)

[Reprinted from *The Explicator*, 34 (April 1976), item 61, by Laurence Perrine.]

A. E. Housman LOVELIEST OF TREES (page 73)

"Loveliest of trees" (*A Shropshire Lad, II*) is a *carpe diem* poem expressing the philosophy that life is short and that one should therefore enjoy it fully while one can, wasting no moment that might be filled with pleasure. The pleasure proposed in this poem is the enjoyment of beauty, especially of natural beauty, as symbolized by the blossoming cherry tree.

In assuming that the natural life span of man is seventy years, the speaker *alludes* to the Old Testament (Psalms 90:10): "The days of our years are three-score years and ten." The speaker is twenty. Normally one would think of a young man at that age as having ample time left for pleasure and enjoyment. His "only" and "little" therefore come as small shocks of surprise, emphasizing how little such time really is for something so wonderful as the enjoyment of nature. This is not verbal irony, for the speaker means what he says, but irony of situation—a discrepancy between what the reader anticipates and what he actually hears.

"Snow" (line 12) is metaphorical, representing the masses of white bloom with which the cherry trees are hung at Eastertide. The critical argument concerning this point is summarized in Laurence Perrine, "Housman's Snow: Literal or Metaphorical," *The CEA Critic* 35 (November 1972): 26–27.

The speaker is not Housman but a Shropshire lad (for Housman was older than twenty when he wrote this poem), but he undoubtedly speaks *for* Housman, or one aspect of him. But this aspect should be contrasted with other aspects, as expressed, for instance, by the speakers in "On moonlit heath and lonesome bank" (page 50) and "To an Athlete Dying Young" (page 284). LP

Langston Hughes **DREAM DEFERRED** (page 73)

Specifically the "dream deferred" is that of full and equal participation of blacks with whites in the political and economic freedoms supposedly guaranteed by the Constitution. Metaphors, because more condensed, are (other things being equal) more "explosive" than similes. The metaphorical comparison of black frustration to a bomb (metonymically representing a race riot or even armed revolution) is therefore appropriately placed in the climactic position. LP

Walter Savage Landor **DEATH STANDS ABOVE ME** (page 74)

The poet depicts death as a huge but not frightening figure bending over and whispering to him softly in a foreign tongue. (The word "low" serves a double function, implying a stooping posture and a quiet whisper.) The poet does not understand the *words* of death's language (which reveal whether or not there is any future life), but he does understand the *tone* (in which there is nothing fearful). Implication: The poet has no fear of death though he has no notion whether it leads to immortality or is final. The phrase "stands above me" indicates death's nearness (Landor was 79 when he wrote this poem). Landor's attitude may be profitably compared to that of Socrates in the *Apology*. LP

6. Figurative Language 2: Symbol, Allegory

Robert Frost   **THE ROAD NOT TAKEN** (page 75)

Since the publication (1970) of the second volume in Lawrance Thompson's three-volume biography of Frost, there have been an increasing number of different interpretations of "The Road Not Taken." These interpretations see the poem principally as an example of dramatic irony rather than of symbol. They are perhaps best summed up in Elaine Barry's discussion (in *Robert Frost* [New York: Frederick Ungar, 1973], pp. 12–13) by her statement that "the poem is a gentle parody of the kind of person whose life in the present is distorted by nostalgic regrets for the possibilities of the past, who is less concerned for the road taken than for the 'road not taken.'" The impetus for these interpretations was provided by Thompson's revelation that Frost himself regarded the poem as a gentle spoof of his English friend Edward Thomas and thought of Thomas rather than of himself as the speaker in the poem (*Robert Frost: The Years of Triumph* [New York: Holt, 1970], pp. 87–89, 544–548). After a careful review of the evidence, both external and internal, I find myself unable to accept these ironic interpretations. (I fall back on D. H. Lawrence's adage, "Never trust the artist. Trust the tale"; and I hope sometime, time permitting, to argue the case in an article.) However, the instructor should know of the existence of these other interpretations, and may wish to raise them for discussion in the classroom.   LP

John Boyle O'Reilly   **A WHITE ROSE** (page 77)

See Robert Herrick, "To the Virgins, to Make Much of Time" (page 43 of the manual).

Robert Browning   **MY STAR** (page 77)

There are, of course, two symbols in the poem: the smallish star in which the poet uniquely sees a special beauty, and the larger planet (Saturn) whose beauty is perceptible to all. The first symbol is enhanced by three similes. The star is like a prism which flashes out different colors when looked at from the right angle (apparently the poet's friends fail to discover that angle); it is like a bird which sings only for the poet (when others listen, it stops); it is like a flower which blooms only for the poet (when others look, it closes).   LP

Archibald MacLeish **YOU, ANDREW MARVELL** (page 79)

The implicit metaphor running throughout the poem compares the coming of darkness to the rising of flood waters. The night comes on steadily, without interruption or pause; the absence of punctuation and the repetition of "and" embody that unceasing, uninterrupted movement in the form of the poem. The substitution of suspension periods for a single period at the end indicates that the movement continues beyond the end of the poem. LP

Robert Herrick **TO THE VIRGINS, TO MAKE MUCH OF TIME** (page 82)

The rosebuds in the first stanza symbolize pleasures. The general meaning of the poem is to enjoy life while one can, for life is short, and the capacity for enjoyment is progressively and sharply reduced in middle age and old age. The last stanza specifies one kind of pleasure—but an important kind: sexual fulfillment in marriage. The use of "virgins" instead of *maidens* underscores the sexual significance.

The meaning of a symbol, like the meaning of a word, is largely controlled by context, and it may be worth pointing out that the "rosebuds" in this poem are slightly different in meaning from the "rosebud" in John Boyle O'Reilly's poem "A White Rose" (page 77). O'Reilly's rosebud is the symbol of an unfolding love: though it includes the idea of marriage and sexual fulfillment, it does not have the generalized meaning of pleasure that Herrick's rosebuds have. O'Reilly's rosebud is made specific in meaning by its juxtaposition with the red rose and the white rose. Herrick's rosebuds are generalized by the author's emphasis on the swift passage of time, and by his use of the plural rather than the singular. *Gathering* rosebuds suggests getting as many as possible, and thus the rosebuds suggest a variety of pleasures—including, of course, the pleasure of gathering rosebuds.

"Smiles" (3) personifies the flower that is dying, thus adding poignance to its death and preparing us for the idea that it is the death of persons, not of flowers, that Herrick is really concerned about. "Race" (7) emphasizes swiftness. "Spent" (11) has the connotation of exhausted or wasted, whereas "use" (13) suggests making a profitable or worthy employment of. LP

George Herbert **REDEMPTION** (page 84)

The first clue that this sonnet is not merely a dramatic narrative is not a forceful one: the title ambiguously refers to a business transaction and to a religious concept. Similarly ambiguous, "Lord" at the end of the first line may refer to a landlord or to God (the capitalization is retained from the first printing of the poem, but there was little consistency in the use of capitals in the seventeenth century). Only in the fifth line does the poem assert the break from superficial meaning, placing the manor house of the lord "in heaven." Even that phrase could be read as a metaphor (the manor house is so grand that it seems heavenly to the tenant) until the contrast in line 8 makes it clear that heaven and earth must be taken literally.

The poem allegorically presents what Herbert and other Puritans of the period called the "New Covenant," or the "Covenant of Grace," between God and man. The old covenant, the "Covenant of Works," had come into effect with the creation of Adam; it left man wholly responsible, and punishable, for his sins, and at Adam's fall it condemned mankind to death. By the Covenant of Grace, God sent his son to offer redemption of sin, a new contract by which man could be gathered into heaven as an act of God's grace rather than by his own deserts.

This allegorical meaning is made clear in a very early commentary on the poem, by George Ryley, at the beginning of the eighteenth century, as quoted by Joseph H. Summers, *George Herbert: His Religion and Art* (Cambridge: Harvard, 1968), pp. 60–61:

> The first lease this great landlord gave to man, his tenant, was the covenant of works, by which man was bound to yeild all the profitts of the land to his landlord's use; the condition being, *he that doth them shall live in them, and the soul that sinneth shall dye.* Man breaking the articles of this once, rendered himself for ever incapable of retrieving that loss, or of keeping them for the future; so by these articles he could never *thrive*, that is, never be *justified. But what the law* (that is, this law of works) could not do, God, sending his own Son, &c. hath wrought for us, that is, our Redemption: making us free from the law of sin and death, and granting us a new *small-rented lease.* This was purchased for us by, and granted to us att, the death of Christ. These premises will lead us into the plain sence of this poem.

The allegorical form permits Herbert to relate the narrative of "history" to the spiritual reality of every person's life. As Summers says, "the speaker is both one man in the present and all mankind from the Fall to the Crucifixion; the search is the search of the Jews until Calvary and it is also the search of every man who wishes to be a Christian; the discovery was made by humanity at one moment in the past, but it is also made by individuals at every moment, present and future" (p. 182).

This explanation helps us to understand the time reference in lines 7–8, "which he had dearly bought / Long since on earth." The event is obviously the Crucifixion, when the lord paid "dearly" (both at great expense, and with great love) to save mankind. As an historical event that occurred in the first century, it was "long since"; but as a continuing redemption, it occurs over and over in the lives of individual people. As Herbert would have seen it, the Crucifixion is a recurring event manifested to the spiritual life of each person, so the concluding image of the poem is both historical and present, and the "ragged noise and mirth" of the multitude re-enacts the scene of the original Crucifixion.

Students who may not have examined the metaphorical texture of Christian terminology may at first be shocked or affronted by Herbert's handling of the action of redemption in commercial terms; they can be led to see that the concept of heaven as *reward*, of Christ's *payment* for the sins of the world, and many others that they might contribute, rest on similar mercantile phrasing, justified by the need to express metaphysical truth in physical terms comprehensible to mankind. TRA

Exercise (page 85)

1. Literal. 2. Metaphorical. 3. Literal. 4. Metaphorical. 5. Literal, metaphorical, and symbolical (see the discussion on page 7 of this manual). 6. Metaphorical. 7. Metaphorical. 8. Symbolical. 9. Symbolical. 10. Symbolical.

All those listed as symbolical are, of course, both literal and symbolical, for a symbol by definition combines literal and figurative meanings—that is, it means itself and something beyond itself. In Tennyson's "Ulysses," for instance, the verbs "hoard, and sleep, and feed" are to be taken literally, but also as indicating that the Ithacans are a materialistic, lethargic, sensual, and unintellectual people—unlike Ulysses, who also eats and sleeps, of course, and presumably stores supplies in his ship against the future. "Sleep," in other words, as applied to the Ithacans, symbolizes a certain quality of life, a lack of aspiration. LP

A. E. Housman REVEILLE (page 85)

In the first two stanzas of "Reveille" Housman uses two extended metaphors for the coming of morning. In the first "the silver dusk"—the half-light between night and morning (some students may think "dusk" refers to evening)—is compared to the incoming tide, the night to a beach, and the just-rising sun to a burning ship stranded on the eastern horizon. In the second the nighttime sky is compared to a dark arch or tent which has been trampled to the ground and replaced by a daytime-sky-covered pavilion. In line 10 the morning is compared to drums, which also wake one up. In line 15 "leather" is a metonymy for boots or shoes. In line 21 "clay" is a metaphor-metonymy for the dead body, "blood" a metonymy for "man alive." ("Belfries," line 14, and "breath," line 22, are also metonymies.) In the last two lines (but not before) "journey" becomes a symbol for life and "sleep" a symbol for death.

Because of the words "Reveille," "tent," and "drums," some students may misinterpret this as a military poem. All three words belong, however, to the metaphorical context of the poem, not the literal. The lad addressed in the poem is not a soldier. He is being invited to rise and follow the life of adventure, not the call of duty. He is presented with a free choice, not a set of orders to follow. He is being called to go his own way, not to march with a regiment. He is being asked to "feast his heart," not to shed his blood.

The poem expresses a *carpe diem* philosophy, but one in which the most enjoyment of life comes through travel and fresh experience rather than through the quiet contemplation of beauty as in "Loveliest of trees" (page 73). LP

Robert Frost **FIRE AND ICE** (page 86)

Scientists have made various predictions about how the world will end, most of them involving either a fiery or an icy terminus. At the time that Frost published this poem (December, 1920), probably the two leading theories were (1) that, as the earth gradually loses momentum in its orbit, it will be drawn by gravity closer and closer to the sun, until finally it plunges into the sun, and (2) that, as the sun gradually cools, or as the interior of the earth itself cools, the earth will get colder and colder, until finally all life is extinguished in a new ice age. Both theories still have many supporters.

Frost makes symbolic use of these theories. Fire becomes a symbol for desire or passion, ice a symbol for hate, the earth a symbol for human or civilized life ("world" means both physical and social world). The poet has experienced enough of desire and hate within himself to recognize that both passion (e.g., desire for sensual gratifications, possessions, or power) and hate (e.g., between nations, classes, or races) are forces strong enough to bring an end to mankind.

The last line is understatement. Instead of saying that desire or hate could ruin, wipe out, or annihilate mankind, he says only that they would "suffice." LP

William Blake **THE SICK ROSE** (page 86)

"Rose," because capitalized, is a girl's name as well as a flower's. The word "bed" suggests a maiden's bed as well as a flower bed. "Crimson joy" suggests the intense pleasures of passionate love-making as well as the brilliant beauty of a red flower. In all these respects the rose of the poem suggests a person as much as a flower; and the "dark secret love" of the "invisible worm" is more suggestive of sexual intercourse than it is of the feeding of a cankerworm on a plant, though it could be either.

The poem has been read by different readers as referring to the destruction of joyous physical love by concealment, jealousy, deceit, or the possessive instinct; of humanity by Satan; of innocence by experience; of imagination and joy by analytic reason; of life by death. Some of these meanings are suggested entirely by the poem itself, some by a knowledge also of Blake's other writings. All are possible.

But the rose must always represent something beautiful or desirable or good. The worm must always be some kind of corrupting agent. The poem cannot be validly read as about the overcoming of something evil by something good. LP

Alfred, Lord Tennyson **ULYSSES** (page 87)

Ulysses represents and recommends a life of continuous intellectual aspiration; he has an avid thirst for life and experience that finds fulfillment primarily in the life of the mind rather than in the life of the senses (his concluding injunction is "to strive, to seek, to find," not "to taste, to touch, to smell"). Geographical exploration in the poem symbolizes intellectual exploration. The key lines for this interpretation are lines 30–32: "And this grey spirit yearning in desire / To follow *knowledge* like a sinking star, / Beyond the utmost bound of human *thought.*" But throughout the poem are words and phrases that reinforce this reading. In line 5 Ulysses characterizes Ithacans as a savage race that "hoard, and sleep, and feed, and know not me" (that is, a people who live a materialistic and physical life and know not the excitement of the intellectual life). In line 13 he says, "Much have I seen and *known.*" In line 46 he addresses his mariners as souls that "have toiled, and wrought, and *thought* with me."

The westward journey has a double symbolism that is also congruent with this reading. In sailing westward (toward the setting sun), Ulysses is sailing toward death (going west is a traditional symbol for death); he is also sailing from what, for the Greeks, was the *known* world (the Mediterranean world) into what was for them the *unknown* world (the world of the Atlantic, beyond the Strait of Gibraltar). The meaning is that Ulysses will continue to seek new knowledge, new discovery, until his death. The continuing nature of this search is also indicated in the images of following knowledge "like a sinking star" and of sailing "beyond the sunset, and the baths / Of all the western stars." One cannot, of course, ever catch up with a sinking star or with the setting sun; no matter how far west one sails, they still set beyond a horizon still farther west. Likewise, no matter how much knowledge one gains, there is still further knowledge to be sought. Thus Ulysses' quest is truly one of continuing aspiration: his thirst for new knowledge will never be satisfied; he will continue to seek new knowledge until he dies. What will become of him *after* death, he does not know (lines 62–64), but his program for life before death is clearly mapped out.

The image in lines 18–21 includes the idea of a horizon that is always to be sought, never to be reached—that is, the idea of knowledge that is never to be exhausted. Lines 26–29 tell us that every hour of life brings new experience, new knowledge. (Grammatically, the subject of "is saved" is probably to be construed as "something more," with a "bringer of new things" in apposition and "every hour" treated as an adverbial modifier; but the ambiguity of the construction suggests the wisdom of saving every hour possible from death, of living as long as possible in order to learn new things.) Thunder and sunshine are symbols for adversity and good fortune. Hearts and foreheads are metonymies for wills and minds (the meaning is "We confronted the thunder and sunshine with free wills and free minds"). The poem celebrates strength of will as much as it does the intellectual quest. The metaphor in line 23 compares a person to a sword or a shield.

In recent years "Ulysses" has been the subject of considerable critical controversy, some of it captious, and some oversubtle. Extreme views are presented by E. J. Chaisson in "Tennyson's 'Ulysses'—A Re-Interpretation," *University of Toronto Quarterly* 23 (1954): 402–09, and by Paull F. Baum, in *Tennyson Sixty Years After* (Chapel Hill: University of North Carolina Press, 1948), pp. 92–95, 299–303. John Pettigrew, in "Tennyson's 'Ulysses': A Reconciliation of Opposites," *Victorian Poetry* 1 (January 1963), pp. 27–45, gives an overview and seeks to reconcile conflicting viewpoints; and Charles Mitchell, in "The Undying Will of Tennyson's Ulysses," *Victorian Poetry* 2 (Spring 1964), pp. 87-95, adds still another point of view. LP

Alastair Reid **CURIOSITY** (page 89)

In its own sardonic and humorous fashion, this poem has much the same message as Tennyson's "Ulysses." Cats and dogs symbolize two different kinds of people: cats, the intellectually curious, the adventurous, and the unconventional; dogs, the incurious, the prudent, and the conventional. Though the parallel is not to be pressed too hard, Ulysses is a cat, Telemachus a dog. The poet's sympathies are with cats. (Tennyson regards Telemachus more favorably, however, than Reid regards dogs.)

The poem utilizes two folk sayings: "Curiosity killed the cat" and "Cats have nine lives." The poem says that curiosity is dangerous, but that one cannot really *live* without it. Curiosity leads to suffering and discomfort; nevertheless, it is the condition of being really alive. Intellectual curiosity is the kind in question.

"Death" in line 3 means literal, physical death. "To die" in line 16 means to die intellectually, emotionally, and spiritually; that is, to exist in a merely physical sense, like Tennyson's Ithacans—or like dogs. "To die" in lines 34-35 means to suffer, and "dying" in lines 41-42 means suffering. Thus "to die" has exactly opposite meanings in lines 16 and 34-35, and these two opposite meanings, being both figurative, are in turn both opposite to the literal meaning of "death" in line 3. These contradictory meanings are not a sign of the author's confusion, as they would be in a logical treatise or in any discursive prose; they are what give life and interest to the poem. Manifested in metaphor, and resulting in paradox, they help the poet probe the real significance of living. He is firmly in control; he knows what he is doing. LP

Alan Dugan **LOVE SONG: I AND THOU** (page 91)

Dugan's "house" is his life, and I classify this poem as allegorical. The speaker swears "by Christ" because Christ *was* a carpenter, and he is pointing up a contrast. Nevertheless, the speaker will be metaphorically "crucified" in his life (that is, he will suffer), as Christ was literally crucified. He needs someone who will "help" him suffer. The word "help" (31) works two ways: the wife will help him to suffer in the sense of causing additional suffering (she will nail his right hand to the right-hand cross-piece); but also, and more important, she will help him *in* his suffering—by sharing it, she will alleviate it, she will make his life supportable, and she will even, by introducing love, bring a little heaven into his life. The word "prime" has at least three relevant meanings: foremost or principal; of best quality (as applied to whiskey); and primitive or original (tying rage in with original sin).

Martin Buber's book has especially influenced the Protestant theologians classified as Christian existentialists. The movement of the poem supports the general tenor of this body of thought. Suffering and imperfection are inescapable conditions of human life ("God damned it. / This is hell"); nevertheless, life is made meaningful as man forms "I-Thou" relationships. Shared suffering is bearable; unshared suffering is not. The speaker in the poem finds that he cannot build a satisfactory life simply as an "I"; he must enter into an "I-Thou" relationship. Essentially the poem begins as an account of the speaker's attempt to build a life for himself and by himself; it ends up as a proposal of marriage. LP

Richard Wilbur   A HOLE IN THE FLOOR (page 92)

The first four stanzas are primarily literal and descriptive; the fifth is transitional; the sixth gives the poem its symbolical dimensions. The poet is drawn by curiosity to look through the hole the carpenter has made in the floor. He is fascinated by what he sees. It is like discovering a whole new world, a buried world. Though he has lived in the house presumably for some years, here is a part of it he has never seen before. It is a dark world primarily (except where the carpenter's hole lets light into it or cracks and chinks between floorboards let in "bits and strokes" of light) and a primitive world (pipes are left unpainted, and there are wood shavings left by the original builders). In stanza 5 the poet draws himself up with a start. Why is he so fascinated by this underneath world? What, in God's name, is he looking for? He makes a couple of whimsical suggestions. Is it buried treasure, hidden there by ancient kings or pirates? Is it some tiny garden such as Alice discovered when she tumbled down the rabbit hole? Or is it the "very soul" of the house, where our memories, conscious and unconscious, of our past lives are stored up? This last suggestion, obviously more serious, though not the answer, leads toward the answer. By speaking of the "soul" of a house, it makes one think of the house in terms of a person. Stanza 6 reveals to the poet and the reader an appropriate symbolic meaning for the area of the house beneath its floor. It is the unconscious mind, the Freudian id, the source of the psychic energies that lie beneath all overt human behavior. Just as the floor-lamp derives its light from the electrical wiring beneath the floor into which it is plugged, so do our actions in the known physical world derive their energy from hidden sources in the unconscious. These psychic energies may manifest themselves in all kinds of behavior, constructive or destructive. The images and connotations of light, bloom, inflaming, love-seat, and danger in the final stanza suggest knowledge, beauty, passion, love, and violence. LP

Jay Macpherson   SUN AND MOON (page 93)

This allegory of the sun and moon as brother and sister employs allusions to mythology as well as to modern scientific theory. The personification of a masculine sun and a feminine moon is ancient, and is found in most primitive mythologies around the world. In some the two deities are lovers or are ritually married, but for the most part the male sun rules and dominates the female moon, who lives only in his reflected light.

Scientifically, the poem makes use of gravitational theory, in which the combination of centripetal and centrifugal forces accounts for the orbiting of the heavenly bodies—forces of attraction and of repulsion, of drawing toward the center and of whirling away from the center.

The ulterior meaning of the poem is contained in these opposing forces, the incestuous attraction of brother and sister as lovers or mates, and in the repulsion for such pairing that forms one of the most prevalent taboos of both primitive and sophisticated societies. That they should yearn for one another and yet obey the compulsion to remain separated is a punishment. (There is also an implied reference, in fire and frost as the punishment, to two of the pains of hell described by Dante, Milton, and others.)

"Ordered heaven" (line 3) implies not only the orderliness created by the gravitational forces which keep heavenly bodies in their orbits, but further suggests a divine commandment that separates the brother from the sister, and provides the appropriate punishment for their desire for union.

Lines 7–8 refer to the moon's light as the sun's reflection, and to the phenomenon of a solar eclipse which results in the sun's being "lost" to earthly view at the same time that the reflected light of the moon's surface disappears; at such a time, when the two heavenly bodies look to be coming together, the light of both is extinguished, another example of the order of heaven that explains both the scientific phenomenon and the prohibition of incest.

The final stanza, projecting a celestial catastrophe in the collapse of the solar system, postpones the lovers' meeting until the end of the world. Until that dire event, the sister moon will eternally pursue the retreating brother sun—eternally, until the end of time as measured by the orbiting of the planets about the sun.   TRA

Robert Browning   FAME (page 94)

The poet's grave is revealed by the title to be a symbol for his fame. Is Browning calling into question the claim so often made in poetry (in Shakespeare's sonnets, for instance) that, though the poet himself may be mortal, his poetry is immortal? Or is he speaking merely of some minor poet, once well-known, whose reputation is beginning to fade? A case can be made for either reading. Though the earlier lines suggest a local setting and therefore a minor reputation, the title is general, and the weathering effect described in the last line happens to even the best-tended graves. LP

Robert Frost   **DUST OF SNOW** (page 94)

William Blake   **SOFT SNOW** (page 94)

"Dust of Snow" describes a literal incident, "Soft Snow," an allegorical incident.

"Dust of Snow," except for the muted metaphor in its title, may be taken quite literally. The beauty of the scene (powdery white snow, black crow), the animation provided by the movement of crow and snow, the suggestions of cheeriness and humor (as if the crow were greeting the speaker or playing a sly practical joke on him)—all combine to give a lift to the speaker's heart and to change his mood from one of sorrow, resentment, frustration, or whatever, to one of delight.

Other readers have read this poem rather differently, seeing sinister connotations in "crow," "dust," and "hemlock." I strongly disagree. If one insists on calling the crow a symbol, it is a life symbol, not a death symbol. In two published notes I have attempted to refute what I consider overingenious and mistaken interpretations of the poem, using my own arguments in one and quoting Frost's remarks on the poem in the other. Whoever wishes to acquaint himself with both sides of this controversy should consult the following: Edgar H. Knapp, in *The Explicator* 28 (September 1969), item 9; Laurence Perrine, in *The Explicator* 29 (March 1971), item 61; Norbert Artz, "The Poetry Lesson," *College English* 32 (April 1971): 740–42; Laurence Perrine, "Dust of Snow Gets in Our Eyes," *College English* 33 (February 1972): 589–90. Whatever its symbolical implications, the *incident* in the poem may be taken literally.

The last line of Blake's poem cannot be interpreted literally, and it forces us to look for a metaphorical or allegorical interpretation of the whole. (I would myself classify "Soft Snow" as allegory—one of the shortest in existence.) The clues to the allegorical meaning are the personification of the snow as "She"; the possible sexual connotations of such words as *soft, play, melt,* and *prime*; the fact that the speaker doesn't play *in* the snow but *with* the snow, or, rather, the snow plays with *him,* after he has first *asked* it ("her") to play with him; the moral judgment implied by "dreadful crime." The snow (in her prime) is a maiden. The speaker asks her to "play" (amorously) with him. The maiden consents and "melts" (yields her virginity). Conventional society ("winter") calls it a "dreadful crime."

It is clear that Blake takes an unconventional stance. He regards sexual desire and fulfillment as natural and innocent. By identifying society with "winter" he suggests that its judgment is cold and harsh, and by identifying sex with "play" and the melting of snow he implies that society's judgment is not only harsh but absurd. Blake expressed similar unconventional judgments in a number of poems; for example, "The Garden of Love," "Ah! Sun-flower," "Abstinence sows sand," and "The Lilly."   LP .

7. Figurative Language 3: Paradox, Overstatement, Understatement, Irony

Emily Dickinson   **MY LIFE CLOSED TWICE** (page 96)

Most readers have little difficulty with the first paradox. The speaker, while living, suffered two metaphorical deaths through the loss of persons dearly beloved by her. Many readers, however, go on to interpret the possible "third event" as another event of the same kind: the loss of another dear friend.

The "third event," however, must be an event of a different order, an event contingent on her own death—for three reasons. (1) The use in line 1 of the past tense (rather than the present perfect) indicates that the speaker is at or near the point of her death: her life has come to its literal close now, and she is therefore in a position to make this definitive statement. (2) The two previous events had been "unveiled" to her by life (losing friends to death is an inescapable part of life); this third event (if it occurs) will be unveiled to her by Immortality. (3) An event of a different order is aesthetically required by the necessity of bringing the poem to a climax: otherwise it could go on forever: ". . . a fourth event . . . a fifth event, etc."

Both interpretations suggested in the first study question for lines 2–6 are viable: (a) The speaker is uncertain whether Immortality awaits her and will unveil a "third event" to her; (b) She does not know whether any "third event" unveiled to her by Immortality can have an emotional magnitude for her equal to that of the two losses she suffered during her life. She suggests, in other words, that the deaths of her two precious friends were so painful to her that even the bliss of her own entry into heaven (or the horror of her entry into hell) may seem trivial by comparison. (Or does she perhaps suggest that Immortality, by separating her from friends still living, may be as painful to her as mortality twice was, by separating her from friends newly dead?)

The last two lines, by using "heaven" and "hell" simultaneously in both their literal and metaphorical senses, sum up the themes both of uncertainty about the future (we do not know whether life on earth will be followed by a continued existence in heaven or hell) and of the tremendous emotional impact of separations suffered during life. Parting is "all we need of hell." Loss of a loved person is so painful that any further suffering for any sins we have committed in life is entirely unnecessary. "Parting is all we know of heaven." This line is subject to two interpretations: (1) The closest we can come to knowing what heaven is is when our friends depart for it, which is to say, we can know nothing of it as long as we are still living and our friends have gone there without us. (2) Though we do not know whether there is an afterlife of bliss after death, we have a foretaste of what heaven will be like (if it does exist) in the emotions we feel at parting from loved ones during life.

Parting is a sweet experience as well as a painful one: it is sweet because, at the moment of parting, one's whole heart flows out to the departing friend; at the moment we feel our love (because we are about to lose its object) more fully and intensely than ever before. Thus, at parting, deep love and deep grief commingle, offering a possible foretaste of heaven and enough of "hell" to be sufficient forever.   LP

Robert Burns   A RED, RED ROSE (page 97)

Richard Wilbur has an excellent discussion of Burns's poem in *Responses: Prose Pieces* 1953-1976 (New York: Harcourt Brace Jovanovich, 1976), pp. 139-45. In *The Poems and Songs of Robert Burns*, ed. James Kinsley (Oxford: The Clarendon Press, 1968), III, 1454-56, the editor presents evidence that his poem may well have been a folk song that Burns collected rather than a poem he composed.   LP

Robert Frost   THE ROSE FAMILY (page 98)

A playful, graceful, and tender tribute to his beloved, Frost's poem begins with a playful allusion to Gertrude Stein's much-misquoted line "Rose is a rose is a rose is a rose" (from "Sacred Emily," *Geography and Plays*, 1922) and derives its central metaphor (line 11) from the first line of Burns's poem, though Burns was hardly the first to use it. Frost is original in combining this poetic metaphor with botanical taxonomy.

The poem opens with a literal statement, confirming Stein's assertion. It goes on to a literal statement of the new scientific theory. The newness and tentativeness of this scientific "truth" (and perhaps of all scientific truth) is indicated in the qualifications with which the statement is made ("The theory now goes" . . . "I suppose" . . . "The dear only knows"). This tentativeness contrasts with the assurance of the poem's final statement. In addition, the gentle colloquialism "The dear only knows" gracefully modulates the discussion from science to love.

In the last two lines the new and tentative gives place to the long and firmly established, literal statement yields to metaphorical, scientific "theory" is replaced by poetic truth. But the breathtaking achievement of these two lines is in what Frost does with "of course" and "But." These two connectives, usually so empty, here become momentous in their implications. On the surface, they make the final assertion so casual as almost to throw it away; deeper down they give it the status of truth so obvious, so assured, so well and long known, as hardly to be worth mentioning.

This is not the declaration of young love. The muted overstatement of "always" embedded in the tonal understatement established by "of course" and "but" reflects a relationship which has been long continued and thus gives to the statement the authority of a truth thoroughly tested. (The volume in which this poem was first included was dedicated to Frost's wife.)

That all ten lines end in the same rime sound emphasizes the unity of rose, apple, pear, plum, and lady as all members of one "family."

[This commentary is abridged from an item in *The Explicator*, 26 (Jan. 1968), 43, by Laurence Perrine.]

Emily Dickinson **WHAT SOFT, CHERUBIC CREATURES** (page 100)

The "gentlewomen" are ladies of gentle birth and breeding, the upper class in their small New England communities, embodiments and arbiters of social fashion and conduct. Proper in their opinions, respectable in their behavior, refined in their manners, tasteful in their dress, they seem so spotless in their virtue that to approach one of them with sexual intent would be as unthinkable as to "assault a plush" (the ultimate in softness and elegance) or to ravish a star (a symbol of lofty purity). With their "dimity convictions" (firmly held opinions about the social proprieties), these women have an abhorrence for anything vulgar, coarse, or "common." They are, the poet begins to suggest, over-refined. They are "ashamed" of "freckled human nature," and thus, though totally unaware of the fact (faithful in church attendance as they undoubtedly are), they are ashamed of "deity"; for Christ, the poet subtly reminds us, numbered laboring class people among his apostles (four were fishermen) and associated with prostitutes (Mary Magdalene). The "gentlewomen," shocked by any unseemly or indelicate behavior—drunkenness, profanity, sexual misdemeanor— are unaware of their own deeper sins against the Holy Spirit: self-righteousness, snobbery, social exclusiveness, lack of true Christian charity. "He that is without sin among you, let him first cast a stone at her," said Christ of the woman taken in adultery (John 8:7); but probably one of Dickinson's gentlewomen had already cast it. In the last two lines, the poet scornfully turns Christ's own words (Luke 9:26) against one of these gentlewomen, thus showing that the adjectives used of them in the first half of the poem ("soft," "cherubic," "gentle-," "refined") were meant ironically. LP

William Blake **THE CHIMNEY SWEEPER** (page 101)

Blake uses dramatic irony here for sympathetic rather than detractive purposes. In line 3 the boy, too young to articulate clearly, is calling out his trade in the streets—sweep, sweep, sweep, sweep—but the poet is telling us that we should weep over his pitiful plight. In lines 7–8 the innocent boy is genuinely trying to comfort his friend and does not recognize, as the poet does, the ironical discrepancy between the comfort he intends and the lack of comfort he actually offers, for losing one's hair is hardly compensation for not being able to have it soiled! In line 24 the boy's words are an expression of a childlike trust that the poet, with more experience of the world, knows to be unfounded: the poem, in fact, is a protest against the harm that society causes its children by exploiting them for labor of this kind. In each case the dramatic irony arises from the poet's knowing more or seeing more than the child does, but in each case also the boy's ignorance testifies to his good heart and likable innocence.

The dream in lines 11–20 is obviously a wish-fulfillment dream, though Blake would not have been familiar with this Freudian terminology. It is also a miniature allegory, capable of two interpretations, one applying to this world, the other to the next. On the first level—most obviously the wish-fulfillment level—the "coffins of black" are the chimneys the boys work in, the Angel who releases them is a wise legislator or rich benefactor (like Oliver Twist's Mr. Brownlow) who releases them from the bondage of their labor with the key of social legislation or of wealth, and the green plains represent a happier future. At this level, the dream represents only a wish or a hope. On the second and perhaps more relevant level, the coffins are real coffins and the Angel is one of God's angels who releases the boys into heaven with the key of death. At this level, the poet is saying that the only release for these boys, under the then existing conditions of society, is through death.   LP

Percy Bysshe Shelley   **OZYMANDIAS** (page 103)

The central theme of "Ozymandias" is the vanity of the claims of human tyrants to enduring glory. It is brilliantly conveyed through irony of situation: the overturn of expectation by fulfillment. After reading the inscription on the pedestal, the second line of which may be paraphrased, "Look on my works, ye mighty (but lesser) kings, and despair of ever equaling them," one expects to look up and see a great imperial city with marble palaces, temples, hanging gardens, monuments, and fortified walls; instead, as far as the eye can reach, one sees only emptiness and sand.

Increasing the irony is the fact that the sole remaining work of this self-proclaimed "king of kings" is a huge broken statue (its hugeness manifesting his megalomania), carved by an artist who saw through the self-deluding egocentrism of the ruler and recorded it in stone, mocking Ozymandias, as it were, to his face. In "the frown, / And wrinkled lip, and sneer of cold command," the sculptor knew that his imperceptive and arrogant master would see only the signs of his awesome authority and power whereas the more perceptive viewer would note the absence of joy, wisdom, compassion, and humility—the marks of true greatness—and see only crude ambition and cruel passions. The insight of the artist has outlasted the power of the conqueror.

The emptiness of Ozymandias's pretentions to everlasting fame is further increased by the fact that this whole account has been related to the speaker by "a traveler from an antique land." That is, the speaker would never have heard of Ozymandias at all had it not been for his chance encounter with a desert explorer. (And most of us, in our turn, would never have heard of Ozymandias had the poet Shelley, another artist, not written a poem about the incident.)

No English reader in 1817 could have read this poem without thinking of Napoleon, who had almost made himself conqueror and ruler of all Europe before he was defeated at Waterloo in 1815 and exiled on the barren island of St. Helena in 1817. In more recent times we may be reminded of Hitler, Mussolini, Stalin, or Mao.

Except for the awkwardness caused by the separation of the transitive verb "survive" (7) and its objects "hand" and "heart" (8), the poem is brilliantly written. In "Nothing beside remains" (12), the word "beside" means both "beside" and "besides." The alliterating *b*'s, *l*'s, and *s*'s of the last two lines put a heavy emphasis on the words that re-create the vast level emptiness, and the final unstopped vowel sound allows the voice to trail off into infinity.

Two pitfalls for the student: (1) The "hand" that mocked the passions of Ozymandias is the sculptor's; the "heart" that fed those passions was Ozymandias's. The passions depicted in the stone visage have outlasted both the artist and the tyrant. (2) The words on the pedestal were not composed by the sculptor. Ozymandias commanded the sculptor to inscribe them there. The sculptor "mocked" Ozymandias by his frank portrayal of the ruler's character in the sculptured visage.   LP

Exercise (page 104)

1. Paradox. 2. Irony. 3. Overstatement. 4. Understatement. 5. Paradox. 6. Overstatement. 7. Paradox ("immortal" is ironical). 8. Overstatement (containing also metaphor and personification). 9. Literal (but "soul" is a metonymy). 10. Paradox.

Richard Lovelace   **TO ALTHEA, FROM PRISON** (page 104)

The central paradox of the poem is that one may be free even when confined, at liberty even when in prison. The paradox is resolved by seeing that the liberty spoken of is a spiritual liberty, while the confinement is physical. Each of the first three stanzas describes a specific liberty that one may enjoy even in prison. The final stanza generalizes. But each of the first three stanzas also describes an additional confinement (not physical but metaphorical) inseparable from its liberty. The poem is therefore not simply one paradox developed, but a nest of paradoxes.

In stanza 1 when Cupid with "unconfinèd wings" brings the speaker's sweetheart to whisper of her love for him through the prison bars, even though he is "tangled" in her hair and "fettered" to her eye, the "birds that wanton in the air" know no such liberty. The comparison of his liberty to that of birds is appropriate to a stanza that begins with a winged Cupid hovering within his prison gates.

In stanza 2 when the speaker and his fellow prisoners gather to drink wine (undiluted by water, for which "Thames" is a metonymy) and to toast the health of their king and of each other, even though their heads are "bound" with rose-wreaths and their hearts with loyal ardor, "Fishes that tipple in the deep" know no such liberty. The comparison of his liberty with that of fishes is appropriate to a stanza that begins with flowing liquids, wine and water.

In stanza 3 when, like caged songbirds, the speaker sings the praises of his monarch, the "enlargèd winds" that stir the ocean up into waves know no such liberty. The poet is "committed" here in a double sense—consigned to prison, dedicated to the cause of his king. The use of the word "enlargèd" (set free) to describe the winds may derive from the Greek myth that Aeolus, their father kept the winds in a cave from which he released them at need. The comparison of the speaker's liberty to that of the winds is appropriate to a stanza that begins with singing, the movement of air from throat to lips.

Stanza 4 expresses the central paradox of the poem in strongly opposed terms: stone walls and iron bars, freedom of the soul. The emphasis here is so much on spiritual qualities and on words which suggest them—innocent and quiet minds, hermitage, freedom of soul, and freedom to love—that the only appropriate comparison is with the freedom of angels, who soar in higher spheres than the birds of stanza 1. LP

John Donne   BATTER MY HEART, THREE-PERSONED GOD (page 106)

In the first quatrain Donne metaphorically compares God to a tinker who is trying to mend a metal utensil such as a kettle. Donne (the kettle) cries out to God that he needs to be made anew, not just repaired. It is not enough for God to "knock, breathe, shine," He must "break, blow, burn," and batter. The parallel series of verbs reflect the three persons of the Trinity. The verbs "knock" and "break" belong to the Father (representing Power); "breathe" and "blow" belong to the Holy Spirit (the word *spirit* comes originally from a Latin word meaning "to breathe"; cf. *respiration*); "shine" and "burn" belong to the Son, a concealed pun on *sun*.

In the second quatrain Donne compares himself to a town "due" to God but "usurped" by Satan (or sin), who has taken captive God's viceroy, Reason.

The "enemy" (10) again is Satan (or sin). LP

John Frederick Nims   LOVE POEM (page 106)

The title may lead us to expect something about moonlight and roses, sighs and a broken heart. Instead, we are given taxicabs, streetcars, coffee, lipstick, and bourbon whiskey. But this is a modern love poem. It is appropriately placed among the realities of modern times (though streetcars have vanished since the poem's publication in 1947), and is more real in its passion because it is so.

Love poems traditionally praise the beloved, and so does this one. But it does not place her on a pedestal. She is clumsy, careless, unpredictable, never on time, "A wrench in clocks and the solar system." In short, she is also real—a human being, not a goddess. We love her the more for it. For her clumsiness with things is balanced by her deftness with people. The poem pivots on this contrast. She is hopelessly inept moving in traffic, but she maneuvers expertly "in traffic of wit." She may break cups, rip cloth, upset coffee, smear lipstick, and spill bourbon, but she knows how to put the nervous at their ease, to make the homeless feel at home, to steady the unsteady, and to join diverse people in a circle of good will, good conversation, gaiety, and love. She merits her lover's praise and devotion.

We may not expect to find wit in a love poem. But Shakespeare and Donne proved long ago that wit and deep feeling are compatible. The lover here, like his sweetheart, is able to maneuver expertly in traffic of wit: to speak of "The drunk clambering on his undulant floor," of lipstick "grinning" on a coat, of the "apoplectic streetcars" (the image is of the streetcar's madly jangling its bell at pedestrians or cars in its path), and of souls floating "on glory of spilt bourbon." Earlier poets loved to write about the soul, but seldom placed it in a context like this.

Overstatement is the traditional language of love poetry. The overstatements in this poem are as extravagant as any, but are used in dispraise as well as praise. The sweetheart is her lover's "clumsiest dear"; beneath her hands *"all* glasses chip and ring"; yet if her hands dropped "white and empty / All the toys of the world would break."

If his sweetheart died, her lover would be heartbroken. This is what the last line means. But it says it so as to make us *feel* it.

[Commentary adapted from Laurence Perrine and James M. Reid, *100 American Poems of the Twentieth Century* (New York: Harcourt Brace Jovanovich, 1966), pp. 165–66.]

Countee Cullen   INCIDENT (page 107)

Good poetry may be simple or complex. This poem relates a simple incident simply, in simple stanza form, without elaboration of metaphor or simile. And yet, in twelve lines, it sums up the poignant tragedy of the black experience in America —friendliness rebuffed, the childish hurt that leaves a scar, happiness turned to ashes.

Simple as it is, we should not regard it as artless. Notice how the four mouth-filling syllables "heart-filled, head-filled" in line 2 are counterpointed against the five skipping syllables of "Baltimorean" in line 3. Because the two hyphenated words are jammed with consonants and separated by a comma, and because they spread two metrical accents evenly over four syllables, they take twice as long to pronounce as the five syllables and three accents of "Baltimorean." The emphasis is appropriate to their emotional importance and gives them the sense of *fullness* required by the meaning. Notice also how the climactic incident of the poem is set off by the rhythm. The other lines of the poem are all to some degree end-stopped; even line 3 is followed by a natural pause. But lines 7 and 8 break in the middle, and line 7 is the one line in the poem which demands that the voice rush on to the next line without pause. Thus the contemptuous action and the contemptuous epithet are isolated by the rhythm. Finally, notice how the significance of the incident is brought home by understatement. We are not told that the speaker's glee was turned to pain, that the contemptuous epithet went through him like a sword or rankled in his consciousness, or that he felt suddenly crushed and humiliated.

We are told only: "Of all the things that happened there / That's all that I remember." Need we be told more?

[Reprinted from Laurence Perrine and James M. Reid, *100 American Poems of the Twentieth Century* (New York: Harcourt Brace Jovanovich, 1966), pp. 190–91.]

Donald W. Baker **FORMAL APPLICATION** (page 108)

Occasion: The poet reads in *Time* that "poets apparently want to rejoin the human race." Perhaps startled to learn that he does not already belong to it, he decides to submit a formal application for membership. Examining recent history (World War II was its central event), he finds that modern man has devoted his major energies to devising ingenious methods of subjugating and destroying other men. The chief qualification for membership, then, is to be a crafty killer. In his application (the poem) he therefore describes the program he proposes for himself in order to acquire the requisite skills.

The poem divides into three equal sections of three three-line stanzas each, marked off by "I shall begin," "Meanwhile," and "Finally." The first section describes how he will master the skill of knife-throwing; the second, how he will acquire the craft of deceit, teaching the birds to trust him; the third, how he will combine these skills to "qualify as Modern Man." He brings his application to a vivid climax in the central stanza of this section through the use of a bold figure of rhetoric in which he addresses the reader as if the reader were actually on the spot, and directs his attention to the "splash of blood and feathers" pinned by his knife to the tree, thus demonstrating that he has already acquired the requisite skills. To identify this gruesome exhibition more closely with other modern artifacts and accomplishments of modern man, he gives it a euphemistic label: "Audubon Crucifix."

The poem as a whole is an exercise in verbal irony. The poet's petition for membership in the human race is a mock-petition. His program for qualifying himself is one that he does not intend to carry out. If the human race is what it appears to be, and if he indeed has the option of belonging or not belonging, he chooses not to belong. In addition, the poem is filled with ironic contrasts between appearance and reality—between the "pleasing (even pious) connotations" of some of its phrases and the brutal realities that lie beneath them. The progress from primitive savagery to civilization implied by the capitalized term "Modern Man" contrasts with the greatly increased scale of terror and destruction actually characterizing the modern world. The technical phrases "conditioned reflex" from modern psychology and "functional form" from modern aesthetic criticism here disguise the nature of the skills they actually refer to. The contrasts between connotation and reality in the terms "Audubon Crucifix," "*Arbeit Macht Frei,*" "Molotov Cocktail," and "*Enola Gay*" are obvious.

The title embodies two distinct meanings. It refers not only to the official petition for membership that the poet pretends to be making, but also to the disciplined effort he mockingly proposes to undertake in acquiring a precise coordination of wrist and fingers in throwing the knife: that is, a rigorous application of himself to the mastery of "form." LP

W. H. Auden **THE UNKNOWN CITIZEN** (page 109)

The title alludes to the "Unknown Soldier." It is ironical because *everything* is known about the "unknown" citizen—except, apparently, his name. The information about him is filed under a code number. The citizen has been reduced to a set of statistics. The loss of his name symbolizes the loss of his individuality. The unknown soldier's *body* had been blown to bits; the unknown citizen's *soul* has been blown to bits.

In the old sense, a "saint" was a person who served God (line 4). In the "modern" sense, he is a person who serves "the Greater Community." The old-fashioned saints, to serve God, often had to defy the world—and in doing so, they found their souls. The modern saint, to serve "the Greater Community," must only do everything he is told to do—and in doing so, he loses his soul. The things "necessary to the Modern Man" are purely materialistic things—"a phonograph, a radio, a car and a frigidaire"—and they are "necessary" not mainly to serve the man but to keep the economy going. The unknown citizen had no opinions of his own, but adopted those of the State—that is, he accepted State propaganda. He "never interfered" with the education of his children: what his children really received was indoctrination, not education, and the unknown citizen never questioned the rightness of what his children were taught.

For Auden himself the questions "Was he free? Was he happy?" are the important questions, not absurd ones, and in his eyes *everything* was wrong. The answers to the questions are that the unknown citizen was *not* free, though he never realized his lack of freedom, and that he was neither happy nor unhappy, for it takes a *man*, with a soul, to be happy or unhappy—and to be a man, one must be free, at least in his soul. The unknown citizen did not live; he existed. He was not a man but a statistic, a comfortable conformist, a pliant tool in the hands of the State.

The satire in the poem is against several tendencies of modern life: its increasing demands for conformity, uniformity, and collectivization; its materialism; and its disposition to do everything by statistics, to exalt the "average," and to put life into the hands of social scientists and managers. The old-fashioned saint was an extraordinary man; the modern one is an average man—if he can be called a man.

Be sure to ask students, "*Was* he free? *Was* he happy?" LP

Robert Frost **DEPARTMENTAL** (page 110)

The poem is a gentle satire—not against mankind or human nature—but against the increasingly departmentalized structure of the modern bureaucratic state, in which all human functions and needs are provided for by the state, with a resultant depersonalization of human relationships, specialization in human interests, and loss of individuality.

The satire is gentle because it is comic, and it is comic partly because the society actually observed is an ant society (we can be amused by behavior in ants that would be unamusing to us in human beings) and partly because of Frost's comic treatment (playful riming, humorous personifications, constant flow of whimsy). But this ant society is symbolic of modern human societies.

"Ants are a curious race" (13)—This generalization coming at the conclusion of the first example of ant behavior (the discovery by an ant of a huge dormant moth) and serving as introduction to the second illustration (the discovery of a dead ant of the colony by another member) is literally true in one sense of the word "curious"; but, ironically, what is curious about them is that, in another sense, they are an extremely incurious race: they have no curiosity about matters unrelated to their own assigned duties in the colony. The ant who discovered the moth "showed not the least surprise. / His business wasn't with such." The ant who discovers his dead fellow isn't "given a moment's arrest— / Seems not even impressed." But both ants pass the word along to the proper authorities, and the second illustration concludes with a "solemn mortician" heaving the dead ant "high in air" and carrying him away. "No one stands round to stare. / It is nobody else's affair."—It is not that ants are apathetic or lazy (each is extremely busy pursuing his own assignment, and the whole society seems to function fairly efficiently); it is just that they are so extremely specialized. (No provision is made for grief, wonder, or personal relationships in the efficiently organized bureaucracy.) Nor is it that ants are selfish or self-centered: the adjective "selfless" (24) implies just the opposite: they devote their whole energies to serving the welfare of the colony (the "Greater Community" of Auden's poem); but, in doing so, they have become self-less in another sense: lacking selfhood. To shift metaphors violently, they are cogs in a machine.

The poem begins with the poet's having just observed the behavior of an ant on his dining table. (The interest shown by the poet in the much smaller ant contrasts with the lack of interest shown by the ant in the much larger moth.) This observation leads him to ruminate about ants in general, and to provide a second illustration of their behavior from past observations. The whimsy in the first observation about "the hive's inquiry squad / Whose work is to find out God / And the nature of time and space" is perhaps a thrust at the departmentalized University. The whimsy in the second illustration about the state burial is clearly aimed at the bureaucratic nation-state. For further discussion, see John Robert Doyle, Jr., *The Poetry of Robert Frost: An Analysis* (Johannesburg: Witwatersrand Univ. Press, 1962) pp. 92–99. LP

M. Carl Holman **MR. Z** (page 111)

M. Carl Holman is a black poet, and "Mr. Z" is the ironic portrait of a black man who attains distinction in life by disowning his own racial and cultural heritage and adapting himself to the manners and values of the white world. He is apparently light-skinned, for he is able to do this quite successfully, and he marries a white woman who, out of a similar motivation, has disowned her Jewish heritage and is adapting herself to the manners and values of the gentile world. The marriage is a marriage of convenience for both of them, for through the marriage, they are both enabled to shake off some of the social stigma of their own backgrounds. There is also the suggestion that neither of them could have acquired a purely white gentile mate of respectable social pretensions: they have had to settle for the second best, which is nevertheless better, in their eyes, than marriage within their own cultures.

In giving Mr. Z only an initial, not a name, the poet suggests that Mr. Z has lost personal identity by disclaiming racial identity. In choosing the last letter of the alphabet for that initial, the poet suggests his own low opinion of Mr. Z. The satire of the poem is directed mainly at Mr. Z and the type of person he represents. But the satire also hits, secondarily, at the snob values of a WASP society that make people like Mr. Z and his wife possible. Mr. Z is clearly a person of considerable ability, and in a healthy society he could have remained himself and still have acquired the kind of recognition he needed.

The obituary notices cruelly reflect the false values of this society by making Mr. Z's distinction relative, not absolute. There is subtle though probably unconscious condescension in the statement that Mr. Z was "one of the most distinguished members of his race." (Implication: He did pretty well for a black person. Further implication: Blacks are inferior.) But the obituary notices are particularly cruel for Mrs. Z, for they implicitly reveal the fact which all their lives she and Mr. Z labored to conceal. This is irony of situation.

There is muted irony throughout the poem: "perfect part of honor" (2), "faced up" (7), "exemplary" (9), "profane" (10), "right" (17), "not one false note" (23). The first ironic note is in the first line, and it might be labeled either verbal or dramatic. The reader realizes, as Mr. Z's "teachers" and Mr. Z do not, that an accident of birth cannot possibly be a "sign of error." (One infers, incidentally, that Mr. Z was lighter skinned than his mother, and that his father may have been white.) LP

Robert Browning **MY LAST DUCHESS** (page 112)

Speaker: The Duke of Ferrara. Time: Late Italian Renaissance, probably mid-sixteenth century. Place: An upper room or corridor in the Duke's palace. Audience: An envoy from the Count whose daughter the Duke plans to marry. Occasion: The Duke and the Count's emissary have just concluded negotiations over the terms of the marriage and the dowry which the Duke expects to receive with his bride. (Students need to know that a duke of Ferrara was a supremely powerful figure, equal in status to a king.) On their way to join the company of guests and courtiers in the assembly hall below, they pass a portrait of the Duke's former duchess, and the Duke pauses to display it for the emissary, engaging him now in what seems purely social talk.

The primary subject of the poem is the character of the Duke, but Browning is interested in his character also as it reflects his period in history (the pride and arrogance of the aristocracy, its system of arranged marriages, its enthusiasm for art and artists). A secondary and pendant point of interest lies in the character of the duchess.

The Duke is characterized, first, by pride—pride of birth and station. He is a duke—let no one forget it!—and one with "a nine-hundred-years-old name!" His dissatisfaction with his former wife (but he refers to her always as his "duchess") is that she forgot it. Instead of being lofty and reserved like himself, saving her smile only for him, thus enhancing the eminence of his station, she treated social inferiors as equals, blushed when they complimented her, was too visibly pleased when they did her favors. She did not comport herself like a duchess! And why didn't he try to correct her? Because to do so would be to "stoop." Even if she accepted his tutelage without making excuses or arguing back (the ultimate humiliation)—"E'en then would be some stooping; and I choose / Never to stoop!" A proud purchaser doesn't haggle over defects in the merchandise; he simply sends it back and demands replacement.

Second, the Duke is cruel. Were it not for the "stooping," the Duke would not hesitate to tell his wife "This . . . in you disgusts me." But since he wouldn't stoop, he "gave commands; / Then all smiles stopped together." What were the commands? Browning doesn't tell us, and doesn't need to, for the very tone in which the words are uttered sufficiently underlines the Duke's cruelty and arrogance. But probably they were to have the duchess put to death. In the opening lines, "That's my last duchess painted on the wall, / Looking as if she were alive," the subjunctive mood implies that she is no longer living—a suggestion repeated in line 47.

Third, the Duke is a connoisseur of art. There is no need to believe that his love of art is not genuine: love of art can coexist comfortably with egotism and cruelty in some natures (read *The Autobiography of Benvenuto Cellini*); and this was a time of great enthusiasm for art and artists. The Duke is a patron and collector of art. He speaks appreciatively of the merits of Fra Pandolf's painting and keeps a protective curtain in front of it which he allows no one but himself to draw. Nevertheless, his love of art is not pure; it too reflects his pride. He is proud of having commissioned work from painters and sculptors of such eminence as Fra Pandolf and Claus of Innsbruck and he carefully drops their names into his conversation ("I said Fra Pandolf by design"). Part of the value of his Neptune taming a sea-horse is that it is "thought a rarity," and that Claus of Innsbruck cast it in bronze "for me!"

Finally, the Duke is shrewd. He knows what he wants, and he knows how to get it. While apparently simply making pleasant conversation about the shortcomings of his former duchess, he is indirectly informing the envoy what he expects in his new duchess, knowing that the envoy will report it back to the Count. Primary evidence of the Duke's shrewdness is his skill in speech. His disclaimer of such skill (35–36) is part of the evidence for it, and should remind the reader of a similar disclaimer by Shakespeare's Mark Antony in his oration on Caesar, which serves a similar purpose. It is a rhetorical trick, designed to throw the listener off his guard. The Duke's momentary gropings after words (21-22, 31-32) by no means support this disclaimer, for the words he eventually comes up with are exactly the right words, and the hesitation in his speech only serves to give them added emphasis. But the conclusive proof of the Duke's skill in speech is the beautifully modulated passage (48–53) in which he couches his demand for dowry. Clearly the dowry is his main motivation in this new marriage (he is driving a hard bargain: his rank and nine-hundred-years-old name for her money), but he is too polished to avow this openly, so he adds, "Though his fair daughter's self, as I avowed / At starting, is my object." The words "I repeat" and "as I avowed / At starting" show that the Duke has mentioned both of these matters before, in reverse order; he is now driving them home in the order of their real importance making sure he is clearly understood. The passage is a masterpiece of diplomatic circumlocution. Though the nature of the demand is made perfectly clear, it is gloved in a sentence softened by a double negative and by a skillfully tactful and euphemistic choice of diction: not "riches" but "munificence"; not "proves" but "is ample warrant"; not "my demand" but "no just pretense of mine"; not "refused" but "disallowed," The hard bargaining is thus enveloped in an atmosphere of perfect courtesy. The Duke's diplomatic skills are also shown throughout in his treatment of the emissary, which is subtly designed to flatter. After the business conference, he gives the emissary a private showing of his prized portrait and chats in a friendly manner about personal affairs. This courtesy, from the man who is accustomed to give commands and who objected to too much courtesy in his Duchess, is apparent throughout the interview: "Will't please you sit and look at her? . . . Will't please you rise?" And when the envoy, having risen, waits respectfully for the Duke to precede him downstairs, as befits his eminence, the Duke tells him, "Nay, we'll go / Together down, sir." And so the envoy walks side by side down the stairway with the possessor of a nine-hundred-years-old name who has just said, "I choose / Never to stoop." How can he do other than return a favorable report to the Count?

So much for the Duke, what about the Duchess? The Duke paints her as being frivolous, trivial, too free in manner, "too easily made glad." The reader's reaction to her, however, is controlled by the genuine pleasure she takes in compliments; by her graciousness to all, regardless of station; and especially by the simple things she takes delight in: the beauty of a sunset, a gift of a bough of cherries, a ride round the terrace on a white mule. Her response to these indicates a warm, sensitive nature which takes joy in natural things rather than in gauds and baubles or the pomp of position and power which attract the Duke.

The poem is a masterpeice of dramatic irony, a dramatic irony which is manifested chiefly in the whole tone of the poem rather than in specific passages. The Duke speaks all the words. He seeks to give a favorable impression of himself (and no doubt succeeds with the envoy, who belongs to his world and has not our advantage of perceiving him through the lens of art) and an unfavorable impression of his last duchess. What Browning conveys to the reader is exactly the opposite. LP

John Hall Wheelock EARTH (page 114)

It may be useful to ask students whether the irony in this poem is verbal or dramatic. It is, of course, verbal. The adverb "drily" (defined in the *O.E.D.* as meaning "with quiet sarcasm or caustic humor") shows the speaker to be fully aware of the implications of his remark. LP

8. Allusion

Robert Frost "OUT, OUT—" (page 116)

A newspaper account would have given us facts—the boy's name, his age, the exact place and time of the accident. The poet, as omniscient narrator in this poem, is interested in communicating experience. The first six lines provide a vivid sense of the setting through combined images of sight (sawdust, stove-length sticks of wood, five mountain ranges under the sunset), of smell (the resinous scent of new-cut timber), and of sound (the onomatopoetic snarling of the buzz-saw as the timber is pushed through it, its onomatopoetic rattling as it waits for the next load). Vivid visual imagery continues through the poem (the boy holding up his injured hand, the boy under ether puffing his lips out with his breath). The poem also provides dialogue (as a newspaper account wouldn't except in the form of a witness's answers to a reporter's questions) and includes the poet-narrator's own comments ("Call it a day, I wish they might have said . . ."; "the saw, / As if to prove saws knew what supper meant, / Leaped out at the boy's hand . . ."; "No more to build on there.").

The role of chance is underscored in the poem in that the boy's death is really a double-accident. The cutting of the hand is caused by a moment of inattention, but moments of inattention rarely have such a dire consequence. The boy's death is caused by shock, but fatal shock infrequently follows such a "minor" accident. The boy does not expect it. The attendants can't believe it. There is indeed a terrible situational irony involved in the swift progression from the boy's first reaction ("a rueful laugh") to his perception that the accident may cost him his hand to the ending that no one anticipates.

The abruptness of the last line-and-a-half misleads some students into thinking the central theme of the poem identical with that of Housman's "Is my team ploughing" (page 21): namely, that life goes on without us when we are gone just as it did before. To be sure, these lines do embroider the central theme with the truth that individual death does not bring human life to a halt. But Frost deliberately leaves the antecedent of "they" ambiguous, and he does not say how quickly "they . . . turned to their affairs." We should not assume that the sister returned to the normal course of her life as quickly as did the doctor, or that the unseen parents immediately resumed their lives as if nothing had happened.   LP

e. e. cummings IN JUST- (page 119)

In this little poem about "Just- / spring"—that is, the very first beginning of spring—cummings captures the perennial delight of the children in a world that is "mud-luscious" and "puddle-wonderful" and in which they can again play outside at marbles and piracies and hop-scotch and jump-rope. The setting is urban, and the whistle of the balloonman advertising his wares in the park or along the sidewalks brings the children running.

The description of the "little / lame balloonman" as "goat-footed" links him (or identifies him) with Pan, half-man, half-goat, the Greek god of nature and legendary inventor of the panpipes. When Pan blew on his pipes in the spring, all the little creatures of the field and wood came running. Thus cummings's city scene reenacts ancient ritual, and the "queer / old balloonman" ushers in the season that begins life anew as he has done each spring since the beginning.

Though the poem is written in free verse, it is organized into alternating four-line and one-line "stanzas" with a floating refrain in the thrice-repeated "balloonman whistles far and wee" each time preceded by an announcement that it's spring. The hyphenated adjectives "mud-luscious" and "puddle-wonderful" express exuberance in the assonance of their principal vowel sounds and echoing *d*'s and *l*'s; the hyphenated nouns "hop-scotch" and "jump-rope" display assonance and consonance respectively; the lines "luscious the little / lame balloonman" glide on alliterating *l*'s; and breathless "eddieandbill" and "bettyandisbel" echo each other in both vowel and consonant sounds. The whole builds up to a celebration of spring and the children's delight in it. cummings called it a "Chanson Innocente." LP

John Milton **ON HIS BLINDNESS** (page 119)

The three parables grouped together in Chapter 25 of Matthew's Gospel teach the necessity of being prepared for the day of judgment, for the coming of the Lord. They emphasize chiefly two aspects of preparedness: that the Lord's arrival will be sudden and without warning, and that the actions of the waiting life are an enactment of the judgment to be made (and, as in the third parable, verses 31–46, that men cannot recognize the meanings of all their actions). The middle parable to which this poem alludes teaches that the state of being prepared for the Lord's return is an *active* state, which insofar as possible requires the servants to perform as their master has performed—even if, to their limited understanding, the master has seemed a sharp dealer more interested in profit than in justice.

The parable of verses 14–30 contrasts the behavior of servants of a lord who in his absence are entrusted with sums of money. Two of them employ the money as their lord had, in trade and usury, and double their sums, while the third buries the one talent he has been given. When the lord returns from his travels, the two who have doubled his money are rewarded, but the one who only has the single talent to surrender back is cast "into outer darkness." The parable has been interpreted to equate the talent with faith, and to mean that one must not merely possess faith, but employ it in the manner God intends. (Taken literally, of course, it seems to teach the value of investing and taking risks, and castigates the person who merely hoards and saves.)

Milton had begun going blind in the late 1640s; this sonnet has been dated variously from 1652 to 1656, while Milton was actively involved in his duties as Oliver Cromwell's "Latin Secretary," a position roughly equivalent to secretary of state, explaining and justifying Cromwell's Puritan regime to the monarchies of Europe. In the sonnet he ponders his future life and work, contrasting the possible use of his literary talent (and his faith) in ways far different from writing public statements and pamphlets supporting the Cromwellian theocracy. The poem seems to report a crisis in his life, examining the alternatives for a writer who wants his gifts to fulfill God's plan for him.

In his blindness (both physical and, momentarily, spiritual) Milton laments that he is not employing his talent, which he supposes useless to do the Lord's work, and fears that when he is confronted by his Maker and made to render his account, he will be cast away. He foolishly is about to ask how a man whose sight has been taken by God can be expected to do the same work as others. But his patience, personified, forestalls the question, telling him that his affliction is not a heavy burden and that his service to God may be merely to "stand and wait" rather than to pursue a life of action.

The word "wait" has several relevant meanings (this poem might be used as the occasion for students to learn to consult the *Oxford English Dictionary*, with its full historical definitions). It may mean to await—that is, to stand in readiness for the master's arrival; or to wait upon—to attend to less active tasks than the "thousands" who range over the world carrying out the Lord's commands, as Milton figuratively is doing for Cromwell. In obsolete meanings current in Milton's time, it also meant to hope or to expect, or—a definition that returns to line 1—to consider. Patience is thus counseling him to accept his less spectacular tasks, to be ready for whatever God intends, to live in Christian hope and expectation of his salvation, and to return to the starting point of the sonnet—to consider again.

In the octave, Milton appears to misunderstand the meaning of the parable, thinking it unfair of God to expect "day-labor" from one who has been deprived of eyesight. But like the verbal echoes of the language of trade, the objection to the parable is literal-minded; properly understood, as Patience instructs him, it teaches him to bear what he must, to stand in readiness, and not to believe that only great activities gain God's grace, for the best service is performed by those who accept their limitations and maintain an active faith.

The word "prevent" is the hinge of the sonnet, occurring at the point separating the octave from the sestet. In its sense of "forestall" it reveals that the ideas of the sestet prevent him from voicing the foolish question which his considerations have led him to. In its further reference to the concept of "prevenience," it suggests that the advice of Patience is an action of God predisposing him toward performing God's will. In both senses, it reveals a circularity in the poem: "as I was about to murmur my complaint, Patience counseled me to consider again." This circularity is also suggested in the obsolete meaning of "wait," to consider. In effect the poem says that a reading of the parable momentarily led the poet to a misunderstanding of God's purposes, but God's prevenience checked him in time to see what those purposes really are. The half-rebellious mood of the octave never turns into open rebellion.

For further discussion of this sonnet, see: Marjorie Nicolson, *A Reader's Guide to John Milton* (New York: Farrar, Straus and Giroux, 1963), pp. 152–55; E. M. W. Tillyard, *Milton* (New York: Collier Books, 1967), pp. 160–62; and Macon Cheek, "Of Two Sonnets of Milton," reprinted in *Milton: Modern Essays in Criticism*, ed. Arthur E. Barker (New York: Oxford University Press, 1965), pp. 125–35. TRA

Emily Dickinson **GOD IS A DISTANT, STATELY LOVER** (page 120)

"In this was manifested the love of God toward us, because that he sent his only begotten Son into the world, that we might live through him." In these words from the First Epistle General of John (4:9)—echoing the more famous formulation in the Gospel According to St. John (3:16)—Emily Dickinson found her grounds for drawing a parallel between Christian doctrine and *The Courtship of Miles Standish.* God (Miles Standish) sends his younger colleague Christ (John Alden) into the world to woo for the love of the human soul (Priscilla). But, asserts Dickinson, God was shrewder than Miles Standish. Lest mankind "choose the envoy and spurn the groom" (as did Priscilla), God has taken the precaution of avouching that He and Christ are identical. Clearly the poet is taking a sly dig at the Christian doctrine of the Trinity, which asserts that in the one God there are three divine Persons—the Father, the Son, and the Holy Spirit—and that, as the First Council of Nicaea declared in 325, the Son is "of the same essence as the Father." This subtle and complex doctrine, intricately worked out by Christian theologians over the course of several centuries, is the object of Dickinson's satire in this poem—not the concept of God, nor of God's love for humanity (though, in other poems, Dickinson can be sometimes skeptical of these broader concepts as well). LP

Alden Nowlan **AUNT JANE** (page 121)

Aunt Jane died intellectually (became senile) at ninety, ten years before she died physically. The last two lines of the poem repeat, with a significant change, the last two lines of the well-known prayer, "Now I lay me down to sleep, / I pray the Lord my soul to keep; / If I should die before I wake, / I pray the Lord my soul to take." This prayer appeared in *The New England Primer* (*c.*1683), a Calvinist school book from which generations of American school children learned to read (in its frequent revisions it is estimated to have sold over five million copies). The change in the prayer makes the poem express the speaker's horror of living on in body, like Aunt Jane, after one's mind (or soul) has completely gone. LP

A. E. Housman **ON THE IDLE HILL OF SUMMER** (page 121)

The speaker is a Shropshire lad recumbent on a hill in summer. Conflict is raised within him by the sound of drilling soldiers. He would prefer to stay where he is, enjoying the lazy pleasures of summer. But the drum, the bugles, and the fife, together with the marching files of men in their scarlet uniforms, seem to summon him to join the colors. He knows that acceptance of the summons may lead to death on some distant battlefield. But the summons is insistent, and in the end he reluctantly submits to it. "Woman bore me," he says in a tone of bitter resignation; "I will rise." He must endure the fate of all mortal men ("Man that is born of woman is of few days and full of trouble," *Job 14:1*); he will rise from his recumbent posture and join the troops—enlist in the army. (The primary meaning of "rise" here is to get to one's feet, but behind it lurks another dictionary meaning, to take up arms, to go to war.)

The movement of the poem is from idleness to action, and the syntax mirrors that movement. The pace of the first stanza is leisurely. Not until the third line does it release the subject-verb-direct object—"I hear . . . drummer"—of its single statement. The rest of the stanza is filled with modifiers. The second stanza is also leisurely. It too makes a single statement, inverted in word order. The verb—"go"—is given at the end of the second line, its subject—"Soldiers"—withheld till the fourth. The third stanza accelerates. It makes two statements. The first occupies three lines, with verb and subject, again inverted, in the second line—"Bleach . . . bones." The second occupies a single line, its subject—"None"—and its verb—"return"—each briefly modified. The fourth stanza, continuing the acceleration, makes five statements. One each, all in normal subject-verb order, is made in each of the first three lines—"bugles hollo," "fife replies," "files . . . follow"—though each line contains modifiers also. The culminating line, in which the speaker makes his decision, consists of two terse statements, both in normal order, both unmodified—"Woman bore me, I will rise." Nothing here remains but the bare grammatical bones: subject-verb-direct object; subject-verb.

Though the movement of the poem is from idleness to action, there is ambivalence of feeling throughout. The first two lines of the poem sound like the beginning of a pastoral idyll; still there is a slightly negative connotation in the adjective "idle," and in the second two lines the peaceful serenity of the first two is intruded upon by the sound of the "steady drummer" in the distance. In his half-trance the speaker hears it, and the sound exerts a hypnotic effect upon him, "like a noise in dreams," both disturbing and compelling. It leads him to think, in the next two stanzas, of the soldiers—all young men like himself—and of their fates. He thinks of the soldiers as "lovely lads," "dear to friends"—men whom he would enjoy as "comrades." But then he thinks of their fates; they are "food for powder" (the phrase, taken from a speech by Falstaff in *I Henry IV*, IV, ii, anticipates the modern phrase "cannon fodder"), and the bones and rotting corpses of *their* comrades are buried "East and west on fields forgotten" (Britain's nineteenth-century wars were fought on foreign soil, mostly on the fringes of the empire). He thinks of these men, with some overstatement, as being fated "all to die" (and so they are, but not all in battle): "None that go return again" (either alive, or to England). The final stanza is filled with the imagery of lively martial music and parading soldiers in their colorful dress uniforms, but again the effect is ambivalent. The bugles "hollo," the "screaming" fife replies, the soldiers follow "gay." There is something highly attractive in this life, but one knows what it leads to. In the last line the speaker assents to it, but assents to it grudgingly, as if bowing to human necessity. All men must die, and many must die in battle. One cannot dwell forever on "the idle hill of summer." LP

William Butler Yeats LEDA AND THE SWAN (page 122)

What this sonnet describes, quite literally, is a rape. The action of the rape is indicated precisely through sexual terms and symbols. The first quatrain describes the fierce assault and the foreplay; the second quatrain, the act of intercourse; the first part of the sestet, the sexual climax; the last part, the languor and apathy following the climax. But this is no ordinary rape: it is a rape by a god, by divine power temporarily embodied in the majestic form of a swan. And so it is described in terms that bring out awesomeness, not sordidness. The divinity appears as a "feathered glory" and its assault is "a white rush." It is also a momentous rape: it has large consequences for the future. And so the climax is described in terms that convey not only the experience of orgasm but also its remote consequences: the destruction of Troy, the death of Agamemnon. And then, after the moment of passion is over, and its results indicated, Yeats asks a question about the significance of the act: "Did she put on his knowledge with his power?"

Neither the word *swan* nor the name *Zeus* is mentioned in the body of the poem. We must rely on the title for our cues to the mythological event. Leda was a mortal princess by whose beauty Zeus, king of the gods, was smitten, and with whom he consummated his passion in the form of a swan. There are several versions of this story, but in all of them Helen of Troy was one offspring of this union, and in the version used by Yeats, Clytemnestra was another. [See William Butler Yeats, *A Vision* (New York: Macmillan, 1956), p. 51.] The later abduction of Helen by the Trojan prince Paris from her husband the Greek king Menelaus led, of course, to the ten-year siege of Troy by Greek forces under the command of Agamemnon and to the ultimate defeat of the Trojans and the burning of Troy by the Greeks. On his return from Troy, Agamemnon was murdered by his wife Clytemnestra and her lover. (It matters little which version of the Leda story we know, the ultimate results are the same.)

In her union with the god, Leda clearly took on some of the power of the godhead, for she bore in her womb the forces that were to shape the future. Did she also take on his knowledge? The question can be formulated in different ways. Can human sexual passion ever foresee its consequences? Can power and wisdom coexist in human life? Can man ever combine the vitality and passion of youth with the knowledge and wisdom of age (cf. "The Coming of Wisdom with Time," page 143)?

The question posed is left unanswered. Critics differ over whether an answer is implied. Some say the question is left open: that it is unanswerable. Others claim that it is the third of three rhetorical questions asked in the poem, all implying a negative answer (lines 5-6: "They can't"; lines 7-8: "It can't help but feel"; lines 13-14: "No."). Others suggest that power and knowledge can be combined in moments of artistic inspiration. This is a rich poem. For three provocative discussions, see Arnold Stein, in *Sewanee Review*, 57 (Winter 1949), 617-20; Hoyt Trowbridge, in *Modern Philology*, 51 (Nov. 1953), 118-29; Leo Spitzer, in *Modern Philology*, 51 (May 1954), 271-76. LP

Edwin Arlington Robinson **VETERAN SIRENS** (page 122)

The "veteran sirens" of the poem are aging spinsters who are unable to accept either their age or their spinsterhood gracefully but continue to invoke rouge, lipstick, nail paint, hair dye, bright clothes, and artificial gaiety in an effort to simulate youth and attract men. They fail to perceive that middle- and old-age can have their own beauty when accepted with dignity and without pretense. The silver hair of age is "a far comelier diadem" than the dyed hair and painted mouth which attempt to conceal age but actually only make it ridiculous. The central irony of the poem is that these women, in attempting to make themselves appear young and attractive, actually make themselves less attractive.

Both allusions work ironically. The sirens were sea nymphs, therefore immortally young, whose song was irresistible to mariners. Ninon is the exception to the human rule—the one woman out of billions who *was* able to defy age for a time and remain sexually attractive to an advanced age. She is hardly a reasonable model for most women. The "veteran sirens" of the poem are almost as "far from Ninon" as they are from the sirens of mythology.

Though Robinson brilliantly exposes the folly and vanity of these women, his deepest feeling toward them is one of compassion. Like the "ghost of Ninon" he "would be sorry" to "laugh at them." He is sorry for their blindness and is constrained from laughter by a charity based on human understanding.

Yvor Winters, in *Edwin Arlington Robinson* (Norfolk, Conn.: New Directions, 1946), p. 33, asserts that this poem is "an expression of pity for old prostitutes who must continue as best they are able at their trade," and Louis Coxe, in *Edwin Arlington Robinson: The Life of Poetry* (New York: Pegasus, 1969), pp. 105, 110-12, endorses this view (but without advancing evidence or argument) against those "obtuse" critics who read the poem otherwise. I am one of these. Winters' interpretation would imply that the prostitutes would like to give up their trade but are forced by economic necessity to keep on. But if they are "unpursued" (16), it is hard to see how they *can* go on economically. Robinson pictures his women as "deceived" by folly and vanity, not as driven by economic necessity. Theirs is a "burning hope" for a husband, not a desperate hope for a customer. I enlarge on this argument in *The Explicator*, 6 (Nov. 1947), item 13. LP

T. S. Eliot **JOURNEY OF THE MAGI** (page 123)

The traditional story tells of the three Magi, journeying from the East, following a star, bearing gifts of gold, frankincense, and myrrh, to worship the child in the stable. When the star stopped over Bethlehem, the Bible tells us, "they rejoiced with exceeding great joy." Eliot's poem undercuts our sentimental anticipation almost immediately. It doesn't mention the star; it says nothing of gold, frankincense, and myrrh; above all, it doesn't represent the experience as one of transforming joy.

Eliot's narrator, one of the Magi, is remembering the journey a long time after it happened, perhaps dictating it to be put in writing by a scribe (33–35). He begins with a description of the hardships of the journey: freezing weather, bad roads, refractory camels, unreliable camel men, hostile cities, unfriendly towns, dirty villages, high prices. Instead of following a star with unwavering confidence and joy, they are plagued by doubts telling them this journey is "all folly." As they near their destination, they encounter indications suggesting hope of something better—a temperate valley, a running stream, a white horse; but these indications are balanced by less hopeful ones—"six hands at an open door dicing for pieces of silver." (The images here anticipate events or symbols connected with the life and death of Christ —the three trees, the three crosses on Golgotha; the white horse, the first of the four horses of the Apocalypse, a symbol of Christ; the vine leaves and wineskins, the wine of the Eucharist; the six hands dicing, the soldiers who diced for Christ's garments; the pieces of silver, the thirty pieces for which Judas betrayed Christ.) When they finally reach the stable, instead of presenting a glorified vision of a haloed Christ child surrounded by adoring shepherds and angels, the narrator can only say, "It was (you may say) satisfactory."

The poem is concerned with the experience of conversion, of spiritual rebirth. Conversion, as Eliot depicts it and as he knew it, is not necessarily a sudden transcendent experience accompanied by light from heaven and "exceeding great joy." It may instead be a slow painful process, accompanied by doubt of its validity, by spiritual agony and perplexity. It means destruction of one's former beliefs and way of life and their replacement by a new, more demanding way of life. "This Birth," the speaker says (he is referring both to the birth of Christ and his own rebirth), was "hard and bitter agony for us, like Death, our death." It made them no longer able to live comfortable lives among their people, whose beliefs they no longer shared. Yes, he would do it again, he says; but he does not say so eagerly. He yearns, in fact, for another death—physical death—to put an end to a difficult, demanding life.

[This commentary is adapted from Laurence Perrine and James M. Reid, *100 American Poems of the Twentieth Century* (New York: Harcourt Brace Jovanovich, 1966), pp. 133–34.]

Anonymous **IN THE GARDEN** (page 125)

If the answer to the question is not immediately forthcoming, it should be possible to elicit it from any class by means of a leading question or two. For example, the instructor may ask: Why does the poet say "the garden" instead of "a garden"? Is any garden so famous that one may refer to it as "the garden" and count on being understood?

It is also useful to ask why (besides for rime) the poet compares the maid to "flowers of the morn" instead of to flowers at noon or flowers at evening, for this question points up the difference between ordinary logic and poetic logic. Morning, noon, and evening flowers are equally fair, but there is a symbolical connection between the morning of a day and the morning of a man's life. Poetic logic calls for as tight a coherence of all details in the poem as possible. Emotional connections are more important than strictly logical ones.

A few students may need to have it explained that Eve was never "born."   LP

9. Meaning and Idea

Anonymous **LITTLE JACK HORNER** (page 126)

"Little Jack Horner," of course, presents an example of dramatic irony—a boy who sticks his thumb in a pie is *not* a good boy. LP

Sara Teasdale **BARTER** (page 127)

Robert Frost **STOPPING BY WOODS ON A SNOWY EVENING** (page 128)

The statement that the reader should be able to enjoy both these poems does not imply that they are of equal poetic value. Frost's poem is by far the richer, more resonant, more tightly structured of the two. Teasdale's poem is unified by its central metaphor of buying and spending. Its first two stanzas, after their opening thematic statement, comprise a brief catalogue of beautiful things, all lovely in themselves, but with no ordering principle beyond that dictated by the rime scheme. Frost's poem has a tight narrative and dramatic, logical, and psychological organization in which no lines or images could be interchanged without loss. There is further discussion of "Stopping by Woods . . ." on pages 139–40. LP

Robert Browning **SONG** (page 129)

Percy Bysshe Shelley **DIRGE** (page 130)

Both poems are brief (eight-line) lyrics which draw their imagery from nature and conclude with a judgment about the world.

Browning's song is from his drama *Pippa Passes*, where it is sung by Pippa, a small girl on her annual holiday from her work in the silk mills. In context it is therefore dramatic, and the last line may be said to reflect Pippa's mind rather than Browning's. The last line may also be viewed as more the expression of a mood than a considered judgment on life. It is the spontaneous reaction of a youthful spirit to a beautiful spring day (anyone who has never felt this way might as well be dead.) In a deeper sense, however, the last line does reflect Browning's own view of life: though he saw plenty of evil in the world, he believed in a divine justification for it.

Where Browning's song consists of a series of declarative statements with verbs in the indicative mood, Shelley's dirge consists of a series of apostrophes leading up to a main verb ("Wail") in the imperative mood. There is also a possible ambiguity in Shelley's last line, where "world's" might be interpreted as a noun in the possessive case or as a contraction of noun and verb. The comma after "Wail," however, favors the latter reading, making the final clause directly opposed in meaning to Browning's. Still, Shelley's generalization is not so sweeping as Browning's (Pippa's), for it does not say that the world is *all* wrong. And again the question arises whether the generalization should be taken as considered judgments on the state of the world or as the expression of a temporary mood. Taken as a considered judgment, the two poems are irreconcilable. As expressions of passing moods they are opposed but reconcilable. The same person might feel each way on different occasions. Both poems truly reflect human feeling.   LP

William Cullen Bryant   **TO A WATERFOWL** (page 130)

Robert Frost   **DESIGN** (page 131)

Bryant's and Frost's poems both begin with an observation from nature and end with an idea about God, but their conclusions are diametrically opposite. Bryant observes the solitary waterfowl at sunset as it flies on its annual spring migration to its summer breeding grounds in the North. Though the air through which it flies is "pathless," empty, and "illimitable," the bird is not lost (Bryant tells us), for there is "a Power [God] whose care" teaches it its way through "the boundless sky" and "guides" it safely to its destination. The poet concludes optimistically that he can safely entrust his own life to the guidance of the same Power.

The connotations in Frost's poem work in two opposite directions. First, there is a series of words and images suggesting innocence—"dimpled," "heal-all," "morning," "right," "snow-drop," "flower," "blue," "innocent," and the five-times repeated "white." Second, there is an equally impressive sequence suggesting evil—"spider," "death," "blight," "witches' broth," "froth," "dead," "night," "darkness," "appall." The collocation of these two kinds of words seems to pose a question.

The design indicated by the title is formed by three things—a white heal-all, a white spider, a white moth. The heal-all, a wild flower with medicinal virtues, is usually blue. Spiders are ordinarily black or brown. What has brought together these three white things, two of them so rarely white? It would seem the work of a conscious artist. But what is the consequence of this artistry? Death. The white moth, lured by the usually protective kindred color of the heal-all, has been trapped by the spider and killed. It is held now "like a white piece of rigid satin cloth" (the image not only describes a dead moth exactly but suggests the lining of a coffin). The three white things are thus "like the ingredients of a witches' broth." The suggestion that these ingredients have been mixed "to begin the morning right" (rite?) is ironical. There is irony also in the connection of the innocent color white with this sinister enterprise of death.

In the eighteenth century, a favorite argument for the existence of God was the so-called "argument from design." The intricate construction of the universe, it was held, with all of its stars and planets whirling in mathematically chartable courses and regulated by the law of gravity, testified to the existence of an infinitely wise creator, for how could there be design without a designer? As the nineteenth Psalm so eloquently expresses it, "The heavens declare the glory of God, and the firmament showeth his handiwork."

Frost's title alludes to this famous argument in a grimly ironical fashion. For the design, Frost points out, in nature is that of "a witches' broth." Thus the poem asks a terrible question,

> What brought the kindred spider to that height,
> Then steered the white moth thither in the night?
> What but design of darkness to appall?—

Perhaps the universe is governed, not by infinite goodness, but by infinite evil. The poem does not assert this proposition as an actuality, merely suggests it as a possibility. And the suggestion is immediately softened, apparently, by the provision of another possibility—that perhaps design does not govern in a thing so small. But the afterthought, tossed in so casually, when examined closely turns out to be not very comforting either. If nature is not governed by design, then it is governed merely by chance, coincidence, anarchy, chaos—certainly not by the traditionally omnipotent benevolent God who is concerned over the smallest sparrow's fall.

Cast in the sonnet form but confining itself to only three rime sounds (the title might refer to the pattern of the poem as well as to the design made by the three white things in nature), Frost's brief poem chillingly poses the problem of evil.

Bryant's use of the verb "guides" (30) and Frost's of "steered" (12) makes Frost's poem seem almost a reply to Bryant's. The waterfowl's instinct in Bryant's poem guides it unerringly to its distant destination. Conclusion: a benevolent God presides over the universe and protects His creatures. The white moth's instinct in Frost's poem steers it unerringly into the spider's trap. Conclusion: perhaps the Power which presides over the universe is malevolent rather than benevolent, evil rather than good. Bryant offers reassurance; Frost offers terror. Frost's terror is more authentic than Bryant's reassurance, for Bryant ignores the fact that many waterfowl do *not* escape the fowler (5). (Whooping cranes were almost extinguished in the nineteenth and twentieth centuries to provide feathers for ladies' hats.)

Bryant's poem has been called a "great lyric" by Yvor Winters [*In Defense of Reason* (New York: Alan Swallow & W. Morrow, 1947), p. 239]; it was greatly admired by Matthew Arnold, and was once enthusiastically described by Hartley Coleridge as "the best short poem in the English language" [John Bigelow, *William Cullen Bryant* (Boston: Houghton Mifflin, 1890), pp. 42–43]. "Design" is surely one of the most powerful sonnets in the language.

[This commentary is partially adapted from Laurence Perrine and James M. Reid, *100 American Poems of the Twentieth Century* (New York: Harcourt Brace Jovanovich, 1966), 46–47.]

In essence the poem is an affirmation of man's spiritual greatness—a greatness that will enable him to survive and transcend any physical destruction of the world. It consists of three stanzas, similar in construction and parallel in thought, whose progression is mainly in the violence and scope of the destruction imagined and, correspondingly, in the increasing force of the counterstatement affirming man's spiritual strength. A generalized paraphrase for all three stanzas might run as follows:

a. What if some natural catastrophe should destroy man's world or even his universe? (four lines)
b. Let it blow (or, what though it blow, smash, or change) fair things into foul, or things of greater into things of lesser worth. (two lines)
c. Man's spirit will survive and surmount this physical destruction. (two lines)

Throughout the poem cummings uses the parts of speech unconventionally, substituting verbs, adjectives, and adverbs for nouns. He strains syntax but seldom beyond the breaking point; he seeks out striking sound correspondences but does not abandon sense for sound. (In line 1, for instance, the word "which," chosen for its alliteration with "What" and its consonance with "much," indicates the materiality of the destructive wind; "which" relates in meaning to "thing" in line 11 and contrasts with "whose" in line 15 and "who" in line 24. In line 9 the word "keen," while it rimes internally with "lean," has a double meaning. As adjective-turned-noun it indicates the sharpness of the wind; as a noun in its own right it means a wailing lamentation for the dead—the sound of the wind, and appropriate for the occasion.)

Stanza 1 imagines a fierce fall wind that exposes as false the gentle aspect of summer. This wind is cosmic in its dimensions. It strips the trees of their blood-colored leaves and sends them whirling against the sun. It displaces eternal stars from their positions in the constellations. If such a storm occurred, it might reduce king to beggar, and queen to a false appearance of one. It might alter friend to fiendish foe (in the fierce struggle for existence) and reduce space (an immensity) to time (a limiting dimension for men). Let it do so, the poet says, for after the worst it can do, the "single secret will still be man." The word "secret" represents what is unknown and ultimately unknowable, because it is miraculous and spiritual.

In stanza 2 the storm imagined is a winter storm—one which "flays" like a whip, "strangles" like a hangman's noose, and "stifles" as Othello does Desdemona with the white bedclothes. The allusion here is not to *Othello*, however, but to the glacial period of earth's history when whole genera of earth's creatures were wiped out. As the storm in stanza 1 was extended in space, so this one is extended in time. What if a new ice age were to come, the poet asks, strangling valleys with ropes of ice, stifling forests with snow? (The adverb-noun "ago" suggests the past by its meaning and snow by its modifier "white.") Though such a storm turn hope into terror and seeing to blindness, turn pity to envy and reduce soul to mind (in his poetry cummings consistently denigrates mind or logic), still those men whose hearts are large

78

like mountains and whose integrity has roots like trees, will survive the catastrope and greet returning spring with joy.

The cataclysmic event of stanza 3 seems less a wind or snow storm than a cosmic explosion: it doesn't just blow things away, it blows them apart. And its action destroys not just the earth but the universe. The stanza begins deceptively with two words that ordinarily in cummings' poetry have positive connotations: "dawn" and "dream." The seasonal sequence suggests returning spring. But the word "doom," thrusting "dawn" and "dream" apart, obliterates these pleasant expectations. This dawn is the beginning of a nightmarish catastrophe—one so destructive that it "bites the universe in two / peels forever out of its grave / and sprinkles nowhere with me and you." This explosion annihilates the universe, it destroys time and replaces life with eternal nothingness, and it blows our bodies to bits and scatters them over the nothingness where the universe was. Nevertheless, says the poet, still undismayed, let it blow "soon" to "never" (may the expected spring never come); let it blow "never" to "twice" ("twice" seems trivial after "never"); let it destroy all physical life and thus make death a thing of the past. In proportion to the number of persons killed in this cosmic explosion (all persons living), the more intense will be the "life" of the indestructible spirit. The human soul will survive the destruction of the universe and of all physical life.

[This discussion is abridged from a commentary by Laurence Perrine in *NMAL*, 4 (Spr. 1980), item 12.]

e. e. cummings **WHEN SERPENTS BARGAIN FOR THE RIGHT TO SQUIRM** (page 133)

The speaker in this Shakespearean sonnet is the poet, speaking for himself and individuals like himself, pronouncing judgment on that collective entity "mankind" (which he elsewhere refers to as "manunkind").

The three quatrains of the sonnet all begin with "when," and the concluding couplet with "then." The general sense is that when natural things and creatures begin engaging in certain kinds of activities peculiar to mankind, only then (and not until then) will the poet "believe" (trust, or have faith) in mankind. But since natural things will never engage in these activities, the poet will never believe in mankind. Mankind is and will remain an "incredible unanimal." "Incredible" means (a) not to be believed or trusted, and (b) so fantastically outrageous in his behavior that one can hardly credit his existence. The word "unanimal" here implies that man's behavior is so unnatural, so far beneath the behavior of serpents, thrushes, and owls, that he is hardly to be classed in the animal kingdom. He belongs in some lower order.

The activities depicted in the three quatrains all manifest mutual distrust, fear, suspicion, and hostility between the segments of mankind. They are also collective activities—that is, actions not of self-affirming individuals but of groups or members of groups relying for support on the common self-interest or the common fears and prejudices of the group. Many of the activities make the naturally superior subject to the mercy or the authority of their inferiors (roses/thorns; thrushes/screech-owls; oak/birch; mountains/valleys; april/march). Contractual arrangements would be unnecessary in a world where men could trust one another. In a truly human (humane) world, men would not have to "bargain" for their natural rights, "strike" to obtain a living wage, make application for permission to sing, or get a license to reproduce; they would not "accuse" or "denounce" or "view" each other "with alarm." Men could rely upon each other to be honest, charitable, and just in their relationships.

"what if a much of a which of a wind" and "when serpents bargain for the right to squirm" are only in apparent contradiction. cummings characteristically divides the human species into two groups: the great-hearted few and the small-minded many. The former poem celebrates only those individuals "whose hearts are mountains, roots are trees" and affirms their eternal survival. The latter poem satirizes collective man or "mankind"—the heartless and soul-less many. LP

Gerard Manley Hopkins **THE CAGED SKYLARK** (page 134)

"The Caged Skylark" is an Italian sonnet. The octave concerns the relationship of the spirit and the body in life, the sestet, the relationship of the spirit and the resurrected body in eternity. The basic analogies may be expressed thus:

1. spirit-in-life : body = caged skylark : cage
2. immortal spirit : resurrected body = wild skylark : nest = meadow down : rainbow

Both a rainbow and a shadow are perfect images for weightlessness, but a shadow suggests evil, fear, darkness, death, whereas a rainbow suggests hope, joy, beauty, God's compact with man in the Bible. Hopkins' rainbow beautifully demonstrates how a poet gets extra dimensions of meaning out of his words and images. LP

Philip Larkin **AUBADE** (page 134)

While the irony in Richard Wilbur's title "A Late Aubade" (page 49) merely overturns a reader's expectation of a poignant dawn parting of lovers, Larkin's irony reaches deeper: his dawn song is not wistful about separating from a mistress, but terror stricken at the prospect of the inevitable parting from life itself.

Larkin does not make that life attractive, but tedious and mundane. It is a life of work, offices, and telephones, with only drink and "people" to relieve the boredom or the lurking fears of death. The emphasis is not on beauty or pleasure or love, all to be lost in the obliteration of death, but on the fear of nothingness. The images associated with life provide the only defense against the thoughts of death, and they are images of social connection, culminating in the last line: "Postmen like doctors go from house to house." All of us, that is, share in the disease of fearing death, and the cure comes in links with other people; but communication is a temporary cure, an alleviation of the *fear* but certainly no defense against death itself or the knowledge of its inevitability.

The time of the poem, four o'clock in the predawn morning, is a time of total darkness and silence. Staring into "soundless dark" is like staring at death, for the two primary senses of hearing and sight have been lost. Deprived of physical sense, the speaker must "see" what his mind knows, "the total emptiness for ever, / The sure extinction."

Neither the rich, elaborate fabric of religion—now tattered and "moth-eaten"—nor the fallacious plausibility of the plainer fabrics of rationalism is sufficient to hide the naked fact of fearfulness; rich or plain, these are mere covers or garments, incapable of disguising the reality at such a time as this.

And "courage is no good" at such times, because it cannot alter the fact the speaker is staring at. Since he defines life in its social connections, "to love or link," courage seems only a matter of social behavior that has value in the impressions one gives to other people. "It means not scaring others" with the horrifying truth that the speaker understands and faces. He does display another kind of courage, though —the courage to acknowledge to himself his fears, and to look into the darkness with honesty.

The final stanza, in which the dawn slowly comes, restores the speaker's physical senses, and leads him to project the resumption of daylight activities. The terror subsides, and the fact of "what we know," though it is as plain and as familiarly unremarkable as a piece of furniture, may be ignored in the workaday world. The knowledge that he has faced when alone can be put aside; the dilemma of knowing that "we can't escape" death and "yet can't accept it" can be postponed another day. TRA

Archibald MacLeish **ARS POETICA** (page 136)

The poet's philosophy of his art is summed up in the opening and closing lines of the poem's third section. A poem is concerned with experience, not with propositional statements. When it is successful, it is "equal" to the experience it creates; the reader properly responds to it by imaginatively "living" that experience, not by judging the content of the poem as right or wrong, true or false. To create experience, the rest of the poem tells us (and illustrates in its telling), the poet must rely upon images and symbols.

"Ars Poetica" has three sections, each of which starts with what seems a paradox or a violation of common sense. Section one declares that a poem should be "palpable" and "wordless." Yet if we run our fingers over this poem as printed on the page, the only palpable thing is the page; our fingers mark no distinction between recipe, advertisement, poem, or blank sheet of paper. And does not MacLeish's statement that a poem should be "wordless" run directly counter to Wallace Stevens's (in "The Noble Rider and the Sound of Words," *The Necessary Angel*) that "Poetry is a revelation in words by means of the words"? No, I think not. What

MacLeish means is that the "experience" or "revelation" created is wordless. When we read a poem, we must be acutely sensitive to the words used, but with the final result that we are drawn into an imaginative experience in which we see "globed" peach or pear, or draw our thumb over an old medallion, or feel the soft moss and worn stone of an ancient casement ledge, or watch a flight of birds crossing the sky.

Section two asserts that a poem "should be motionless in time, / As the moon climbs," which seems contradictory in itself, for how can something be "motionless" and yet climb? Yet the moon "climbs" so slowly that its motion is imperceptible except when it can be related to some earthly object, such as the horizon or a "night-entangled tree," and watched for some time. What is this section saying about a poem then?—That when we read it, we are so caught up in the experience created that we are unconscious of the passage of time? Or that the experience it creates lingers in the mind and fades from memory slowly and almost imperceptibly? An excellent case for the latter reading is made by Edwin St. Vincent, in *The Explicator*, 37 (Spr. 1979), 14–16, through a detailed analysis of the difficult syntax of this section.

And so we come to the summary third section which says that a poem should be "equal to: / Not true," and "should not mean, / But be." Does this mean that a poem should be meaningless? No, only that its "meaning" (what I have called in this chapter its "total meaning") is an *experience*, not an idea or propositional statement, and is expressed through images and symbols. The symbolic image of an "empty doorway and a maple leaf" (suggesting absence, loneliness, and the transitory quality of life) creates "all the history of grief," and the images of "leaning grasses and two lights above the sea," (suggesting perhaps a summer field where two lovers might lie overlooking the ocean) creates the experience of love.   LP

10. Tone

W. H. Davies   **THE VILLAIN** (page 140)

Emily Dickinson   **APPARENTLY WITH NO SURPRISE** (page 140)

The title and the image in the last two lines of Davies' poem both suggest stage melodrama, and therefore a kind of theatricality exaggerated or remote from reality.

Dickinson's poem may profitably be compared with Frost's "Design" (page 131), for both poems raise similar issues, and both (like Melville in *Moby-Dick*) make the color white, usually associated with purity and innocence, take on exceedingly sinister connotations.   LP

William Butler Yeats   **THE COMING OF WISDOM WITH TIME** (page 143)

Yeats associates youth with "leaves," "flowers," and "sun," which are agreeable, and with "lying," which is disagreeable. He associates age with "truth," "wisdom," and "oneness," which are agreeable, and with "wither," which is disagreeable. Thus he carefully balances youth and age as to favorable and unfavorable qualities. Yeats is neither exulting over a gain nor lamenting a loss; but he *is* lamenting the fact that one can't have everything at once—beauty, vigor, and enthusiasm, *and* wisdom. Life is never complete: one gains some desirable qualities at the expense of losing others. LP

Michael Drayton   **SINCE THERE'S NO HELP** (page 143)

From the first eight lines of this sonnet it seems apparent that the speaker (the male, as we shall see) and his beloved are breaking off their relationship. Does the speaker want to break it off? He asserts quite positively, perhaps too positively, that he does (3–4), but even in these first eight lines this assertion is undercut by the implication that he is acting under constraint ("Since there's no help") and by the suggestion that at any future meetings they may have difficulty disguising their still-existent feelings for each other. If any doubt remains that he does not really want to break off, it should be dissolved by the sestet, especially the last two lines, where he declares that she could still bring their love back to life, if she only would. He obviously hopes that she will. The rich allegorical and poetic language of the sestet, as opposed to the clipped, prosaic language of the octave, indicates that his true feelings come out here, feelings that he deliberately falsified in the octave. The exclamation point at the end is additional evidence.

Does *she*, then, want to break off the relationship? Although she is given no words in the poem (he is the speaker throughout), the "Nay" beginning in line 2 is a clear signal that this line is spoken in response to some gesture or word of protest made by her against his pronouncement in line 1. She does not want to "kiss and part." A further clue to her feelings is provided by his including her along with himself in his forecast of the difficulty *both* will have in concealing their feelings at future meetings.

But if neither of them *wants* to break off the relationship, *why* are they breaking it off? To answer this question, we must examine the allegorical death scene depicted in the sestet. When asked how many figures are involved in this scene, students initially answer four. But do we then have two dying figures, two deathbed scenes? Or are not "Love" and "Passion" two different names (suggesting the spiritual and the physical aspects) for one dying figure? Clearly they are one person, most fittingly called "Love-Passion." There is only one deathbed (11), and the dying figure is referred to by a singular pronoun in each of the last four lines ("his," "his," "him," "him"). The masculinity of the pronoun suggests that the dying Love-Passion is *his* (the speaker's). The logic of the situation suggests that the two attendants at the bedside, Faith kneeling in prayer, Innocence pulling down the eyelids of the presumably dead figure, are *hers*. By a subtle associative logic these two attendants, ostensibly present to ease the death, are made to appear the causes of the death. Her innocence is closing up the eyes of his passion; her faith (religious scruple) is assisting at the bedside. Yet, he asserts, if she would, she might at the very moment of death—"Now"—in an instant—bring his love-passion quite suddenly back to life. Surely, the situation is clear. Though the woman wishes to retain his love, she also values and wishes to preserve her innocence (her purity, her chastity); her faith tells her that fornication is a sin. He claims that, by refusing to satisfy his passion, she is causing both it and his love (they are one and the same) to die. LP

A. E. Housman FAREWELL TO BARN AND STACK AND TREE (page 144)

The story told goes back to that of Cain and Abel, and this association and extension back through time deepens its pathos. How long will brother kill brother? we ask. In its fundamentals human life shows little change through time.

The speaker, in a sudden quarrel or outburst of anger, has killed his brother on the hill they had been mowing together and is about to go into self-imposed exile. He is bidding farewell to the places and things he has loved, and, most specifically, he is saying goodbye to his close friend Terence. He takes thought for the future loneliness and despair of his mother, who "had two sons at break of day," and who tonight—one son dead, the other fled—will be alone. In offering his hand to Terence he is acutely conscious that the blood of guilt on it has replaced the sweat of honest toil, and in taking leave of Terence he wishes him the things he has himself lacked—the strength of emotional self-control, a sweetheart to keep him steady, and good luck. The "long-will-wait" repetitions of the final stanza are eloquent understatements, for his absence will be not long but forever. The hayrick and the sheepfold are metonymies for the farmland he has known and loved, and the "empty plate" and "dinner" especially eloquent metonymies for the comforts and security of the home he will never know again.

The poet's attitude toward the speaker is one of pity and compassion, not of aversion or accusation or blame. He shows this by his characterization of the speaker as a person of deep human affections and attachments, who will suffer a lifetime of exile from the things and places and people he has loved simply because of a moment of weakness. (The detail of the "half-mown hill" shows the suddenness of the outbreak.) The speaker exhibits no meanness or cruelty of character and expresses no satisfaction over his brother's death, only a full realization of its consequences. He is seen and shown by the poet not as evil but as a victim of human frailty and bad luck. LP

Tony Connor **ELEGY FOR ALBERT HUBBARD** (page 145)

"Elegy for Albert Hubbard" laughs at its subject, though not ungently, and singles out all his faults, though not bitterly. The poet makes one feel that a "character" has passed away, and that, though the new man will do better work, some color and interest will have passed out of life with Hubbard's passing. But the tone of the elegy is ironic: the word "elegy" makes us think of "Lycidas," "Adonais," and "Thyrsis," and leads us to expect praise and lamentation. The tone of this elegy disappoints these expectations: it is detached and gently satiric. Chiefly, the poem presents a graphic sketch of a "character." LP

Robert Frost **THE TELEPHONE** (page 146)

The poem is a dialogue between two lovers at the close of day upon his return from an all-day walk set out on in the morning. Whether the lovers are a married couple or are still in the courtship stage of their relationship is uncertain, but he has returned to the "here" (2)—home, summer hotel, village, or whatever—where both are living. At the farthest point of his walk, there had been an hour "all still" (probably about noon) during which he had felt a strong urge to be with his beloved and had felt intuitively that she was feeling a simultaneous wish to have him with her; now he is back and is trying to confirm the truth of that intuition. He goes about it playfully but delicately, inventing a fanciful story of her calling him on her telephone—the flower on the windowsill—and his receiving the call on a telephone—a flower—in a field where he was resting. (Early telephones were comparable in shape to daffodils, and the two flowers may, though need not, be taken as daffodils.) But of course he has made up this fantasy, and, as soon as he says "I heard you talk," he interrupts himself to say "Don't say I didn't," in order to keep her from denying it before he has well begun. Then, because he does not want to embarrass her or himself by putting words in her mouth that she might be forced to deny, and because he really wants to hear from *her* lips the confirmation that he was wanted, he breaks off from telling her what he heard her say, to ask, "Do you remember what it was you said?" But she is cautious too, unwilling to commit herself to the role until she knows more fully the part he has imagined for her. "First tell me what it was you thought you heard," she says. So the lover elaborates on his story, completing the metaphor of the telephone call; but again, when he gets to the crucial point, he hesitates to put words in her mouth and still wants *her* to say them, so he turns again to questions—"What was it? Did you call me by name? Or did you say—" And then he sees how to handle the problem—by saying what he wants her to admit having felt, but without himself putting the words in her mouth: "*Someone* said 'Come.'"—It works. "I may have thought as much," she confesses, "but not aloud." Then joyously and triumphantly (though quietly) he affirms the truth of his fiction: "Well, so I came."

"The Telephone" is a poem of subtle dramatic interplay, delicate fancy, shared feeling, and deep tenderness. The two lovers are dramatically differentiated—the male ardent, fanciful, playful, but also diffident; the female more down to earth but open and responsive. Whether a telepathic message has actually been communicated between the two lovers—as he wants to believe, and as the title perhaps implies—is left open for the reader to decide for himself. It is, in any case, not unusual for two lovers simultaneously to wish to be together.

[This discussion is adapted from an item in *Notes on Contemporary Literature*, 10 (May 1980), 11-12, by Laurence Perrine.]

John Wakeman LOVE IN BROOKLYN (page 147)

The man—middle-aged, fat, lonely, employed by a large Brooklyn business firm at a desk job which requires him to write correspondence. The woman—younger, physically attractive, sent up from the Payroll Department within the year to be the man's secretary-typist.

The man, smitten, inexperienced with women, vulnerable, has after several months summoned up courage to invite the woman out for a drink and to declare his feelings for her. He does so ineptly, blurting out the words, addressing her by her last name, blowing his nose. The woman, though neither insensitive nor unintelligent, is hard and experienced, has undoubtedly been propositioned many times, and has developed defensive tactics. Her immediate response, splashing her drink, is "The hell you say." But then she senses there is something different about this case; she lights a cigarette, thinks hard, and explains a difference she has probably not had occasion to put in words before: there is a difference between loving a woman as a person and mere sexual desire combined with gratitude for good typing.

But she has underestimated his feeling. "You wanna bet? You wanna bet?" he blurts out in protest against her suggestion that he has just "drunk" his drink "too fast." Then, trying to articulate his feelings, he makes an almost grotesque comparison. Seeing her swing round on her typing chair made him "shake" like his first seeing, in World War II, a tank slide through some trees "like it was god." Somehow the very grotesqueness of the double comparison testifies to its sincerity. He means it.

Her response, conditioned by past behavior, is jocular, fending the propositioner off in a kind of ritualized game which she must not take seriously. Playfully she swings full circle on her bar stool, mimicking the motion of her typing chair which had "shaken" him so. "You think I'm like a tank, you mean?" she says, deliberately misinterpreting his meaning; "Some fellers tell me nicer things than that." But then she sees his face and realizes that this is no time to kid. The man is not only earnest, he is highly vulnerable.

The last four lines express the depth and hopelessness of the man's emotion, and the pity she is capable of beneath her hard outer shell. Though there is little prospect that she can return this man's feeling, she recognizes its extent and helplessness, and she presses his trembling hand hard to express her pity.

This, according to the poet, is love "in Brooklyn." In contrast to Frost's poem, Wakeman's is deliberately unromantic, even antiromantic. The bar setting, the crude colloquial language, the grotesqueness of the man, the hard outer shell of the woman— all remove it from the delicate pastoral world of "The Telephone." Even the girl's name, Horowitz, is chosen for its unromantic connotations. Though probably common in Brooklyn, it is decidedly uncommon in poems about love. The man's feeling for the girl is not one based on a mutuality of mind and spirit, as in "The Telephone"; yet it is a powerful and sincere gut feeling which is a good deal more than an itch. The poem portrays genuine feelings: the hopeless if grotesque yearning and vulnerability of the fat man have pierced the woman's defensive armor and moved her, if hardly to a reciprocated feeling—at least to profound pity.   LP

Emily Dickinson   **ONE DIGNITY DELAYS FOR ALL** (page 148)

Emily Dickinson   **TWAS WARM AT FIRST LIKE US** (page 149)

The theme of "One dignity delays for all" is that all of us, no matter how humble, will one day be honored and treated like nobility—namely, on the day of our burial. In the second stanza the funeral procession through the streets of the village is compared to the progress of a king, duke, or bishop through his domain. The hearse is a carriage, the casket is the royal chamber, the undertaker and his assistants are footmen, bells toll in the church towers, crowds stop to watch on the sidewalks or follow behind the hearse. In the third stanza the procession stops at the graveside, the officiating clergy ("dignified attendants") conduct a funeral ceremony (like a coronation ceremony or an official welcome to a visiting prince), and everyone takes off his hat as prayers are read and the casket is lowered into the grave. (The above account may be overspecific in its point-to-point comparisons, but the general meaning is valid.)

"Meek escutcheon" combines oxymoron and metaphor. Metaphorically it represents our humanity. Just as a coat of arms entitles its bearer to ceremonial treatment on all occasions, so our common humanity entitles us to ceremonial treatment at death. We may all look forward to this moment of grandeur. It "delays" (waits) for all.

"'Twas warm at first like us" describes the changes that take place in a body between death and burial. The poem begins its description at a point a split-second after the instant of death. Though still warm, the body has already become an "It," is no longer a *he* or *she*. Then, in almost clinical detail, are shown the loss of body warmth, the vanishing of expression from face and eyes, the stiffening of rigor mortis, the increasing and finally utter separation between the worlds of the dead and the living. In the final stanza, as it is lowered into the grave, the corpse is a mere thing, a weight, unable by any sign to assent or demur to what is happening. The final word "adamant" underscores its stoniness.

Written in Dickinson's characteristic elliptical style, the poem demands for grammatical completeness that we supply an *it* at the end of line 2, an *if* after "as" in line 12, and a completing verb (*show? manifest? manage?*) at the end of line 12. But the meaning is clear without these additions. Dickinson's omissions simply compact her meaning.

There may be a latent irony in the fact that the "dignity" that "delays for all" does not occur till we can no longer be conscious of it, but in the poem this irony is muted. The tone of the poem is generally one of excited anticipation, marked by the exclamatory elation of the last two stanzas, and by words like "dignity," "mitred," "purple," "crown," "state," "grand," "pomp," "surpassing," "ermine," and "escutcheon." Death in this poem is not the great democratizer, leveling all ranks, but the great "aristocratizer," elevating all to the status of nobility.

The tone of "'Twas warm at first like us," on the contrary, is one of unrelieved and increasing horror. Concentrating not on the funeral ceremonials but on the physical facts of death, it projects not an elevation in status but a reduction in status, from human being to thing. Its tone is determined by words like "chill," "frost," "stone," "cold," "congealed," "weight," and "dropped like adamant." Instead of "pomp surpassing ermine," it presents us with a dead body crowding "cold to cold."   LP

Alfred, Lord Tennyson   **CROSSING THE BAR** (page 149)

Thomas Hardy   **THE OXEN** (page 150)

Despite the fame and popularity of "Crossing the Bar," students often have difficulty with it, and it is well to make sure that they understand it. The two complementary sets of figures used to express approaching death are the coming of night and setting out on an ocean voyage. The momen of death in the first set is the disappearance of the last light of day: the arrival of "the dark." In the second set it is the moment of "crossing the bar": leaving the harbor, which belongs to the land,

and setting out on the ocean. As the land represents temporal life, the ocean—"the boundless deep"—represents eternity. "That which drew from out the boundless deep" is the soul: in Tennyson's thought the soul comes from eternity, takes fleshly embodiment during life, and returns to eternity upon death. Tennyson wants no "moaning at the bar"—no lamentation over his death—for his soul is returning "home," is passing on to eternal life, and will see its "Pilot" (God) "face to face" after death. The occasion should therefore be one for joy rather than for sadness.

The whole poem expresses Tennyson's faith in immortality. Despite its popularity, which stems largely from its message, the poem is a good one. An oversubtle cavil about the image of the pilot, raised by Brooks and Warren in their manual for *Understanding Poetry*, 3rd ed. (New York: Holt, Rinehart & Winston, 1960), is satisfactorily answered by G. Geoffrey Langsam in *The Explicator* 10 (April 1952): 40. For a debate about the tone of the poem, see James R. Kincaid, "Tennyson's 'Crossing the Bar': A Poem of Frustration," *Victorian Poetry* 3 (Winter 1965): 57-61, and Laurence Perrine, "When Does Hope Mean Doubt?: The Tone of 'Crossing the Bar,'" *Victorian Poetry* 4 (Spring 1966): 127-31.

"The Oxen" divides exactly in the middle, the first two stanzas presenting a scene from the speaker's childhood, the second two, one from his adult life. If we take the speaker as Hardy himself, or as a contemporary of Hardy, the two scenes are divided by Darwin's *Origin of Species* (1859) and by the dramatic decline of religious faith that it accelerated. In the poem the superstition of the kneeling animals is symbolic of the whole system of Christian belief that Hardy was taught as a boy and that he gave up as a man, but that, like Matthew Arnold (see "Dover Beach," page 258), he never ceased to regret. Though he can no longer subscribe to Christian doctrine or to its world view, he regrets the loss of the emotional security and comfort provided by that world view.

In emotional tone the two halves of the poem differ sharply. In the first two stanzas, there is a sense of warmth, of comfort, and of community. Young and old sit "in a flock / By embers in hearthside ease," and the speaker uses the plural pronoun "we." In the last two stanzas, there is isolation and darkness. The speaker uses the singular pronoun, refers to the barton as "lonely," and with the word "gloom" refers not only to the darkness of the night but also to the spirit of the times—the desolation caused by the loss of religious faith. The superstition of the kneeling oxen—and with it the divine birth and the resurrection—is dismissed as a "fancy," one that few people any longer accept, but that was nevertheless "fair" (attractive).

The word "hope" in Tennyson's poem and in Hardy's has opposite meanings relative to the expectations involved. Tennyson's *hope* expresses expectation without real doubt. Hardy's expresses a wish without real expectation. Tennyson's poem expresses confident faith that it will be so. Hardy's expresses a wistful yearning that it might be so. Hardy does not say that he would go out to the barton to see the oxen kneel. He says (in effect), "I *feel* I would go *if* someone asked me." But no one will ask him, and it doesn't occur to him to go alone. Moreover, if someone did ask him, he wouldn't really go. The feeling is an ephemeral one that would not survive the invitation. Hardy (or the speaker) is an intellectually sophisticated twentieth-century man who would feel himself a goose to go on such a fool's errand. To put this point across to a class, it might be useful to ask: Would Hardy go if someone asked him? Would *you* go? Today Charlie Brown may wait in the pumpkin patch on Halloween to see the Great Pumpkin, but he won't when he is five years older, and no one of high school or college age in America today would be caught dead waiting for Santa Claus to come down the chimney. Hardy's "hope" is a wistful yearning, not a hope.

Reading Tennyson's poem aloud, one should read the word *hope* very quietly, without emphasis, for to emphasize it is to express doubt, and the serenity and beauty of the preceding imagery indicate absence of doubt. One need not, in reading Hardy's poem, put artificial emphasis on "hoping": the inversion of accent (a trochee instead of an iamb) forces an emphasis on it. Hardy's poem, in its own way, is as quiet and as beautiful as Tennyson's, but the quietness comes from resignation rather than from faith. (For further comment, see the discussion of "The Darkling Thrush," page 179 of this manual.)   LP

Anonymous   **LOVE** (page 151)

There is a brief comment on these verses on page 225.   LP

Alexander Pope   **ENGRAVED ON THE COLLAR OF A DOG WHICH I GAVE TO HIS ROYAL HIGHNESS** (page 151)

The *speaker's* tone is plain enough: it is one of supreme *hauteur.* The *poet's* tone is more complex. Is there a bit of pride expressed in the title at being on such close terms with the King? A bit of flattery for the King in the implication that no higher honor could befall a dog than to belong to him? But surely some irony too in having dogs take pride in the station and birth of their owners. How much more snobbish can a creature get! Yes, a sly dig at snobbery in any station of life.   LP

11. Musical Devices

Ogden Nash **THE TURTLE** (page 153)

One might also ask why Nash chose to write about a turtle rather than a tortoise. The anatomical problem is the same for each. LP

W. H. Auden **THAT NIGHT WHEN JOY BEGAN** (page 155)

The two people in the poem have been disillusioned by their experiences with love. They have found that it is not lasting and that it ends in disappointment They have been "burnt" by it. Thus they are deeply skeptical about their present affair. It begins, as have past affairs, in the joy of sexual excitement; they are prepared to find in the morning that their attraction has little or no other basis. But in the morning they are still in love; days pass, then weeks; they begin to realize that they have found a true human relationship, one rooted in something deeper than sexual attraction.

The basic metaphor presents two foot travelers cutting across fields that they hope are the public fields of love where all may travel but that they fear my be private lands where they will be shot or apprehended for trespassing. The metaphor in lines 3–4 beautifully combines the visual image of the sun's horizontal rays awakening them from their dream and the metaphorical idea of the landowner's shooting them for trespassing—that is, destroying their temporary illusion of love. But as they hike for additional miles (days), they outgrow their nervousness and begin to believe in spiritual peace, for they are not reproached for trespassing and they can see in the future (through love's field glasses) nothing that is not genuine and lasting love.

The rime pattern:

Lines 1 and 4 (of each stanza): alliteration and consonance
Lines 2 and 3 (of each stanza): alliteration and consonance
Lines 1 and 3 (of each stanza): assonance
Lines 2 and 4 (of each stanza): assonance

In line 10 the last syllable must be thought of as beginning with *r* rather than with *p* to preserve the integrity of this pattern, and in line 12 the final syllable must be thought of as including the final *s* (really a *z*) of *his.* The whole is ingeniously worked out, along with the extended metaphor, and the poet's pleasure (and ours) lies partly in the working out of this design. LP

The theme of the poem might be stated in some such words as these:

The natural world is filled with the beauty and energizing power of its Creator. But men, ignoring God's authority, through their commercial and industrial activities have despoiled and polluted this beauty and separated themselves from its spiritually regenerating power. Nevertheless, this power is never used up; through God's love for his world, nature's beauty is continuously renewed.

How pale and flat this prose statement is as compared to the poem's "grandeur"!

In line 1 the word "charged" because of its associations with electricity and gunpowder, has many times the force of *filled*. In line 2 the image is of crinkled metallic foil (gold, tin, silver, or lead) being shaken in the sun and flashing light-reflections from each of its multifold creases and facets. In line 4 "rod" is a metaphor or symbol for God's authority and chastening power. In lines 7–8 the soil is "bare" because man has pitted it over with his heaps of coal and iron ore and paved it over with streets and walks; and man cannot feel the grass underfoot anyway because his feet are cased in shoes. (We need not assume that Hopkins denounces the wearing of shoes, though he may indeed think it good sometimes to walk barefoot in the grass.) Pavement and shoe leather serve the poet here as symbols for man's twofold separation from nature. In lines 11–12 the image of the sun's light disappearing in the west only to reappear next morning in the east is a symbol for the perpetual renewal of nature. And this renewal springs from the love of the Holy Ghost (third member of the Trinity) in His traditional metaphoric embodiment as a dove (symbol of gentleness and tenderness) brooding over the world (as over a nest) with warm breast and bright wings. The word "bent" means both that the earth is curved (as suggested by the preceding image of the sun's apparent travel around it) and bent out of shape from man's misuse of it.

Just as the world is charged with the grandeur of God, so this sonnet is charged with a rich verbal music appropriate to its subject. In its end-rimes it follows the strictest and most demanding pattern for the Italian sonnet (four rime sounds). Alliteration is apparent in almost every line, perhaps most briliantly in the three two-word clusters of line 14 (world *br*oods—*w*arm *br*east—*br*ight *w*ings). Assonance is especially apparent in line 11 (bl*a*ck-l*a*st, W*e*st-w*e*nt) and line 13 (H*o*ly Gh*o*st *o*ver). Consonance is prominent in line 1, where each stressed syllable ends with a *d* (worl*d*-charge*d*-gran*d*eur-Go*d*). In the question in line 5, where nine short monosyllables (all but two of them stressed) are spat out in rapid succession like bullets from a machine gun, there is internal rime (men-then), alliteration (now-not, reck-rod), and assonance (not-rod, reck-men-then); except for the initial "Why," each stressed syllable in the series gets into the act once if not twice. In line 6 the triple repetition of a whole phrase ("have trod") emphasizes the repetitiousness of the action described. In lines 6–7 two sets of internal rimes (seared-bleared-smeared; wears-shares) combined with three *sm-* alliterations (smeared-smudge-smell) put such an emphasis on words of disagreeable meaning as to give one a feeling of almost physical revulsion. But we leave this analysis incomplete; the reader's patience will be "spent" long before the poem's "music" is.

An interesting thematic comparison may be made between this sonnet and Wordsworth's "The world is too much with us" (page 316).   LP

A. E. Housman   **WITH RUE MY HEART IS LADEN** (page 158)

The poem is an expression of grief for all good friends the poet had who died in their youth. Though neither the word *died* nor *death* is used in the poem, the fact is conveyed through "had," "are laid," and "are sleeping." The brevity and apparent simplicity of the poem make its poignancy seem almost magical. It results from an exquisite choice of diction and a classical perfection of form. The compound adjectives "rose-lipt" and "lightfoot" are both particularized and universal in their application to the blooming beauty and athletic vitality of the maidens and youths they modify. Their reversed repetition in the second stanza, attached to different nouns, balances the two stanzas against each other and binds them together in a pattern of parallelism and opposition The word "rue," meaning sorrow, is also the name of an herb with bitter leaves, which readers of *Hamlet* may remember as one of the flowers distributed by the young Ophelia in her mad scene (IV, 5) shortly before her death. The connotations of "golden"—precious, bright, shining, pure, true, young—are enriched and deepened for the reader who recalls the dirge from *Cymbeline*, addressed to another youth who has died young.

The landscape of the second stanza is not literally that of the churchyard cemeteries where these lads and girls are buried; the point is that after death *all* brooks are too broad for leaping and that in the grave *all* beauty fades.

The ear picks up much of the rich alliteration in the poem on a first reading. Analysis discloses that every stressed word or important syllable (I include the unstressed halves of the two compound adjectives) in the poem except one alliterates with another:

> rue (1), rose- (2), rose- (7), roses (8);
> heart (1), had (2);
> laden (1), -lipt (3), light-, lad (4), leaping (5), light-, lads, laid (6), -lipt (7);
> golden (2), girls (7);
> friends (2), -foot (4), -foot (6), fields, fade (8);
> many, maiden (3), many (4);
> brooks, broad (5).

The one exception is "sleeping," and it, of course, is a rime word. Though the full extent of this alliterative network is apparent only on analysis, its presence contributes to the beauty of the poem.   LP

Gwendolyn Brooks **WE REAL COOL** (page 159)

The placement of the pronouns in this poem gives its rhythm a syncopated effect appropriate to the jazz culture of the speakers.

The critic who called the poem immoral was oblivious to its dramatic irony (its tone). The poet does not share the opinion of the speakers that they are "real cool," nor does any moderately good reader, which obviously the critic was not. LP

Barton Sutter **SHOE SHOP** (page 160)

The central contrast of the poem is between "image" (in the public relations sense of the word) and substance; between shoddy work (with a high gloss) and honest craftsmanship. The cobbler is a man who knows and values craftsmanship, and who cares nothing for "image." In his shop there are no "displays," boots and shoes lie "tumbled" in heaps; there is a smell of real leather, nothing pretends to be what it is not. He himself is without the ingratiating smile and slick manners of a salesman. He gives the work in hand more attention than he does his customer, "as if he held a grudge against business." There is double meaning here, for he does have a grudge against "business" in the sense of large-scale production, corporate enterprise, "factories," everything brought in by the industrial revolution. For him good craftsmanship is hand craftsmanship, not the product of assembly-line techniques, not the creation of advertising. His values are directly opposed to those of much of the modern business world, as seen in his ironical statement of its creed: "Cut the price. / Advertise! Never mind the merchandise." He is, he realizes, an anachronism in this world. His pride is "steeped in bitterness," and he knows that his "guerilla warfare" (his fuming and bitching) is hopeless. Yet, paradoxically, he derives tremendous satisfaction from his work. He has pride in his own workmanship; but, even more importantly, he can find physical and emotional release from his frustrations by whacking the tacks with his hammer—as if each were one of the enemy!

The poem begins when the speaker closes the door on "the racket / Of rush hour traffic" where the sleek machines of the modern world speed by, and steps into another world: an older world, like a blacksmith's; a more human world, like a barber shop (not a "hairstyling salon") where the workers (one to a customer) fill the air with talk and sharpen their nonelectric razors on leather strops; a world opposed to modern values, yet not a "front" for agitators (or anything else), for there is no back room. (The word "front" suggests a false appearance, like the "fronts" on a movie lot.) What the speaker finds in the shop is reality, respect for craftsmanship, and contempt for illusion. No wonder that when he steps into the street again, back into a world of illuminated billboards and dancing city lights, the whole city looks as "flimsy" and as false "as a movie set."

Except for the concluding couplet, the poem is written in a series of four-line stanzas with mostly approximate rimes, masculine or feminine, arranged in an *abba* pattern. In the first stanza, however, both sets of rimes contain a *k* sound which helps to magnify the noise of the onomatopoetic first rime "racket." In the second stanza, similarly, all lines end with a sharp *p*, reinforcing the onomatopoetic "whip-persnap," in which the sound occurs twice. There is also onomatopoetic reinforce-ment in the riming of "satisfaction" with "whack it" in the final full stanza. In line 27 an almost perfect internal rime contained in the first and final metrically similar words, is combined with assonance in the middle word, with an alliteration of *m*'s, and with a pair of unstressed "-ver" syllables plus a stressed "mer-," to make the line sound, ironically enough, like the perfect advertising slogan it almost is.   LP

John Updike   **WINTER OCEAN** (page 161)

The central figure of speech is apostrophe.   LP

John Crowe Ransom   **PARTING, WITHOUT A SEQUEL** (page 162)

The disappointment of first love bears a slightly comic aspect when viewed from the outside or when looked back on over a perspective of years, but to those who are actually suffering it, it is undiluted tragedy. We may try to talk "wisdom" to the disappointed youngster, but how can she understand? Or how can *we* understand? "She just doesn't realize," the oldsters say; "this will be nothing to her in a few months or years." "They just don't *know*," the youngster thinks; "how can they know what I feel?"

John Crowe Ransom catches both the comedy and the tragedy in this wryly poignant little poem. Observing the termination of a first attachment from a point of view partly inside and partly outside the heartbroken girl, he is able both to *feel* the tumultuous suffering of the girl and to note its theatrical exaggerations and its humorous ambivalences. The comic aspects are reflected in the double and triple rhymes, many of them slant; in the melodramatic triteness of the phrase describing the girl's attitude toward her letter "which he so richly has deserved"; in her gloat-ing satisfaction with the letter's crushing language ("And nothing could be better"); in the stagy *hauteur* of her command as she delivers it to the messenger boy—"'Into his hands'"; in the solemn pretentiousness of the epithet for the messenger boy—"the blue-capped functioner of doom"; in her mixed feelings as she watches the messenger boy ride off (hoping at once that he will deliver the letter promptly, which will put her errant lover in his place, and that it will get lost, allowing one more chance for reconciliation); and in her exaggeration of the episode's significance —"the ruin of her younger years." It is also reflected in the title, where the phrase "Without a Sequel" suggests the theatrical component of the affair ("Final Parting" would have been more straightforward).

But if we allow ourselves amusement at the girl's expense, we must also bleed with her. The parting *hurts.* We are moved to pity as the blood drains from her face and she goes to seek comfort from her father. The fourth and fifth stanzas are ambiguous. Is it her father or a tree she goes to? Either reading is possible. The "oak" may be a metaphor for her father, chosen to connote his strength and pride. Or it may be literally an oak, one perhaps that her father has planted by the front door ("lintel") of the house, a tree which embodies his strength, and through which his spirit seems to speak. At any rate the father, or the father's presence in the oak, tries to calm the daughter, gently reproaching her for the foolishness of her despair. In vain, of course. His talk is like the sound of leaves as it ceases and begins again. There are several double meanings here. The word *sere* means old and dry, but also suggests wise (*seer*). Is there something dry and meaningless in the wisdom of the father? The word *vaunting* applied to a tree would mean large and spreading; applied to a man, proud. Combined with *sere-seer* it suggests a gently wry ironic comment on the father's "wisdom." Wisdom comes easily to an old man who is himself past the storms of youth.

The use of figurative language is imperative if we are to be faithful to the full truth and complexity of human feeling. The bitterness of the girl's feeling is summed up in the marvelous metaphor of the last stanza comparing the tread marks of the bicycle tire to the track of a snake (and to the pattern on the back of the snake). Both visually and emotionally the metaphor is exact. The girl has been venomously bitten by her disappointment and hopes that her letter, whose characters are also snakelike, will bite the offending young man. The physical effects of the bite (i.e., of her emotion) are accurately conveyed through the paradox of the last two lines: "she stood there hot as fever / And cold as any icicle." Logically the statement is contradictory and impossible, but in the epistemology of human feeling it is not only true but could be conveyed in no other way.

[This commentary is reprinted, with a slight alteration, from Laurence Perrine and James M. Reid, *100 American Poems of the Twentieth Century* (New York: Harcourt Brace Jovanovich, 1966), pp. 139–41.]

Winthrop Mackworth Praed **SONG** (page 163)

A drinking song should be rollicking and jovial, for it is sung by men gathered for fellowship as much as for drinking. A drinking song for soldiers must also be morale-building, for it is sung by men engaged in a bloody, dangerous, and unpleasant business. It may therefore be excused for a good deal of bravado and for celebrating the pleasures of "killing" as well as of "swilling." (It will seldom celebrate the pleasure of being killed.) A drinking song may have no single speaker, for it is composed to be sung in unison. All we know about the speakers (singers) in this poem is that they are English soldiers, possibly Cavalier soldiers (supporters of the king during the English Civil War, 1642–1649).

The rollicking, jovial tone of this drinking song is sustained by its spirited rhythm (anapestic tetrameter), by its light and ingenious double riming (Roundhead, abounded; flagon, drag on); and above all by its brilliant word-play. This brilliance is displayed most prominently in the linking of words somehow similar in sound but

96

opposed in meaning (one word pertaining to war, the other to drinking). Such linkage occurs in every stanza (in most, several times); by lines: pints, pike-staves; pistols, pottles (1); trooper's, toper's (2); battles, bottles (3); casks, casques (8); flag, flagon (9); war, wine (11); can, cannon (13); full quarts, free quarters (14); drink sack, sack cities; whet, wet (17); bowls, bullets (19); swilling, killing (21); wine-cups, wars (24). The linking of war and drinking is also made by puns: in lines 5–6 by the use of the verb "taps" literally with "the wine of the vintner" and metaphorically with "the blood of the Roundhead"; in line 16 by the play on "grape" (a metonymy for wine) and *grapeshot*; in line 17 by the two meanings of "sack." In lines 23–24, phrases that apply literally to guns and shooting are applied metaphorically to glasses and drinking. Instead of being asked to fill our glasses to the brim with wine, we are told to "charge" them "to the muzzle" (as with powder); and instead of being invited to drink a toast, we are instructed to "fire off a salvo." Finally, any disheartening effect from the one line in the poem that suggests an unfavorable aspect of drinking and fighting is immediately canceled by the brilliance of the double pun in which it is expressed: "We're not always fond of the charge of the host" (20).   LP

William Stafford   **TRAVELING THROUGH THE DARK** (page 164)

Line 3 makes clear that it is not unusual for dead deer to be found on the Wilson River road. The only inference to be drawn is that they are hit by autos as they cross the road on their way to the river, but that most drivers, after the impact, leave the carcass where it falls and drive on. That the speaker stops—even though he was not the one who hit the deer—shows him to be an unusually responsible person. He has carefully driven around in front of the animal, has turned down his headlights—another responsible action—but has left the motor running, hoping to make quick work of pushing it over the edge, not stopping too long on the dangerous unlit road.

That he recognizes an ethical dilemma when he discovers the unborn fawn still living inside the dead doe particularly marks him out as a thoughtful person concerned with the preciousness of all life; and that he hesitates—thinking hard "for us all"—again reveals his deep sense of involvement. Who are the "us all" for whom the speaker thinks? Himself surely, the unborn fawn surely, other motorists traveling the Wilson River road, and, beyond that, all humanity, perhaps all life, which needs relationships with other forms of life in order to exist.

But what are his options? There is no way he can deliver the unborn fawn: he is hardly equipped to perform a Caesarean in the middle of the road. Nor could he mother the fawn, were it born. He must either take responsibility for killing the fawn by pushing its dead mother over the edge, or walk away and leave the dead doe there, endangering other lives—motorists who might be killed while swerving to miss the body. There is no choice really. The second alternative would be equivalent to washing his hands of moral responsibility—like Pontius Pilate in the Bible. The fact that he hesitates, however—considering the options—makes us like him. That one "swerving" from what should and must be expeditiously done—makes him fully human.

97

Many of the images have symbolic implications, though perhaps not of the kind that benefit from being pinned with a label and spelled with a capital "S." The image of "Traveling through the dark" (how different in effect from "Driving at night"!) suggests the difficulties of living life and having to make moral decisions with only limited knowledge and with no certain moral guidance. The cold of the doe's body and the warm spot in its side are *signs*, not symbols, of death and life. The car, its steady engine purring, its parking lights "aimed ahead," suggests a kind of automated life which never hesitates, does not make decisions, and is always ready for action. Its purring engine contrasts with the stillness of the wilderness (and of the unborn fawn), which has its own claims on the speaker, and which seems to "listen" (16), as if for his decision. The red taillight of the car is a conventional symbol of danger, and "the glare of the warm exhaust turning red" in which the speaker stands (15) almost symbolizes his dilemma. He must choose between spilling the warm blood of the unborn fawn over the edge of the canyon or endangering the lives of other human beings.

"Canyon" (3) is the only line-end in the poem without any correspondence in sound to another line-end in its stanza, and even it alliterates with the first line-end in the following stanza, just two lines away.   LP

Robert Frost   **NOTHING GOLD CAN STAY** (page 165)

The paradox in line 1 is to be explained by the fact that, when leaves first bud in the spring, they have a golden tint, more gold than green, which they lose as the leaves grow larger.

The paradox in line 3 has been explained by Alfred R. Ferguson as referring to much the same thing: "The earliest leaf unfolds its beauty like a flower," but I believe it refers to something different. Some trees and shrubs blossom in the spring before they bear leaves (the plum, for example; also the redbud and some species of peach and cherry). In botanical language, however, the term *leaf*, in its broadest sense, includes all foliar structures of the higher plants, including the sepals, petals, pistil, and stamens of a flower: all parts of the blossom, technically, are modified leaves. For trees like the plum, therefore, it is literally true that the "early leaf's a flower." That it remains so only "an hour" is an overstatement, but the blossoming period of these trees is brief at best; then the flowers drop off and the ordinary leaves begin.

Frost's poem, then, lists four things that have an early but brief period of perfect beauty (or happiness): the foliage of trees; the plants which blossom before they bear leaves; the course of human history (as storied in the Eden myth—or other myths of a "golden age"); and a day (which begins with the fresh gold-tinted air of sunrise). It ends with a generalization: "Nothing gold can stay." But by this time Frost's examples have assumed the force of symbols: they remind us as well of the year (which begins with spring), of the individual human life (which blooms in youth), and perhaps of love (most blissful in its early stages). Frost's "gold" is a symbol of perfection, and his theme is that most things reach their moment of perfection early and retain it briefly. His poem is about the transiency of beauty, bliss, youth, spring, and the transport of early love.

For another treatment of this theme in Frost, see his poem "The Oven Bird." For additional perspectives on "Nothing Gold Can Stay," see Lawrance Thompson, *Fire and Ice* (New York: Holt, 1942), pp. 169–70; Charles R. Anderson, in *The Explicator*, 22 (Apr. 1964), item 63; Alfred R. Ferguson, in *Frost: Centennial Essays* (Jackson: Univ. Press of Mississippi, 1974), pp. 436–39; and John Robert Doyle, Jr., *The Poetry of Robert Frost* (Johannesburg: Witwatersrand Univ. Press, 1962), pp. 174–76. For a possibly fuller analysis than you may want of the musical devices in the poem (and *their* perfection), see John A. Rea, "Language and Form in 'Nothing Gold Can Stay'," *Robert Frost: Studies of the Poetry*, ed. Kathryn Gibbs Harris (Boston: G. K. Hall, 1979), pp. 17–25. LP

Joshua Sylvester   AUTUMNUS (page 165)

A man given up to materialistic pleasures or pursuits ("worldling") may find in autumn a mirror ("glass") in which to view his own fading, wasted life ("face").

The adjectives in line 3 ("warped and wrinkled-up") alliterate for the eye only (since the second *w* is silent), but the two *p*'s furnish a linkage between them, as the *t*'s and *n*'s do to the adjectives in line 2. Perhaps the most remarkable line is 6 with its three parallel sequential monosyllabic two-word phrases woven together by *g*'s and *n*'s. The chief structural device of the poem, however, is rime, approximate in lines 1–3 and 6–7, perfect in 2–4 and 5–8. LP

12. Rhythm and Meter

A Note on Scansion

English meter is still a matter of considerable controversy—perhaps it is becoming more so—and I do not expect everyone to agree with my own scheme. In fact, I do not agree with part of it myself. But I believe that the *serious* student of poetry needs some familiarity with traditional terms. If he doesn't know what iambic pentameter is, he will be handicapped in reading about poetry.

Many writers, for purposes of scansion, prefer to use x for an unstressed syllable and an accent mark ($'$) for stressed syllables. I find this system clumsy for classroom use. The x's take too long to write on the board (two strokes instead of one), and the accent marks get confused with uprights dividing the feet. An additional merit of the horizontal stroke for stressed syllables is that the stroke may be lengthened to indicate heavy stresses, shortened to indicate light stresses.

Some metrists include the pyrrhic ($\smile\smile$) and the amphibrach ($\smile - \smile$) among the kinds of feet, but I don't find them necessary or helpful. The notion of a foot without an accent violates my definition of a foot. Where scansion might seem to call for a pyrrhic, one syllable will nearly always be slightly heavier than the other and thus can be regarded as bearing a light stress. As for the amphibrach, one gets it only by dividing the feet in an unusual and unwarranted way.   LP

George Herbert   VIRTUE (page 168)

Three stanzas presenting sweet things that die are contrasted with a fourth presenting the one thing that does not die. The first three stanzas parallel each other: each is an apostrophe beginning with the word "Sweet" and ending with the words "must die." The fourth stanza, which is not an apostrophe, reserves "sweet" for the third position in the opening line, and ends with the word "lives." The first three stanzas are interconnected and build to a climax because the "day" of the first stanza may be thought of as containing the "rose" of the second, while the "spring" of the third stanza contains them both. The ordering is also marked by the opening words of the fourth lines: "For thou . . . ," "And thou . . . ," "And all . . . ."

In stanza 1, the day is presented in an apt metaphor as the "bridal" (wedding) of the earth and sky, uniting them in light; the metaphor connotes a beginning, brightness, and hope. The dew is fittingly chosen to mourn the death of the day, for dew is associated with evening. The dew is both a personification and a metaphor, both the weeper and the tears that are wept. The words "to night" function both as adverb and, because the hyphen has been omitted, as prepositional phrase in which the noun is a traditional symbol for death.

In stanza 2, through a bold metaphor, the crimson rose is compared in color to the face of an angry man, and, in an even bolder overstatement, is described as so bright that it causes tears in an observer who rashly gazes at it without shielding his eyes (like looking directly at the sun). Yet, despite this dazzling brilliance, it too is doomed to die. Its "root" is ever in its "grave" (a metonymy for earth). The rose's death is a condition of its birth: it dies back into the very soil from which it sprang; its root is "ever" there.

In stanza 3, the spring is compared metaphorically to a box where "sweets" lie compacted. (For the seventeenth-century reader the connotations would suggest, not a box of candy, but a box of perfumes—rose petals, lavender, cedar sprays, etc.). But the poet's "music" shows that the spring also has its "closes" and must die like the rest. The "music" may be read literally as well as metaphorically (Herbert was a musician as well as a poet). The word "closes" has three relevant meanings: the spring ends or terminates, the metaphorical box shuts, and a "close" in music is a cadence or concluding strain.

Stanza 4 presents a contrast. A "sweet and virtuous soul," it declares, is immortal. Like "seasoned timber" it never "gives" (*buckles* or *snaps*). Even should the whole world "turn to coal" (*cinders, ashes*), it would survive. Spiritual in its origin, and having preserved its purity and strength through virtuous discipline, it will live even more intensely after the destruction of everything physical.

Two thoughtful brief discussions of this poem, by Louis L. Martz and M. M. Mahood, may be found in *Metaphysical Poetry*, ed. by Malcolm Bradbury and David Palmer (London: Edward Arnold, 1970), pp. 109-10 and 143-44. There is an extended discussion in Helen Vendler, *The Poetry of George Herbert* (Cambridge, Mass.: Harvard Univ. Press, 1975), pp. 9-24. LP

Exercises (page 177)

1. a. Iambic pentameter (rimed); b. Free verse; c. Free verse; d. Blank verse; e. Blank verse; f. Free verse; g. Free verse; h. Iambic, irregular line lengths; i. Blank verse; j. Blank verse.

Rudyard Kipling **SEAL LULLABY** (page 178)

The word "flipperling" was coined by Kipling for this poem. It is made from *flipper* (in this context a metonymy for a seal) plus the dimunitive suffix *-ling* (cf. *duckling, gosling, nestling, nursling, sapling, stripling*).

The meter is anapestic tetrameter, but an iamb is regularly substituted in the first foot, and the odd-numbered lines regularly have an unaccented syllable left over at the end. If the left-over syllable is combined with the iamb beginning the following line, it makes it an anapest, thus increasing the anapest flow of the verse.

The first syllable of "swinging" is demoted by the metrical pattern, but its weight still serves to slow down the line at this juncture.   LP

William Blake   "INTRODUCTION" TO *SONGS OF INNOCENCE* (page 178)

The child upon the cloud substitutes for the traditional Muse. The Lamb symbolizes innocence. The poet is first inspired by an emotion or idea (stanzas 1-2), then finds words to express that experience (stanza 3), then writes down or publishes his poems for all to read (stanzas 4-5). (In the poem he fashions a pen from a hollow reed and dyes water to make ink.) In this "Introduction" Blake indicates the source of inspiration for his poems—childhood; their subject matter—innocence; their intended audience—both children and adults (the last line indicates that "Every child" may joy to hear them; but line 14 indicates that the book is for "all" to read); and their tone—pleasant (2), merry (6), cheerful (6), happy (10), joyous (20). (Actually they are all these and more.)

Lines 1-2 and 8-10 establish a regular tetrameter pattern with accents on both the first and last syllables of the line. (In scansion the pressure of the pattern forces us to promote the initial prepositions (*On, In*) and the conjunctions (*And, So, While*) to accented status. *Every* (20) is pronounced essentially as two syllables. Dividing the feet *after* the stressed syllables produces one monosyllabic foot and three iambs in each line. Dividing the feet *before* the stressed syllables produces three trochees and one monosyllabic foot in each line. It is obviously duple meter, but whether one calls it iambic or trochaic is a purely arbitrary decision: it is no more one than the other.   LP

William Whitehead   THE "JE NE SAIS QUOI" (page 179)

The initial "Yes" indicates that the speaker is answering a question or responding to an allegation. He readily confesses that he is in love with Celia though he is hard put to explain it. The poem's basic paradox is that Celia is an utterly charming creature yet has no distinguished features. Her face is plain, her figure poor, her manner common, her sense "only chat," her voice and touch pleasing but not extraordinary. Yet "Celia altogether" is captivating. There is a "je ne sais quoi" about her. The whole is much more than the sum of its parts.

"Love" (5) is the direct object of "creates." Students not brought up on poetry (or grammar) often have trouble adjusting to the inversions of normal word order that earlier generations took for granted (the "poetic license" allowed poets who worked in strict meter and rime).

The extra unaccented syllables that were a variation of the basic pattern in lines 9 and 11 of "Virtue" (page 168) are here *part* of the basic pattern, and any description of the poet's meter beyond mere labeling must take them into account. The feminine endings add appropriate lightness and grace to the verse, and the regular use of feminine approximate rimes (an innovation in the poet's day) echoes the uncertainty indicated in the title and third line of the poem.   LP

e. e. cummings   **IF EVERYTHING HAPPENS THAT CAN'T BE DONE** (page 180)

The subject is love. The season is spring. The tone is ecstatic. cummings is a romantic poet for whom, if there is anything more wonderful than being a live individual with a heart and feelings of one's own (a ONE; not a cipher, a blank, a nothing, an emotionally dead person), it is being one of two such individuals (two ONES) who achieve identity through love. But being a ONE is prerequisite, and the poet devotes the first two stanzas to establishing that "there's nothing so something [so important] as one." Being a ONE, for cummings, is a function of feeling, not of intellect. The analytic reason (symbolized throughout the poem by "books" and in stanza 2 by analytic terms such as "why," "because," and "although") for cummings deadens and kills, whereas feeling (symbolized by "buds" and "birds" and "trees") enlivens and vitalizes ("buds know better than books" and "books don't grow," to expand cummings' telescoped phrase). The consummation of natural feeling comes with the mutually realized love of two individuals; and the love theme (introduced in the third stanza with "so your is a my") is explicitly stated in the fourth stanza ("now i love you and you love me") and receives its triumphant expression in the fifth (where all the pronouns have changed to "we's"), especially in the poem's final line, which incorporates, with a neat bit of word play, the mathematical equation for this identity ("we're WONderful ONE times ONE"). When such miracles happen (when "everything happens that can't be done"), as they regularly do in the spring, then even "the stupidest teacher" (representing the intellect again) will dimly guess the miraculousness of individuality, feeling, spring, life, and love.

cummings has constructed his poem on an intricate pattern. Each stanza is linked to the one that follows (like persons holding hands) by the repetition of its last word as the first word in the next. Lines 2–4 of each stanza contain a parenthesis in which life and feelings are contrasted with intellect. Lines 6–8 of each stanza contain a second parenthesis showing the participants in the poem to be engaged in a spontaneous joyous dance. Each stanza is additionally organized by a pattern of approximate and perfect rimes in which lines 1, 4, 9 rime together, and lines 5, 8. The prevailing meter is anapestic (freely mixed with iambic and monosyllabic feet, which give it spontaneity and variety), in which the nine lines of each stanza have four, two, one, one, four, one, one, two, and three feet respectively.

Had cummings printed the two parentheses of each stanza as one-line rather than three-line units, he would have had a simple five-line stanza with all lines riming (anapestic aabb^{4}a^3). But by breaking up the parentheses, he introduces into them two additional rhetorical (line-end) pauses which, without altering the meter or slowing it down, give it additional spontaneity, variety of movement, a bit of a swirl, reinforcing the dance-like quality of these lines. Indeed the joyous tone of this poem is as much the result of the meter as of the words. Notice, moreover, that line 28, which states the subject of the poem, the cause of its joyousness, consists of four regular iambic feet. Had the poem been printed, as proposed above, in five-line stanzas with the parentheses compacted into one line each, line 28 would be the only one in the poem without a single anapestic foot. This slowing down of line 28, through the use of exclusively duple feet, gives it an emphasis appropriate to its thematic importance in the content of the poem.

[This discussion is adapted from the essay "A Look at Rhythm and Meter" in *The Art of Total Relevance: Papers on Poetry*, by Laurence Perrine (Rowley, Mass.: Newbury House, 1976), pp. 70–73.]

A. E. Housman   **OH WHO IS THAT YOUNG SINNER** (page 182)

The poem is a satire against the prejudices that cause men to hate and persecute each other for superficial and accidental differences between them. The color of one's hair, having nothing to do with intrinsic human ability or worth, symbolizes any such difference. When I first read the poem I identified it in my own mind— because of my American experience with racial conflict—with skin color. I have since learned that the poem was occasioned by the conviction and imprisonment of Oscar Wilde for homosexuality. Either reading of the poem is legitimate, and so probably would be such religious or racial differences as presently divide Protestant and Roman Catholic in Northern Ireland and Moslem and Jew in the Middle East.

I would call the irony verbal, for the poem gives me no sense of a dramatic speaker different from the author.   LP

William Butler Yeats   **DOWN BY THE SALLEY GARDENS** (page 183)

The meter is basically iambic heptameter, but the fourth accent regularly falls on a pause—except that in lines 3 and 7 it *might* be taken as falling lightly on "as." By the former option, the fifth foot in these two lines is anapestic; by the latter, iambic. LP

Walt Whitman   **HAD I THE CHOICE** (page 184)

Robert Frost   **THE AIM WAS SONG** (page 184)

Walt Whitman defends free verse (in unrimed free verse); Robert Frost defends metrical verse—"measure" (in rimed iambic tetrameter). The verse form, in each case, is perfectly chosen for the subject matter. This may seem elementary, but what would have been the effect if Whitman had defended free verse in meter, and Frost, meter in free verse?

In Whitman's poem even the greatest poetic art is seen as pale and inferior when set beside nature. The implication for poetry is that the most desirable poetry will be that which is most natural, most *like* nature. The further implication is that free verse is natural and that metered, rimed verse is artificial. Still another implication is that metaphors, similes, and contrived paradoxes ("conceits") are artificial.

In Frost's poem successful poetry is seen as an improvement on nature. Though it uses natural materials, it orders them, imposes form on them, and thus gives them a power which they do not have in their natural state. In repeating the words "by measure" in line 13—and placing a period after them—Frost gives the phrase tremendous emphasis. Song, he insists, is "measured"; rather than taking form from nature, it gives form to nature. Thus nature is made humanly meaningful.

Readers must judge the two philosophies by their own standards. But the fact is that great poetry has been written both in meter and in free verse. LP

Samuel Taylor Coleridge **METRICAL FEET** (page 185)

Coleridge's verses are about feet both literally and metaphorically. The personified Trochee "trips," the Spondee "stalks," the Iambics "march," the Anapests proceed with "a leap and a bound." LP

13. Sound and Meaning

Anonymous **PEASE PORRIDGE HOT** (page 186)

This verse has been described as a "clapping game" for children. LP

William Shakespeare **SONG: HARK, HARK!** (page 187)

Even with onomatopoetic words, we must not assume an *identity* between sound and meaning. The French equivalent of "cockadoodle-doo" is *co co rico*; in German it is *ki-ke-ri-ki*; in Spanish it is *kikiriki*; and in Shakespeare's original (un-modernized) text it was *cockadiddle-dow*. LP

Carl Sandburg **SPLINTER** (page 188)

"Thin" and "splinter" (also "cricket") are phonetic intensives, and in line 4 their effect is reinforced by the short *i*'s in "singing" (and, though their effect on the ear is slight, by those in "It" and "is"). The consonance of "last," "first," and "frost" also adds to the effectiveness of this miniature. LP

Robert Herrick **UPON JULIA'S VOICE** (page 189)

"Silvery" (literally *like silver*) suggests something precious, beautiful, smooth to the touch, softly gleaming in color. Julia's voice is smooth, soft, agreeable, and precious to the speaker. "Amber" (a fossilized resin) is a translucent substance that glows with soft rich golden-yellow light. Julia is singing and accompanying herself on a lute made of wood but finished with an amber-colored varnish. More impor-tantly, the sound of the lute under her fingers is softly and richly resonant, golden-toned, the perfect complement to her voice. It is as if the melodious words she sings each melted into a purely translucent amber lute. LP

Robert Frost **THE SPAN OF LIFE** (page 192)

No one who has ever been greeted at the door by an affectionate and enthusiastic puppy can miss the image implicit in the second line, which is all the more effective because of Frost's *understatement* (almost *un*-statement) of it. [Actually the Greeks, whose versification was based on duration rather than on accent, had a name for the second foot in the first line (it was called a *molossus*) but we see no reason to

106

burden English students with it.] Frost's title universalizes the subject of the poem, making the dog a symbol of human as well as of animal life. LP

Exercise (page 194)

The letter in parentheses indicates the superior version.
1. (a) ("Independence") The linkage in sound of "*g*uide" and "*g*uar*d*" (alliteration and consonance) emphasizes their syntactical parallelism in an iambic pentameter couplet. Version *b* takes more words (and an extra foot) to make a less forceful connection. (The Biblical allusion is to Exodus 13:21.)
2. (b) (*Comus*) This blank verse passage, after the generalization in line 1, calls for harshness in line 2 and musicality in line 3. The three hard consonant sounds of "*crabbed*" crowding around one vowel are much harsher than the soft consonants in "*r*ough" (pronounced *ruff*); in addition, two accents coming together on "dull fools" emphasize these words (as do their repetition of *l*'s) and strain the meter (a monosyllabic foot replaces the expected iamb in the fourth position), whereas "foolish men" is pleasant in sound and regular in meter. The name "Apollo," with its final open vowel and its mellifluous *l*'s (picking up *l*'s in "musical" and "lute") is far more melodious than "Phoebus."
3. (b) ("Mid-Winter") The core of each version is "crows croak hoarsely" with its suggestion of raucous cawing. The three sharp *k*-sounds in "*c*rows *c*roa*k*" are supported in version *b* in "out-*c*ast" and "a*c*ross"; and the hissing *s* of "hoarsely" is reinforced in "out-ca*s*t," "acro*ss*," and "whitene*ss*" (with the addition of three sharp *t*'s). In version *a*, "fleeing" and "over the snow" are rather pleasant in sound.
4. (b) (*Tristram*, VI) The gaps in "Your _____ how bells of singing gold / Would sound at _____ over silent water" must be filled with pleasant, musical sounds. In version *b* "low voice" is soft and lovely, "tells" provides an internal rime with "bells," and "twilight" a half-rime with "silent." In version *a* "talk attests" is noisy; "evening" is softly pleasant but provides no rime.
5. (b) (*The Princess:* "Come down, O maid") The blank verse of version *a* is metrically regular throughout. In version *b* the superfluity of unstressed syllables in line 1 (MYR-i-ads of RIV-u-lets HUR-ry-ing THROUGH the LAWN) gives the effect of speed; and the onomatopoetic words "moan" and "murmuring" are reinforced by the *m*'s, *n*'s, and *r*'s in "*m*yr*i*ads," "i*mmemor*ial," "el*m*s," and "i*nnum*erable."
6. (a) (*Romeo and Juliet*, III, 5) The effect wanted is a harsh unpleasantness. The nasal "sings so" is less pleasant and less flowing than "warbles." The metrical irregularity of "STRAIN- ing HARSH DIS- cords" strains the meter and puts heavy emphasis on harshness, whereas the smooth regularity of "with HARSH dis-CORD-ant TONES" mutes it. "Unpleasing sharps" is without the pleasant assonance of "tones and doleful."

7. (b) (*Don Juan*, VII, lxxviii) The flowing rhythm and euphonious sound of version *a*—its liquid *l*'s, *r*'s, and *m*'s and its soft *f*- and *v*-sounds—make it beautiful to listen to; but this beauty is highly inappropriate to the subject. The sharp monosyllables, the clogged meter, and explosive *b*'s and *d*'s of version *b* make it far superior.

8. (a) ("Reconciliation") The repeated *s*-sounds in "sisters," "incessantly," "softly," and "soiled" provide the repetition called for and perhaps even the sound of hands sloshing repeatedly in sudsy water.

9. (b) ("Elegy Written in a Country Churchyard") In line 1 "tolls," like "knell," is onomatopoetic. In line 2 a spondee appropriately slows down the line by bringing three accents together (the LOW- / ing HERD / WIND SLOW- / ly O'ER / the LEA /). In line 4 a light accent on "and" in the fourth foot requires a slight compensatory pause before it (as if there were a comma after "darkness"), thus isolating the final pronoun and preparing for the meditative nature of the poem. (In version *a* lines 3 and 4 are absurdly swift for solemnity of the subject.)

10. (b) ("Epistle to Dr. Arbuthnot") In line 1 the succession of short monosyllables with sharp endings ("let," "flap," "bug," "wings") spits out the spite of the speaker at the subject of his satire, and line 2 adds another ("child"). But the manifest superiority of version *b* is the superiority of "stinks and stings" to "smells and bites." The alliterating *st*'s, the assonance of the short *i*'s, and the sharp final consonants link these verbs in sound as well as in syntax and give them a force that the soft word "smiles" lacks (though "bites" has it). LP

Alexander Pope **SOUND AND SENSE** (page 195)

Introducing his topic with the general observation that good writing is the result of art (it looks easy, but mastery is acquired only by long practice), Pope then states the thesis of his passage in line 4: In good writing "The sound must seem an echo to the sense." He elaborates and demonstrates this thesis (simultaneously) through a series of five examples, each included within an iambic pentameter riming couplet. When a poet writes about a gentle west wind and a smooth-flowing stream, Pope begins, the verse should also be soft and smooth. (The following scansions represent my sense, and may be modified to fit yours.)

SOFT is / the STRAIN / when ZEPH- / yr GEN- / tly BLOWS, /

And the SMOOTH / STREAM / in SMOOTH- / er NUM- / bers FLOWS. /

The reversal of stress in the first foot gives additional emphasis to "Soft," which is the key-word in the first line. Most of the words in the line are soft in sound, especially "Zephyr," whose *z-f-r* combination of consonants is softer than the *w-est-w-nd* of *West wind* despite the latter's alliterating *w*'s. The *g* in "gently" is a *j*. The explosive *b* of "blows" is gentled by the following *l* and long vowel sounds. "Soft" and "strain" contains a gentling *f* and *n* respectively. In the second line the key-word "smooth," itself a smooth-sounding word, is emphasized (a) by the meter, which joins it with "stream" (also smooth in its long vowel sound and concluding *m*), and (b) by its repetition in "smoother." The fourth foot contains the soft consonants *n* and *m*. The fifth combines the soft *fl-* with a long vowel. The repeated *s*'s in these two lines (I suspect) take on the color of their surroundings.

But WHEN / LOUD SURG- / es LASH / the SOUND- / ing SHORE, /

The HOARSE, / ROUGH VERSE / should LIKE / the TOR- / rent ROAR. /

It is arguable whether the key-word "loud" is a loud sound (its vowel, of course, is a diphthong, and is the sound we use for a cry of pain—"ow!" or "ouch!"), but it is inarguable that the meter puts a stress on it appropriate to its importance in the sentence, and that its effect is intensified by its near-rime with "sounding." The onomatopoetic "roar" is emphasized by its anticipation in "shore," "hoarse," and "torrent." The alliteration of "loud" and "lash" and the consonance of "hoarse" and "verse" gives emphasis and linkage to these two pairs of words. Though none of the words in these two lines is particularly harsh in sound (the roughness and hoarseness we may imagine in "rough" and "hoarse" disappear from *ruff* and *horse*), the meter by bringing three accents together in "hoarse, rough verse," puts extraordinary emphasis on words that are hoarse-meaning and rough-meaning, and pushes together three syllables that form "a mouthful"—do not articulate easily. The grammatical pause contributes to this lack of articulation.

When A- / jax STRIVES / SOME ROCK's / VAST WEIGHT / to THROW, /

The LINE / TOO LA- / bors AND / the WORDS / MOVE SLOW. /

It is not just the five stressed syllables in a row that slow down the first line and give it such a sense of strain and muscular effort, it is the impossibility of sliding these words easily off the tongue, the muscular effort required in the reading. The mouth has to be reshaped for each word in the series. Even in a single word like "strives," effort is required, for we must pronounce five distinct consonant sounds *s-t-r* and *v-s* with only one vowel sound between them (*v-s* is harder than *s-t-r*). In the second line the two spondees, bringing three stresses together at two points in the line, slow the line down.

NOT so, / when SWIFT / Ca- MIL- / la SCOURS / the PLAIN, /

FLIES o'er / the un- BEND- / ing CORN, / and SKIMS / a- LONG / the MAIN. /

In each of these lines the reader has the choice of stressing the first or the second syllable in the opening foot. I have elected to stress "Not" because (a) it signals the change from the grunting effort of Ajax to lift his rock to the effortless ease of swift Camilla running, (b) the two unstressed syllables following it speed up the line, and (c) the increased distance separating the first two stresses gives added emphasis to the second stress—"swift"—which is the key-word in the couplet. The name "Camilla" (like "Zephyr") fits Pope's purpose perfectly, so easily do the syllables flow together. (Contrast the effort and speed involved in saying the three syllables of "Camilla" and of "rock's vast weight.") The assonant short *i*'s of "swift," "Camilla," and "skims" quicken these words, as well as link them in meaning. In the second line I have chosen to stress the initial "Flies," again because the reversed stress gives added emphasis to the more important word in the meaning, and because the unstressed syllables succeeding add speed to the line. (The three unstressed syllables together were not allowed by the strict rules of Pope's day, however, nor the two consecutive vowel sounds in "the" and "un-". Pope's unmodernized text— *th' unbending corn*—blends "the" and "un-" together in one syllable.) The notable variation here, however, is the introduction of a six-foot line (called an "Alexandrine") into the pentameter pattern. The extra foot, making it possible to divide the line into two three-foot segments (separated here by a comma), gives the line additional lightness (see discussion in Exercise 1, page 177).

HEAR how / Tim- O / theus' VAR- / ied LAYS / sur- PRISE, /

And BID / al- TER / nate PAS- / sions FALL / and RISE! /

With no other text than that before us, the reader with a sensitive ear can confidently declare that Pope put the accent on the second syllable of "alternate." With the accent on the first syllable, the meter goes smash. Put on the second syllable, the line perfectly alternates unstressed and stressed syllables (it is the most regular line of the whole fourteen), thus echoing the alternation of passions of which Timotheus sings. (British usage, as opposed to American, even today stresses the second syllable of *alternate* when used adjectivally, as we do with the word *alternative*.)

Pope's passage is a brilliant display of technical virtuosity.   LP

Emily Dickinson   **I LIKE TO SEE IT LAP THE MILES** (page 196)

The basic metaphor of the poem compares a train to a horse, though neither train nor horse is named in the poem. The subject is a train because it laps miles and valleys up, feeds itself (takes water) at tanks, peers (with its headlight) into shanties by the sides of roads, hoots (with its whistle), is punctual, and stops "docile and omnipotent" (obedient to the engineer but tremendously powerful) at its stable (station or roundhouse). It is a horse because it laps, licks, feeds, steps, peers, has ribs, crawls, complains, chases itself, neighs, and stops at a stable. It is a whole train rather than just a locomotive because it chases itself downhill.

The most unusual technical feature of the poem is that each of the first three stanzas ends with a run-on line. These run-on lines give the poem, or the train, a continuous forward motion (there are no periods until the end of the poem), a forward motion that finally grinds to an abrupt halt on the word "stop" (line 16). The stop—it must be a strong one to stop a train—is made strong in a number of ways: first, the word *stop* itself stops suddenly, ending with an explosive consonant; second, though in a normally unstressed position, the word receives a strong metrical stress (with the partial exception of the preceding line, which slows the train down, this is the only line in the poem stressed on the initial syllable); third, it is followed and preceded by grammatical pauses; fourth, it is followed and preceded (on the other side of the grammatical pauses) by stressed syllables, with one of which it has assonance and with the other of which it alliterates. All these features emphasize or isolate the word *stop* in a remarkable way. The phrase that follows—"docile and omnipotent"—is a beautiful expression of power at rest.

But before the train comes to a stop, it makes a variety of motions and sounds. In the first two lines the regular meter and the predominance of *l*'s give the train speed, while at the same time the monosyllabic words ending in *p* or *k*, found throughout the first stanza, give it the clippety-cloppety-clackety sound of iron wheels going over joints in the rails. In line 4 the big word "prodigious," set off between commas, slows the line down as the train slows down to "step" around a curve—an effect that is repeated in line 5. The division of what would normally be line 9 into two lines, comma-interrupted, again slows the train down, this time to a crawl, as it goes through a tunnel, tooting its whistle each inch of the way. The three trochaic words in succession—"horrid, hooting stanza"—convey the regularity and repetition of the whistle's sound, intensified by the narrow walls of the tunnel. The onomatopoetic word "hooting" sounds like *tooting* but alliterates with "horrid," thus emphasizing the repetitiveness of the sound while also retaining the metaphoric sense that this is a creature rather than a machine.

This brief analysis by no means exhausts the adaptation of sound to sense in this poem, but it perhaps indicates the chief features.

The poem employs approximate rime (consonance) in its even-numbered lines. Lines 8 and 16 contain overstatement. LP

Ted Hughes **WIND** (page 197)

The poem describes a house and the surrounding countryside during a hurricane. The wind is accompanied by rain during the night (stanza 1); the rain ceases with morning, but the wind continues throughout the day. In the last two stanzas the poet and his companion sit before the fire, presumably that evening, but can concentrate on nothing but the tremors of the house and the sounds of the storm. Throughout the poem the poet uses violent images to convey the violence of the storm.

Many of the images are sound images, and these are reinforced by the use of onomatopoetic words ("crashing," "booming," "drummed," "bang," "flap," "rang," "shatter") and effective use of sound repetitions. In the first stanza, for instance, the alliteration of *w* ("woods," "winds," "window," "wet") is accompanied by a remarkable series of repeated *d*'s ("woods," "darkness," "winds," "stampeding," "fields," "window," "floundering," "astride," "blinding"), *k*'s ("crashing," "darkness," "black"), and *b*'s ("booming," "black," "blinding"). The *w*'s are appropriate to the whoosh of the wind, the *d*'s, *k*'s, and *b*'s to the thudding, crashing, booming, and banging noises caused by it. In line 14 the onomatopoeia is reinforced by assonance ("bang," "vanish," "flap"). In lines 15–16 rhythm also contributes in a remarkable way, the series of stressed syllables in "BLACK- / BACK GULL BENT like an I-ron BAR SLOW-ly" reinforcing the visual slowness. Similar effects may be observed throughout the poem.

The poem uses various kinds of rime, mostly very approximate, following the scheme *abba* except in stanza 3, which is *abab*. The rhythm moves very freely around what is basically a five-beat line. LP

Gerard Manley Hopkins HEAVEN-HAVEN (page 198)

The speaker is a nun taking the vows that commit her to the cloistered life of the convent. This life, dedicated to religious meditation and the worship of God, is metonymically represented by "heaven" and metaphorically represented as a "haven" or sheltered place. In the extension of the metaphor, the sea represents life in the outside world and the storms are especially violent commotions in that life—passions, desires, appetites. The "havens" are pictured in the first stanza as gardens or sheltered fields (as inside a convent wall), in the second stanza as harbors protected from the ocean swells. "Springs" (2) refers both to springs of water—sources of pure refreshment—and to the mildest season of the year, free from wintry storms. "Lilies" (4), because of the pure white color of Easter lilies, are a traditional symbol of purity, chastity, religious worship, absence of sexual passion. Be sure your students realize that "blow" (4) here means "blossom," *not* "sway in the wind."

The basic stanza pattern is iambic $a^3 b^2 b^5 a^3$, but there are many variant feet. In the last line the substitution of anapests for iambs in the last two feet gives the line a swinging motion that imitates its meaning. The effect is enhanced by the use of monosyllables, by the extreme lightness of the unstressed syllables, and by the alliteration of "swings" and "sea." LP

Wilfred Owen ANTHEM FOR DOOMED YOUTH (page 198)

The octave has its geographical setting on the battlefield (since this is a World War I poem, in France). The sestet has its geographical setting back home (since Owen was an English poet, in England). The octave concerns the death of soldiers in battle. The sestet concerns the bereavement of friends and families back home. The imagery of the octave is primarily auditory. The imagery of the sestet is primarily visual. The tone of the octave is angry and indignant. The tone of the sestet is tender. (Line 8 is transitional: the "sad shires" are back in England. This line connects the deaths to the bereavement and shifts the geographical locus from battlefield to home.) Both octave and sestet are introduced by questions.

Octave and sestet are unified by the central metaphorical image of an Anglican funeral service. Neither the literal terms of this metaphor (battle and bereavement)

nor the figurative term (church funeral service) is named, so this is a metaphor of the fourth form (see page 59). The terms of the central metaphor are arrived at, as it were, by adding up the subsidiary figures and drawing a total. In the octave, at least, the central metaphor emphasizes contrast more than similarity, for the point is that these soldiers will never have a church funeral. Instead of the items in the second column of the list below (the figurative terms), they will have only the items in the first column (the literal terms):

literal	*figurative*
Owen's poem	anthem
monstrous anger of the guns	passing-bells
rapid rifle fire	orisons
wailing shells	choirs singing
bugles calling	voices of mourning
glimmers of good-byes in boys' eyes	candles held by altar boys
pallor of girls' brows	pall-cloth on coffin
tenderness of patient minds	flowers
dusk coming each evening	drawing-down of blinds

The last metaphor on this list does not belong to the funeral service image, but it too is associated with the formal observance of death. (In addition to the metaphors, the octave uses considerable personification: guns are angry, rifles stutter and patter out prayers, shells wail and are demented, bugles call, shires are sad. Words like "monstrous," "stuttering," and "demented" suggest that the noises of battle are like those of a madman.)

Students will have their greatest trouble with lines 10–11. Many will identify the "boys" with the "doomed youth" and read these lines as referring to the gleam in the eyes of the dying soldiers on the battlefield. Candles at a church funeral, however, are not held by the dead man but by attendants (altar boys). The logical organization of the sonnet, moreover, places this scene back home rather than on the battlefield. The boys and girls of the sestet are younger brothers, sisters, sweethearts, or other persons close to the dead.

The main point of the poem is that a church funeral service would be a "mockery" for these dead soldiers. Funeral services are a means of ritualizing or giving dignity to human death. These soldiers, however, did not die a human death; instead, they were slaughtered like "cattle." The dignity of a funeral service would be inappropriate to the indignity of their death. Owen's poem, though a tribute (an "anthem") to the dead soldiers, is mainly a bitter attack on modern war. It expresses horror, indignation, and anger at the senseless slaughter of human beings by mechanical means. Modern warfare, it implies, is mass slaughter: a mockery of human dignity. Death in modern warfare is an animal death, not a human death.

In the octave, sound is adapted to sense chiefly by the use of words and phrases whose sounds imitate meaning. The onomatopoetic series "stuttering . . . rattle . . . patter" is reinforced by the *t*'s in "cattle," "monstrous," and "hasty." The onomatopoetic "wailing" is reinforced by the *l*'s in "bells," "shrill," "shells," "bugles," "calling." ("Bells" and "shrill" may perhaps themselves be considered onomato-poetic.) The phrase "rifles' rapid rattle" is given speed by its pronounced trochaic rhythm (the phrasing corresponding with the meter)* and by the alliteration of the liquid *r*'s, but the hard *p* and *d* of "rapid" reinforces the staccato quality of "stutter-ing . . . rattle . . . patter."

In the sestet, sound is adapted to sense chiefly by the linking together through similarity in sound of words logically connected to meaning, e.g., "candles . . . hands," "glimmers . . . good-byes," "pallor . . . pall," "dusk . . . drawing-down." LP

*The basic meter of the poem is iambic pentameter, and in *scansion* line 3 would be divided as follows:

ON - ly / the STUT- / ter- ing RI- / fles' RAP- / id RAT- / tle.

In *reading* the line, however, we hear "rifles' rapid rattle" as three trochees.

Robert Browning   **BOOT AND SADDLE** (page 199)

Thomas Westwood   **NIGHT OF SPRING** (page 200)

Browning chooses a triple meter to express swift riding, Westwood a duple meter to express slow riding. These choices are appropriate; but even more important is what each poet does with the meter he has chosen. If we divide Browning's opening line into feet at the natural pauses (rather than arbitrarily), we get a monosyllabic foot, a trochee, an iamb, and an anapest:

BOOT, / SAD - dle, / to HORSE, / and a - WAY! /

The line starts from a standstill with the monosyllabic foot, gets into motion with the trochee, picks up speed with the iamb (because it follows the unaccented syl-lable in the trochee and moves us toward the basic meter of the poem), and is gal-loping at full speed with the anapest. The rhythm beautifully expresses the slowly gathering speed of the rider. Then, because the two lines that follow this initial comma-interrupted line are without punctuation, the galloping sweeps us on to the first chorus line with breathless urgency.

Although Westwood's basic meter is duple, his opening line (like Browning's, used as a refrain) has two monosyllabic substitutions:

SLOW, / HOR - ses, / SLOW. /

The scarcity of unstressed syllables, the long vowels in the stressed syllables, and the grammatical pauses marked off by commas all slow the line down to a slow walk. The second line of the refrain, though it picks up the duple meter, continues with long, open vowel sounds in *through* and *go*. (Because these vowels, like the vowel

114

in *slow*, are "open"—that is, unstopped by a final consonant—the voice holds on to them longer in reading.)

That Browning's poem utilizes only one rime sound perhaps adds to its sense of insistent urgency. LP

A. E. Housman **EIGHT O'CLOCK** (page 201)

"They hang us now in Shrewsbury jail," comments the speaker in "On moonlit heath and lonesome bank" (page 50), and we can fancy the execution of the lad in this poem as taking place in the courtyard of that site.

The clock is one of those that plays a four-note tune at a quarter past the hour, extends it to eight notes at the half hour and twelve at three-quarters past, and then plays a full complement of sixteen notes before beginning the bong, bong, bong that announces the new hour. The young man, strapped and hooded, with a noose around his neck, sees nothing, but he hears the sixteen notes (the four "quarters") of the clock's tune "tossed" down upon the town, then the noises of the clock machinery as it tightens its springs (almost literally collecting its strength) before beginning the series of eight monotone strokes, at the first of which the trap will be sprung beneath him, and he will drop the distance (carefully calculated according to his weight) sufficient to break his neck.

The stanzaic form is iambic $a^3 b^5 a^5 b^2$, with the *a*-rhymes all feminine, but with considerable metrical variation. The second line, for instance, with its initial trochee and its very lightly accented "on" in the third foot, brings together a number of unstressed or lightly stressed syllables that give it a speed consonant with the indifferent brightness of the tune played by the chimes. In contrast, the two internally punctuated spondees that begin line 3 and the internally punctuated first foot of line 5 followed by an initially stressed trochee, slow these two lines dramatically in consonance with the subjective experience of the protagonist. Of particular importance is the series of sharp *k*-sounds beginning in line 6: "*c*ounted . . . *c*ursed . . . lu*ck* . . . *c*lock *c*ollected . . . stru*ck*," and the heavy *str*-alliteration of "*str*apped" (5), "*str*ength" and "*str*uck" (8). The syntactical displacement of "its strength" from the expected position immediately following the verb places the alliterating monosyllables "strength" and "struck" together in the final line, where the final word "struck" culminates both the *str*- and *k*- series of repetitions. In addition, the heavy metrical regularity of this line, with its internal comma isolating the final verb, gives "struck" enormous force (the result of alliteration, consonance, rime, syntax, meter, and punctuation), thus putting a heavy emphasis on its double meaning. Not only does the clock mechanically strike the hour, but it (or perhaps the whole clock tower), personified as an executioner, brings down its axe with a powerful blow on the neck of the victim, striking out his life.

The use of "morning" and "nighing" as adjectives is unusual enough that one may detect a suggestion of *mourning* and *sighing* behind them. LP

James Joyce **ALL DAY I HEAR** (page 201)

The central purpose of the poem is the evocation of mood, the objectification of inner feeling. The mood is one of sadness or desolation, and the poet projects it through both imagery and sound.

He *hears* the noise of waters and the cry of the winds. The waters seem to be "making moan" in a "monotone"—a single sustained sound. He compares himself to the sea-bird which in memory, in imagination, or in fact he *sees* "going / Forth alone," and which he assumes is sad because it is alone (as he is). He envisions the winds as "grey," not a cheerful color. He *feels* the winds as well, and they are "cold."

The dominant musical device is the repetition of the long *o* sound, phonetically linked with melancholy or sorrow (page 188). The six short lines all end in rimes containing this vowel; the six long lines end alternately with the word "waters" (three times) and with rimes containing the long *o* (three times). The sound also occurs internally in "forth" and "cold." All of these *o*'s support the poem's one onomatopoetic word, "moan."

The speaker does not tell us the cause of his desolation, but the imagery, emphasizing loneness, monotone, and lack of warmth, strongly suggests that loneliness, isolation, separation from a loved one, may be the cause.

The meter is iambic, alternating tetrameter with dimeter lines.   LP

William Carlos Williams **THE DANCE** (page 202)

The repetition of the first line of the poem as its last line gives the poem a circularity of form, which is emphasized internally by the repetition of the word "round" (2, 2, 5), "around" (3), and its rimes "impound" (6), "Grounds" (9), "sound" (10), plus the assonant "about" (8). [The poem lacks end rime, but is rich in internal rime, exemplified in the above; in "prance as they dance" (11); and in such approximations as "squeal"-"tweedle"-"fiddles" (3–4), "tipping"-"thick"-"hips" (5–7), "bellies"-"balance" (7), "about"-"butts" (8–9), etc.] The abundance of participial verb forms—"tipping," "kicking," "rolling," "swinging," "rollicking"—contributes also to the sense of vigorous motion. The triple meter gives this motion speed, but is subject to occasional jolting irregularities (as in 5, 6, 8) which remind us that these are thick-shanked, big-bellied, heavy-butted peasants dancing, not a graceful group of nymphs on Mount Olympus. The great majority of the lines are run-on (only the last ends with a full stop, and 1 and 6 with partial stops), thus giving the poem a sense of continuous motion, especially when the lines end with such traditionally unlikely words as "and," "the," and a hyphenated "thick-," where the reader is thrown forward into the next line without even a pause to observe the line-ending. This fact is further enhanced by the fact that all but three of the lines (5, 6, 11) have feminine endings, so that the meter as well as the grammatical incompleteness throws the reader forward. A highly unusual feature of this poem is that all but

116

three ("around," "impound," and "about") of the words of more than one syllable (there are twenty-six of them) are accented on the first syllable; and this also contributes to the sense of continuous motion. The exceptions to the foregoing observations occur just frequently enough to keep the reader a bit off-balance, like the peasants themselves.

Three onomatopoetic words provide the music for all this motion—the "squeal," "blare," and "tweedle" of the bagpipes, bugle, and fiddles. LP

Ben Jonson **TO FOOL, OR KNAVE** (page 202)

The speaker allows himself neither to be flattered by the praise nor stung by the dispraise of fools or knaves. The effectiveness of Jonson's epigram derives from its beautiful grammatical balancing of contrasting meanings emphasized by similarity of sound. In the opposed verbs "stroke" and "strike" only the vowel sound is different. LP

14. Pattern

When read in the two ways suggested, cummings' poem reveals a multiplicity of patterns. First, a rime pattern (*abcbac*), repeated in each stanza, utilizing both approximate and perfect rimes. Second, a metrical pattern, built on an anapestic base (five lines of dimeter and one of monometer), in which the corresponding lines of each stanza match each other exactly. Third, a sound pattern which relates the two chief words of each first line by assonance ("greedy"-"people"), alliteration ("timid"-"tender"), or rime ("chary"-"wary"). Fourth, a syntactical pattern which matches the corresponding lines of the various stanzas, putting identical grammatical structures and parts of speech in corresponding places. (The second line of each stanza, for instance, is always a parenthesis in which the framework "as _____ as can _____" is filled in by words related in form but opposed in meaning.) Fifth, and most important, a structural pattern, in which the meaning of the first four lines of each stanza is countered by the last two, and within which words of similar or related meaning and form are balanced neatly against each other (such pairings as "sell" and "buy," "don't" and "do," "when" and "how" are obvious).

The cummings trademark comes out in this poem in his imaginative transformation of the parts of speech, particularly in the final word of the fourth line in each stanza, in which conjunctions ("because"), pronouns ("which"), verbs ("seem," "must"), and prepositions ("until") are made to serve as nouns. "Because" (4) for cummings represents the cold sterility of abstract reason as opposed to the warm life of instinct and emotion (Faith asks of materialism, "Why?"). "Which" (10) is a thing rather than a person ("Who"). "Seem" (16) indicates a mere illusion of existence as opposed to real existence ("Be"). "Until" (22) represents an indefinite future as contrasted to the living present ("Now"). "Must" (28) represents the restrictive authority of artificial social conventions and rules as opposed to the permissiveness of nature ("May"). cummings concludes his poem with a triumphant pun, for "May" is not only the auxiliary verb of permission; it is that season of the year which stands for youth, for growth, for nature, and for life.

The two nouns in line 1 of each stanza represent undesirables in cummings' vocabulary ["people" (1) stands for *masses* rather than *individuals*; "tender" (25) is probably meant in the sense of *tender-minded* rather than *tender-hearted*]. Of the two variables in line 2 of each stanza, the first always represents something undesirable, the second something desirable ["you're" (14) is a plural as opposed to a singular "i'm"]. The activities depicted in lines 3–4 of each stanza are undesirable ["work" (27) represents materialistic drudgery as opposed to creative play; "pray" (27) is directed toward an authoritarian god (a "must") rather than toward a God of love].

118

In summary, the poem opposes states of unbeing and being. The first four lines of each stanza pass in review those people who feverishly pursue materialistic goals and whose lives are governed by greed, anxiety, prudence, convention, and conformity. In the last two lines of each stanza, the steeple bell, moon, stars, sun, and earth offer a laconic comment on these people's foolishness.

[This commentary is adapted from Laurence Perrine and James M. Reid, *100 American Poems of the Twentieth Century* (New York: Harcourt Brace Jovanovich, 1966), pp. 156–57.]

Anonymous **THERE WAS A YOUNG LADY OF NIGER** (page 206)

> Don't think of this tale as distressing.
> The tiger (from gout convalescing)
>> Had had nothing to eat
>> For a month. What a treat
> Was fresh meat with some palm leaves for dressing!
>
> ——
>
> (And he didn't forget to ask blessing!) LP

John Keats **ON FIRST LOOKING INTO CHAPMAN'S HOMER** (page 207)

The octave is concerned with exploration, the sestet with the experience of discovery.

The octave is an extended metaphor in which travel is the figurative term for reading, and "the realms of gold" for literature. The "goodly states and kingdoms" are various kinds of literature, and the "western islands" are specifically poetry, the domain of Apollo, god of poetry and inventor of the lyre (from which the term "lyric" is derived). Though geography should not be pressed too hard, these islands are probably called "western" to associate them with the West Indies, where many of the early English and Spanish explorers sought for gold.

The sestet consists of two similes conveying the thrill of discovery. First, the speaker compares himself to an astronomer looking through his telescope when "a new planet swims into his ken." Anyone who has looked through a good astronomical telescope can testify to the "swimming" or quaking motion that an observed celestial body has as it enters the field of vision. The word "ken" is also beautifully effective here, for it not only means "range of vision" but is associated with knowing or knowledge; and the excitement here is generated by the astronomer's discovering a planet—a whole new world—previously unknown to man.

The second simile partly derives its force from the fact that the early explorers, seeking a shorter route to the East Indies and Cathay, at first thought they had found it and did not realize that what they had actually found was a new continent separated by another whole sea from their destination. Balboa's discovery of the

Pacific thus came as a surprise and vastly expanded European ideas about the size of the earth. Keats captures the exact awe-struck moment when the explorer and his men first encounter this vast, shining, and unguessed-at new ocean while crossing the mountains of a land they did not know to be an isthmus.

One would prefer poets to be historically accurate, and it would be folly to pretend that nothing is lost when they are not. Yet Keats's subject is not history but human experience, and when one contemplates the consequences of substituting the three syllables of *bal-BO-a* for the three syllables of "STOUT COR-tez," one may even be glad for the blunder. The first loss is the adjective "stout" which, along with "eagle-eyed," gives strength and stature to the discoverer. The second loss is one of sound and rhythm which support this strength. "STOUT COR-tez" with its three *t*'s, sharp *k*-sound, and two stresses, gives the adventurer just that intrepid quality which is needed, while *bal-BO-a* softens its *b*'s with a liquid *l* and trails off into two vowel sounds suggestive more of grace than of strength. The heroic description of the discoverer matches the heroic verse and voice ("loud and bold") of Chapman's translation, which for Keats first captured the heroic qualities of Homer's epic narratives.

But if this poem were only about Keats's discovery of Chapman's translation, it would be of limited interest. What gives it enduring value is Keats's transformation of his discovery into a symbol for all discovery, his magnificent success in conveying the excitement that may attend any discovery, made by any of us, whether it be of universal or only personal significance.   LP

William Shakespeare **THAT TIME OF YEAR** (Sonnet 73) (page 208)

In this sonnet an aging speaker, constantly aware of his approaching death, addresses a beloved person considerably younger than himself.

The structure of thought in the sonnet is perfectly matched to the formal divisions marked out by its rime scheme. In each of the three quatrains the speaker makes a metaphorical statement of his increasing age and nearness to death, and in the concluding couplet he makes a counterstatement of his beloved's increased love for him. This structure is formally expressed in the language of the poem. Its opening line contains the words "thou mayst in me behold"; the second and third quatrains each begin "In me thou see'st"; the concluding couplet, before making its counterstatement, summarizes what has preceded in its opening words "This thou perceivest."

In the opening quatrain the speaker compares himself to "that time of year" (late autumn or early winter) when "yellow leaves, or none, or few" hang upon the trees. In the second stanza he compares himself to the dusk of day, fading from sunset into night. In the third he compares himself to a sinking fire, whose glowing embers are about to be extinguished by the ashes of the fuel which once "nourished" it. Though the quatrains (each a sentence) make parallel statements, they are arranged in a climactic order and could not be rearranged without loss. First, they are concerned with diminishing periods of time (a year, a day, the length of time that a fire will burn), and thus they bring us metaphorically closer and closer to the thought of death (weeks, hours, minutes). In addition, the first quatrain emphasizes coldness ("bare" boughs "shake against the cold"); the second emphasizes darkness (twilight fading into "black night"); the third combines cold and dark in the image of the sinking fire which is losing both warmth and light.

Each central metaphor is complicated by an additional metaphor or metaphors. In the first, the tree's leafless boughs are called "bare ruined choirs." A choir is that section of a church or chapel containing wooden choir stalls, and the sight of "bare ruined choirs" would have been familiar to every reader of Shakespeare's time because of the confiscation of Roman Catholic monastic properties throughout England by Henry VIII some half-century earlier and the subsequent spoliation of the monasteries by Reformation landowners. Through this association of thought the "sweet birds" become not only the songbirds which have migrated south for the winter, but the choir singers who once sang in the now-ruined monastery churches. The image of desolation is thus intensified. In the second quatrain, "black night," because of its association with sleep, is called "Death's second self"—a kind of twin or surrogate of Death "that seals up all in rest." In the third quatrain, the ashes of the fire become the deathbed on which the fire's personified youth is expiring, paradoxically "consumed" (in a third metaphor) by the food which once "nourished" it.

Against the three quatrains with their metaphorical statements of declining life and approaching death, the speaker opposes a concluding counterstatement concerning love. He throws human love, as it were, into the teeth of death. That the couplet is a counterstatement is metrically signaled by the inversion of stress in the opening foot. It begins, however, as a summarizing statement—"This thou perceivest"—where "This" refers for its antecedent to all of the images in the preceding quatrains (that is, to the grammatical objects of the verbs indicating seeing or beholding). The speaker then asserts his belief that the friend addressed throughout the sonnet loves the speaker all the more intensely because of the friend's realization that the speaker must soon die. The friend's increased love compensates for the speaker's impending death. Death's negative is countered by an affirmation of love.

Or so it would seem, on a first reading. On a second reading, we may be less sure of the strength of the affirmation. The speaker, we notice, is a person who needs to be loved. He does not conclude:

This thou perceivest, which makes my love more strong,
To love that well which I must leave ere long.

That is, he is not primarily concerned with giving love but with receiving it. We may then ask what evidence he has for his final assertion and perhaps question whether he is asserting a belief, expressing a hope, or making a plea. We may also begin to wonder whether he is actually as old as the metaphors in the quatrains suggest, or whether he does not mix considerable overstatement with these metaphors, perhaps as a play for the beloved's sympathy. The poem, seemingly simple on the surface, becomes increasingly complex and ambiguous as we delve into it. Some readers will read it for moral profundity; others will find it more notable for psychological profundity. [The questions raised here are more likely to rise in the mind of a reader who has read more of Shakespeare's sonnets than in that of a beginning student who reads the sonnet out of context. Such a student, however, may be asked to recall Sonnet 138—"When my love swears that she is made of truth" (page 34), where the speaker, surely not far past thirty, also refers to himself as "old" and quite clearly feels insecure in his relationship with a younger beloved.] LP

Anonymous A HANDFUL OF LIMERICKS (page 210)

The limerick can be useful for giving students personal experience with versification. Give them a first line ("A freshman who snored in his sleep") or part of a first line ("There was a young man from _____") and offer a prize for the best completion, taking into consideration both successful handling of the form and cleverness of the punch line. (Be sure, if you give them the first line, to provide one with ample riming opportunities.) Note that, though the basic meter is anapestic, iambs may be freely substituted in the first foot (but only in the first foot) in any line. Rarely, if ever, are the first feet in a limerick all anapests; but often (as in "There was a young lady of Lynn") they are all iambs. LP

Dylan Thomas POEM IN OCTOBER (page 211)

In tone this poem is rhapsodic. It begins on a note of delight and anticipation, climbs steadily to joy, leaps into an exalted state of visionary experience and recollection, then lapses slightly back into joy and hope. There are contrasts of tone in the poem, but they are not sharp contrasts. The whole poem is pitched at a high level of exultation. This exultation comes from the poet's relationship with nature, not only its beauty, but a sacredness he senses in it, akin to what Wordsworth found in it a century and a half earlier.

The poet celebrates his birthday by rising early in the morning (he hears the morning beckon him to set forth) and walking beyond the gates of the town and up the mountain that lies behind it. He climbs so high that he gets above the weather. The month is October, and it had been raining in the town, but high on the mountainside the sun is "Summery," birds are singing, and he only hears "the rain wringing / wind blow cold" in the woods "faraway" under him. From this height the town church seems small as a snail with its "horns" (its two towers) rising through mist. Where he stands, however, "all the gardens / Of spring and summer" seem to be blooming, and it is a fit spot to "marvel" his birthday away—"but the weather turned around." We must be careful not to put too much emphasis on that "but" or to read the following clause literally. The weather does not turn from rainy to

122

sunny or from fall to summery: these changes had already occurred as he climbed the mountainside. The weather metaphorically and psychologically turns "around" in that the poet's mind is carried in vision and in time away from the "blithe" summery scene presently before him where he could "marvel" his birthday away, back to his childhood days when he felt an even intenser and completer identification with the "wonder of summer." He remembers the forgotten mornings when "He walked with his mother / Through the parables / Of sun light / And the legends of the green chapels" (the woods), and "the mystery / Sang alive / Still in the water and singing-birds." In the final stanza the first three lines are a recapitulation of lines 38–40, not a new turning; nevertheless, this final stanza brings him slowly back to the reality of the present with its full recognition that the "true / Joy" of his visionary experience had been that of a "long dead child," that it is now his "thirtieth / Year to heaven" (a recapitulation of the opening line), and that the town below him is wearing its autumn foliage. The poem ends with the poet's prayer that on his next birthday he may still be capable of such visionary experience.

Though less explicitly philosophical, "Poem in October" in several ways resembles Wordsworth's "Tintern Abbey." The adult poet is a lover of nature, responsive to its beauty, and a believer that it somehow embraces the divine (as shown by Thomas's use throughout the poem of "sacramental imagery" and language: "thirtieth year to heaven," "heron / Priested shore," "water praying," "the blue altered sky"—with its concealed pun, "parables / Of sun light," "legends of the green chapels," "mystery"). Yet the poet regrets the loss of the even intenser involvement with nature that he enjoyed as a child when he felt the divinity of nature (his "true / Joy") less consciously in the intellect but more fully through his whole being.

A minor difficulty in this poem is caused by Thomas's omission of the hyphen from such compound adjectives as *mussel-pooled, heron-priested, net-webbed, rain-wringing, lark-full,* and *blue-altered.* The involved syntax of the first stanza has also caused difficulty. Its skeleton is "It was my thirtieth year to heaven [that] woke to my hearing the morning beckon myself to set foot in the town and set forth." Thomas has omitted the relative pronoun between lines 1 and 2. "Woke" is an intransitive verb modified by the prepositional phrase beginning with "to"; the object of the preposition is the long gerund phrase "my hearing the water beckon . . . etc." The object of the gerund is an infinitive phrase with "the morning" as its subject and "[to] beckon" as its verb. For fuller discussion, see *The Explicator,* 27 (Feb. 1969), item 43. LP

Matsuo Bashō / Moritake TWO JAPANESE HAIKU (page 213)

Just as the limerick is a useful form for giving students experience with versification, the haiku is a useful form for initiating them into original *poetic* composition (experiential rather than merely clever). The brevity of the form forces them to practice verbal economy; its nature, by delivering them from the hampering notion that meter and rime are essential to poetry, frees them to concentrate on other dimensions—particularly imagery. The essence of haiku poetry is that it suggests rather than states. It strives to give the reader some unique perception of nature, or some immediate insight into the nature of things, without intervention of the abstracting intellect. It accomplishes this, most frequently, either by presenting a single sharply observed image, or by juxtaposing two images which parallel or contrast with each other in significant and suggestive ways. So essential to the form is brevity that many writers of haiku in English have abandoned the traditional 5-7-5 syllabic pattern and written poems even briefer. The haiku composition assignment may therefore be made in various ways. If you wish to give your students the discipline of working within a prescribed form, insist on their adherence to the 5-7-5 pattern. If you wish to free them from all constraints of form, ask for a poem of not more than three lines. If you want to stress chiefly verbal economy, let them write a poem of any number or arrangement of lines but contaning no more than seventeen syllables. The important stipulation should be that the poem purvey its perception through imagery rather than through abstract statement. LP

A. E. Housman **WHEN I WAS ONE-AND-TWENTY** (page 214)

In form the two stanzas are practically identical: iambic trimeter riming *xaxaxbxb* with the unrimed lines regularly having an extra unstressed syllable at the end. In thought structure the first six lines of each stanza are almost identical—the first lines exactly the same, the second lines practically the same, then four lines of quotation which in the second stanza explain the advice given in the first. The meaning and effectiveness of the poem emerge from the contrast of content in the last two lines of stanzas parallel in form and, until line 15, perceived as being parallel in thought. The changes between lines 7 and 15 are few and slight—sufficient to signal the revelation of the last line without giving it away. An initial conjunction "But" (implying contrast with what has preceded) gives way to "And" (implying addition to what has preceded). The tense of the verb is changed from past to present. The speaker is one year older (by "birthday" age, not necessarily by calendar years. Since the speaker heard the wise man's advice twice when he was twenty-one, lines 14 and 15 may be separated by only a few months or days in time). Not until the last line— with its exclamatory "oh" and its twice-repeated "'tis true," do we get the full force of the speaker's switch from total rejection to full confirmation of the old man's "wisdom." The poet does not tell us, nor does he need to, what has happened to cause this change of attitude. The speaker has been jilted by his sweetheart. The emotional impact of the poem derives largely from its adroit patterning and its leaving to the reader to infer what has happened.

The heartbreak of disappointment in first love is so poignant a subject and so common an experience as to make it attractive to poets. For other treatments, see Yeats's "Down by the Salley Gardens" (page 183) and Ransom's more complex "Parting, Without a Sequel" (page 162).

The "wisdom" of the old man's advice may well be left to the student. The answer depends partly on the statistical validity of the wise man's generalization "The heat out of the bosom" is *"never* given in vain") but mostly on how one judges his advice against such an opposing opinion as Tennyson's *"'Tis better to have loved and lost, / Than never to have loved at all."* (Tennyson was speaking about the loss of his dearest friend by death; but the quotation out of context may be twisted to fit the present situation.) But of the poem's emotional truth to the young man's feeling, there can be no question. LP

John Crowe Ransom **PIAZZA PIECE** (page 214)

This sonnet is unusual among sonnets in having two speakers—one in the octave, another in the sestet. The first speaker is Death, as identified by the connotations of "dust" in the name of his garment, by his age, by the roses dying in his presence, by his association with a "spectral" moon, and by the young woman's terrified reaction to him and his "dry" words. The poem is a modern variation of the traditional Death-and-the-maiden theme, notably treated in art by Albrecht Dürer, Hans Baldung-Grien, and Edvard Munch, and in music by Franz Schubert. (Schubert's famous song on the subject is a musical setting of a poem by the German poet Matthias Claudius.) The subject is macabre, and Ransom makes it more so by domesticating it on the veranda of the woman's house, by referring to Death as a gentleman, and by casting it in the sonnet form—used so frequently for love poems.

Ransom varies the traditional Italian form by repeating the first line of the octave in its last, and the first line of the sestet in its last (and by using three rimes rather than only two in the octave). By cutting off the sentence-ends of the repeated lines, he gives them a wider and more terrifying range of possible meaning. Line 8 suggests that Death is "trying" to obtain the young lady's maidenhead or life. Line 14 may mean that the young lady has resigned herself to waiting for death.

An interesting poem to compare and contrast with this is Emily Dickinson's "Because I could not stop for death" (page 271). LP

William Shakespeare From *ROMEO AND JULIET* (page 215)

Since *Romeo and Juliet*, except for a few brief prose passages, is written throughout in iambic pentameter, and since much of it also rimes, the lines riming sometimes alternately and sometimes in pairs, it is not surprising that 14 lines, from a total of almost 3,000, should fall into the rime pattern of an English sonnet. That this excerpt does so from design, rather than from coincidence, can, however, be definitively demonstrated.

1. The passage has four kinds of unity: grammatical, situational, metaphorical, and tonal. First, the passage begins at the beginning of a sentence and ends at the end of a sentence. It is grammatically self-contained. Second, the passage covers a self-contained episode or situation: it begins with the first words of Romeo and

Juliet and ends with their first kiss. Third, the passage is unified by a single extended metaphor, one in which a pilgrim, or palmer, is worshiping at the shrine of a saint. Fourth, the religious nature of this metaphor—employing words like *profane, holy, shrine, sin, pilgrims, devotion, saints, palmers, prayer,* and *faith*—combines with the delicious punning wit of the dialogue to give the passage unity of tone: a tone of earnest delicacy and delightfully charming gravity which forces us to take seriously an episode we might otherwise take cynically. Romeo, we feel, is not simply a fresh young man on the make and Juliet an easy mark: this is genuine love at first sight. "Dear saint, let lips do what hands do" is tonally a great deal different from "Gimme a little kiss, honey, won'cha?"

2. In structure as in form, the excerpt is organized into three quatrains and a final couplet. In the first quatrain Romeo, initiating the basic metaphor, apologizes for taking Juliet's "holy" hand in his unworthy one, but humbly offers to make up for the offense by giving the hand a gentle kiss. In the second quatrain Juliet reassures Romeo, telling him that he has done no wrong but shows mannerly devotion in taking her hand, for pilgrims quite properly touch saints' hands, and pilgrims "kiss" by clasping hands. She thus simultaneously encourages Romeo to hold her hand but with maidenly delicacy indicates that there is no need for him to kiss it. In the third quatrain, however, emboldened by this reassurance, Romeo decides to play the long shot and ask for a kiss on the lips. But he puts the request delicately and charmingly. Do not pilgrims and saints have lips as well as hands? he asks. Translated, this means, why should we not kiss with our lips instead of merely with our hands? Juliet, still modest, yet keeping to the metaphor, replies that pilgrims' lips are for praying with. Then Romeo brilliantly seizes his opening: "Let lips do what hands do." The line has two meanings. Hands not only kiss, they also pray. Lips not only pray, they also kiss. So Romeo, shaping his hands into the attitude of prayer, prays also with his lips; but what he prays for is a kiss. In the final couplet Juliet, not unwillingly defeated in this contest of wit (for what can a saint do when a faithful pilgrim prays to her?) gracefully surrenders: she grants the kiss, thus answering Romeo's prayer. The first quatrain is Romeo's apology; the second is Juliet's reassurance; the third is the plea; and the couplet is the plea granted. Structure follows form.

3. In Shakespeare's time the sonnet form was used primarily for the treatment of love. His play concerns a pair of "star-crossed lovers." The episode in the excerpt concerns their first meeting and their first kiss. What more appropriate than that Shakespeare should deliberately cast the episode into the form of an English sonnet?

[This discussion is abridged from the essay "When Form and Content Kiss, / Intention Made the Bliss," in Laurence Perrine, *The Art of Total Relevance: Papers on Poetry* (Rowley, Mass.: Newbury House, 1976), pp. 75–77.]

The speaker is a mother with two children—a boy, six; and a girl, five—and in the poem she expresses a wish that every loving mother sometimes feels—that she could keep her children just as they presently are—inexpressibly precious; protected against the changes and calamities that the future will bring. This wish runs counter to the wishes of the children: unaware of the burdens of adult responsibility, they want desperately to be older, to enjoy the independence or the privileges that their present status denies them. It also runs counter to the law of life—that everything changes; time stops for no man or mother.

But this mother is also a poet—a "magician"—and in her poem she has found "the one abracadabra" (36) or "charm" (1) capable of suspending the children in time—of keeping them forever as they are now, "the boy at six / and the girl fast at five"; while outside the poem they are able (as the mother ambivalently also wants them) to grow, sing, fly, do what they're here for (39).

Unlike the sonnet, which often inspires talent and has produced a rich array of masterpieces, the sestina more often smothers talent. The repetition of the same end-words seven times, even though varied in order, tends to result in monotony. Few sestinas are memorable. But this "magician" has had the originality (a) to abandon fixed meter and line length (a usual concomitant of the form) for free verse, thus making the exact reappearance of the end-word less predictable and allowing the poet greater freedom in maneuvering her lines to meet the end-word requirement, (b) to choose for her end-words the first six cardinal numbers (not to my knowledge done before), and (c) to vary the use, meaning, and form of the end-words so inventively through puns, split-off syllables, etc., as to make us actually look forward to the ingenuity with which she will meet the successive challenges. Yet the poem is no ᵢₑere exercise in ingenuity, but is rich in human insight, authentic in its depiction of the mother's feelings and of the children's behavior. The form, with its six-line stanzas, is unusually well-adapted, given the poet's choice of end-words and of ages for the children, to her subject.

The structure of the poem, counterpointing rather than paralleling its form, further helps the poet overcome monotony. The mother speaks to herself in the first seven-and-a-half lines. In thought she addresses her son from the middle of line 8 to the middle of line 26, her daughter from the middle of line 26 through line 36, and both of them in the envoy.

Notes: "I'll be one / again" (6-7) may have a double meaning. The "feathery totem" (a symbolic and sacred family representation; i.e., the poem) which the speaker is tattooing "against time" may make her "one" (integrated, whole) again, even when her children have grown up and left her to be "one" (alone) again. The son's "five / finger exercises" (he is taking piano lessons) predict no easy waltz-time future for him but a troubled life of "symphonic storms" (10-16). If the son has two children, he will "make three / journeys upstream" (15-16), one for each of the children, one for himself—as the mother has herself done. The son, embarrassed at six to seem dependent on his mother, no longer holds on to her fingers at drugstores, and is forever running into sharp corners where a year earlier he had met graceful curves (16–19). Yet the mother, humorously, half-ironically, and ambivalently urges him to maintain this independence and not let himself be seen tied to his "grotesque three / headed mother." Humorously but sadly she predicts, in an allusion to Peter's three denials of Christ (Mark 14:29–30, 66–72), that he will deny her "more than three / times" (25–26). She knows and wisely accepts the fact that children in growing up must rebel against their parents in order to attain their own selfhood. "Everyone / draws your lines" (29–30) may mean "holds you back as with harness traces" or "draws lines you must not overstep." The girl is so eager to be six because she envies the prerogatives of her brother, and is shut out of the three o'clock "male rendezvous" (33) when the boys get out of school. Her mother, in a paradoxical overstatement, says she is trying so hard to grow up that she'll be fourteen before she's six (35–36). LP

Anonymous **EDWARD** (page 217)

The story told in "Edward"—a dark domestic tragedy of greed, guile, murder, and remorse—is unfolded gradually through dialogue, question, and answer. Not until the third stanza do we learn what Edward has done. Not until the last do we learn why he has done it. The tension of the poem mounts steadily through the first climax to the last.

A man of noble birth and heir to his father's estate, Edward has killed his father because of the "counsels" of his mother, who had hoped to get control of these properties into her own hands. To accomplish this end, she has been willing to subvert her own son. Crafty, manipulative, greedy, and entirely lacking in natural affections, she has somehow worked on her son's feelings through hint, suggestion, and insinuation, until he has felt it his duty or his interest to kill his father. But the psychological dimensions of the story exist largely between the lines.

Why does the mother, if she put him up to it, have to ask why Edward's sword drips with blood? She is perhaps surprised to see Edward "sad" rather than rejoicing, and needs to confirm her hopes. Why does Edward lie about what he has done? Since doing the deed, he has undergone a revulsion of horror and remorse, and is lying more to himself than to his mother. He cannot admit to himself what he has done. The mother calls his bluff, presses her question; Edward lies again, and is again detected; but the mother reveals something about herself. One steed is the same as another to her, and she does not understand that a man might have a peculiar affection for a particular steed, especially an old one (like his father). When Edward finally admits the truth, the mother shows no emotion; it is what she had secretly known and hoped for. In her question about what penance Edward will do for his deed, she cunningly washes her hands of any share in the guilt. Edward, overcome with guilt, sees exile from home and family and all he has loved as the only possible penance. The next question—what will Edward do with his towers and hall?—brings us to the center of the mother's interests. But Edward cares not a whit for the towers and hall: they

128

are the witnesses of his dreadful crime. Failing of the answer she wanted, the mother shrewdly digresses in her next question, disguising her main concern. Edward's reply to what he will leave his wife and children does not indicate that he is uncaring, but only that he is so emotionally overwrought that he feels any provision made for them can only contaminate them with his own guilt. In her final question the mother returns to her main concern: "And what wul ye leive to your ain mither deir?" In that final phrase we glimpse the mother's manipulative method. Twice in the poem she has addressed Edward as her dear son (12, 28); now she reminds him that she is his own dear mother. But she is totally unprepared for the switch in parental allegiance that Edward has undergone since the killing. Edward uses the word "dear" in the poem only in speaking of his dead father (21, 23).

Edward's final outburst comes with a shock to the reader as to the mother. For the reader it is a double shock—that of hearing a son deliver the curse of hell on his mother and of learning that he killed his father at his mother's suggestion. Yet the reader is left, most likely, with a feeling of pity for Edward and of horror for the mother. The emotional Edward suffers torments of horror, guilt, and remorse for what he has done; the crafty and unnatural mother feels nothing but greed.

The narrative kernel of each stanza (lines 1, 4, 5, 8) is in ballad stanza. The two refrains ("Edward, Edward" and "Mither, mither") keep the crucial family relationship constantly before us. The repeated lines prolong the suspense and add immensely to the emotional power. LP

Maxine Kumin **400-METER FREESTYLE** (page 220)

Although the poem pays tribute to stamina and "heart," it primarily celebrates a mastery of form achieved by discipline and hard training: "Thrift is his wonderful secret; he has schooled out all extravagance." The economy of motion that eliminates any wasted movement is "schooled." The swimmer's feet "know the lesson" of steady cadence, and the lungs "know" not to list for air.

Thrift is the poet's virtue, too, and this poem drives steadily forward from "The Gun" which starts the race to the announcement of the winner's "TIME: 4:25:9." There is minimal punctuation, and there are no wasted words.

The sixteen horizontal lines of the poem match the sixteen lengths of a Junior-Olympic-size (25-meter) pool that have to be swum in a 400-meter race. The three-letter vertical arcs connecting the lines imitate the flip-turn used in modern competitive swimming. As the swimmer approaches the end of the pool, he ducks his head under, and in one continuous movement he brings his legs out of the water, knees bent, slaps the soles of his feet against the end of the pool while executing a half twist, pushes off hard, and glides underwater (as the spectators watch "for signs") before resurfacing and resuming his stroke.

For about one month in 1958, 4 min. 25.9 seconds was the world's record (men's) for this event. The poem was published in 1961. Maxine Kumin has herself been a competitive swimmer. LP

William Burford   **A CHRISTMAS TREE** (page 221)

The pattern of this poem is metrical as well as typographical. The lines have respectively one, two, three, four, five, one, and two feet. The poem's meaning is reinforced visually not only in the Christmas-tree shape but also in the word
"huddld," where the omission of the letter *e* huddles four tall-stemmed letters together. The rime scheme is *aabcxb*, the *b* rimes being approximate.   LP

15. Bad Poetry and Good

Exercise (page 226)

I should arrange these as follows: d. (Browning); e. Melville: *Moby Dick*); a. (Thoreau: *Walden*); c. ("Thirty days"); f. (J. S. Mill: *Three Essays in Religion*); b. (algebraic equation).

The passage from *Moby Dick*, though not metered, uses the rhythms, the musical devices, the images, and the metaphors of poetry. In the assonance and half-rime of "handclappings . . . rapture," an onomatopoetic nucleus is intensified; in a sequence like "warningly waving . . . hoveringly halting . . . longingly lingered," alliteration and consonance are combined with rhythmical and syntactical similarity.

The passage from *Walden*, though less obviously lyrical, is stately in its rhythm and gains its force from a highly imaginative and effective metaphor.

"Thirty days" is doggerel: it has meter and rime but no other poetic quality. It does not create experience; it exhibits neither feeling nor imagination.

The philosophical definition of Nature is entirely abstract, but it is at least composed of words.

The algebraic passage represents the ultimate of abstraction.   LP

Arthur Hugh Clough   **SAY NOT THE STRUGGLE NOUGHT AVAILETH** (page 227)

Walter D. Wintle   **THE MAN WHO THINKS HE CAN** (page 228)

Students often oversimplify the theme of Clough's poem. It does not say that you will succeed if you don't give up—this would be a sentimental and grossly false assertion to make about life, though it is often made in the shallower examples of "inspirational" poetry ("every cloud has a silver lining"). Clough's poem says that at the moment when things seem darkest, you *may* be on the brink of success—so don't give up. It is worth stressing for students that the phrase "may be" is repeated —in lines 5 and 6. Clough offers no assurance of success for the persevering man.

Clough develops his theme through three images: a battle (stanzas 1–2), the incoming tide (stanza 3), and the rising sun (stanza 4)—all presenting instances where appearances may be or are deceptive. Again, students may misunderstand these images. Stanza 3 is not about creeks flowing into the sea, but about the sea flowing into creeks—as the tide comes in. The subject of "comes" (12) is "main." (It may be worthwhile to have students rearrange lines 11–12 in normal prose order, to clarify their understanding of its grammatical structure.) As measured by the rise of water against a vertical cliff, the coming in of the tide may be imperceptible, but in low places, like creeks and inlets, the water spreads out, quickly covering large areas of land that were previously dry. Stanza 4 presents the phenomenon of the sun's lighting up the sky even before it rises. If we look east to watch the sun rise, it seems to rise very slowly; but if we look west, we see the land flooded with light when the tip of the sun is barely over the horizon. The three images are parallel in their implication; each makes the point that, though victory or success in one's own locality seems to be lost or doubtful or slow, elsewhere it may be complete.

Poetically, Clough's poem gets progressively better, each stanza being superior to the one that precedes it. The biblical language of the first stanza ("availeth," "faileth") was poetically archaic even in Clough's day, but Clough drops it in the second stanza, and the kind of poeticism represented by "e'en" in stanza 2 does not reappear in stanzas 3 or 4. The battle image of the first two stanzas is a trite one, but in stanza 2 Clough develops it sufficiently to make it his own. The images in stanzas 3 and 4 are both fresh and imaginative, and in syntactical and rhetorical structure, stanza 4 is an improvement over stanza 3.

Clough's genuine poetic skill is manifested not only in his images but also in his extraordinarily skillful handling of meter. His basic pattern is iambic tetrameter with an unstressed extra syllable at the end of lines 1 and 3 in each stanza. Clough adroitly varies this meter throughout, avoiding monotony. More important, by his departures from perfect regularity, he has reinforced his meaning. In line 16, for example, the grammatical pauses on either side of "look" have the effect of isolating that word and giving it an increased emphasis appropriate to its function in the dramatic context of the poem. In line 5 the trochaic substitution in the third foot, following a grammatical pause, puts a very heavy emphasis on "fears" which again is appropriate to the meaning. (The line is much more forceful than if Clough had written, "If hopes were dupes, so fears may cozen.") In line 3 the spondaic third foot "faints not," following the very light stress on the final syllable of "enemy," receives a much heavier emphasis than the idea it expresses would have received if Clough had written, "The foeman fainteth not, nor faileth." In these examples the reinforcement is achieved by the metrical emphasis placed on words or phrases important to the meaning. An even more dramatic reinforcement of meaning occurs when the metrical movement corresponds to the movement indicated by the content. In line 15 Clough could have written a metrically regular line:

in FRONT / the SUN / a- RIS- / es SLOW- / ly.

But this line, so written, *moves* fairly quickly. Accordingly, Clough has slowed the line down in several ways. First, he has substituted spondees in the last two feet, thus forcing five stressed syllables together. Second, he has introduced two grammatical pauses, indicated by the commas. Third, he has thrust sounds together which are difficult to pronounce quickly. (The three syllables of "arises" glide easily off the tongue, but the sounds of "climbs slow how" cannot be uttered swiftly.) In making these changes in movement, Clough has repeated the key word "slow." The result is a line in which sound and movement correspond beautifully to meaning:

in FRONT / the SUN / CLIMBS SLOW, / HOW SLOW- / ly.

A similar effect is achieved in line 9.

"Say not the struggle nought availeth" is didactic poetry. "The Man Who Thinks He Can" is didactic verse. It takes a commonplace idea—Self-confidence is essential to success—and repeats it, in commonplace language, *nine* times (lines 1, 2, 3-4, 5, 6-8, 9, 10, 11-12, 13-16). It expresses this message in a jigging iambic-anapestic meter (trimeter in lines 1, 2, and 4 of each stanza; tetrameter in line 3) that undercuts any seriousness the message might otherwise have. The lines are without fresh images; indeed, almost without images at all. The metaphor "life's battles" (13) is left, like the theme of the "poem," an undeveloped cliché.

The "battle" metaphor, used in both poems, demands further consideration. In "The Man Who Thinks He Can" it apparently represents the struggle for personal advancement. The poem is concerned with how to "rise" (10) "in the world" (6), with how to "win a prize" (12), the prize being "Success" (7), and its achievement depending on individual effort and self-confidence. In "Say not the struggle nought availeth," however, the "battle" cannot be simply dismissed as "the battle of life," for life is not an enterprise in which there is a definite victory, and the details of the image do not function meaningfully in this interpretation. Who are the comrades, who are the foes, in the battle of life? How can the battle of life be won for one by one's comrades, when in one's own area he is losing? No, the "battle" must here represent the struggle for some social cause, in which one group of human beings are striving for goals which are opposed by others. It might be, for instance, a struggle for democratic government, for human rights, for racial justice, or for fair labor laws: it stands undoubtedly for some idealistic kind of effort. In brief, Clough's poem is not only better written, it is also concerned with a nobler subject.   LP

Anonymous   **GOD'S WILL FOR YOU AND ME** (page 228)

Gerard Manley Hopkins   **PIED BEAUTY** (page 229)

The poetic deficiencies of "God's Will for You and Me" are not far to seek. Its literal language is trite ("when things go wrong," "God knows best"). Its figurative language is trite ("willing feet," "our daily key"). Its remaining imagery is feeble ("song," "dark or bright," "child"). Fourteen of the poem's sixteen lines repeat the phrase "Just to," ten times followed by "be." These three words constitute almost 40 percent of the poem. The rest is mostly a string of abstract adjectives—"tender," "true," "glad," "merciful," "mild," "trustful," "gentle," "kind," "sweet," "helpful," "cheery," "loyal"—strung together in no particular order. Worst of all, the poem's tripping triple meter and childish repetition of "Just to be" make God's will for you and me seem simple, undemanding, and easy to carry out. In truth, no man could do it successfully for one whole day. The poem not only fails to create experience; it falsifies it.

Though both poems concern God, their themes are quite different. "God's Will" is didactic verse instructing us how God wishes us to live our lives, "Pied Beauty" is, first, a hymn of praise to God for the variegated, changing beauty of the natural and human worlds, and, second, a contrast between this variegated, changing beauty of the created world and the uniform, unchanging beauty of the Creator. (The theme has its Biblical base in James I: 17: "Every good gift and every perfect gift is from above, and cometh down from the Father of lights, with whom is no variableness, neither shadow of turning.")

The first theme is stated in the title and first line of the poem and is developed and exemplified in the next eight. "Glory be to God," the poet exclaims, for the beauty of things that are pied, dappled, couple-colored, brinded, stippled, plotted and pieced, fickle, or freckled. With one exception these terms all apply to things that are of more than one color. The exception, "fickle," referring to variation in time rather than space, ties in with "swift, slow" and reminds us that this various beauty is in constant motion and is constantly changing. The white clouds move and change in shape across a brightening or darkening blue sky; the decoratively rose-mole-stippled trout swim in a changing current. In line 5, which introduces human activities into the poem, farmers alter the landscape by laying it out in plots of grazing, fallow, and plowed land.

The concluding two lines of the poem summarize the first theme and introduce the second. The praise for this diverse, changing beauty is due to a Creator whose beauty is "past [beyond] change." The poem thus brings into contrast multiplicity and unity, constant change and changelessness, plenitude and amplitude, with the implication that the latter are greater. If the wonders of the created world (which varies "who knows how?") pass understanding, how much more so must the beauty of their Creator!

The achievement of the poem lies, first, in its packed, vivid imagery. Line 4, for instance, in six words introduces three separate vivid images (two literal, one figurative). There are "finches' wings" (black and gold) and "chestnut falls" (fallen chestnuts beneath a tree, glowing in mahogany browns), these latter compared by a compound adjective to fresh firecoals glowing golden and umber in a grate. Though the imagery of the poem is chiefly visual, the opposition of "sweet, sour" reminds us that the world is variegated in its appeal to the other senses as well. Second, the poem is remarkable for its rich use of sound: patterned end-rime; paired alliterations linking words parallel or opposed in meaning ("swift, slow"; "sweet, sour"; "adazzle, dim"), or simply the complex orchestration of such a line as 4 (with the alliteration of *Fresh-fire-falls-finches*; the assonance of *fresh-chestnut* and *finches' wings*; the *l*-consonance of *coal-falls*). Third, the poem is remarkable for its concentration. In line 4 every word is image-bearing; in line 6 all words but the initial "With" carry a full freight of meaning (contrast such lines with the slackness of "Just to be tender, just to be true"). Finally, "Pied Beauty" is notable for its freshness of diction. The four adjectives in line 7 are all apposite yet unexpected; the adjectives in "God's Will for You and Me" are as predictable as those in the Boy Scout oath. LP

Robert Francis **PITCHER** (page 229)

George E. Phair **THE OLD-FASHIONED PITCHER** (page 229)

   The first poem celebrates pitching as an art, the second as a feat of endurance. This is their difference of intention at the literal level—and the second poem has only a literal level.
   "The Old-Fashioned Pitcher" is a familiar exercise in sentimental nostalgia for "the good old days." Its one cleverness lies in its imitation of a more famous poem of the same sort, "The Bucket" by Samuel Woodworth (1785–1842). Woodworth's first stanza begins "How dear to my heart are the scenes of my childhood" and ends by referring to "The old oaken bucket, the iron-bound bucket, / The moss-covered bucket which hung in the well." Comparison of their stanzaic pattern, and of their opening and concluding lines, shows that Phair's poem is a conscious allusion to Woodworth's. Aside from this element of parody, "The Old-Fashioned Pitcher" has little to recommend it. The adjective "old" before "village green" (2) is an obvious sentimentalism designed to elicit a stock response of warm affection for former times. The phrase "ducks from the scene" (4) is trite and slangy. Line 7 is a blatant example of "padding" (the use of unnecessary words to fill out the metrical requirements of the line): "That is the reason" could be reduced to "that's why" or "therefore"; "hanker and long for" uses two verbs where one would suffice. The nouns "hurler" and "twirler" are used so often in sports pages simply as variations for "pitcher" that it is difficult to know whether the poet here intended to differentiate them. They can be differentiated, of course. A "hurler" relies upon strength and speed simply to "fire" the ball past the batter. A "twirler" puts a spin or twist on the ball, causing it to curve or break in a manner deceptive to the batter. The former relies upon strength, the latter on skill. Since throwing curve balls puts a greater strain on the muscles than throwing fast balls, the "twirler" suffers more often from a sore arm than the "hurler." Does the poet recognize this distinction? Does he mean to confess "I prefer strength to skill—Goliath to David"? Or is he not rather saying simply that "men aren't what they used to be"? Evidence favors the latter surmise. If the old-fashioned pitcher was "iron-armed," what need had he to be "stouthearted"? It seems unlikely that this poet was thinking about such distinctions. Sentimental gush and critical thought are seldom bedfellows.
   "Pitcher" celebrates the skill and subtlety of the good pitcher. His "art" is to be off-center. His "aim is how not to hit the mark he seems to aim at"—the batter's bat, or the dead center of the strike zone (directly over the center of the plate and halfway between the batter's knees and shoulders). (Notice how the two "aim's" vary slightly in meaning.) He must "avoid the obvious"—the pitch that goes exactly where it seems to be going, but he must "vary the avoidance" lest the batter learn what to expect. The other players on the team—infielders and outfielders—throw to be understood (the shortstop throwing to first base does not want to fool the first baseman); but the pitcher throws "to be a moment misunderstood" by the batter (so that the batter will swing too low or too high, or too soon or too late, either

hitting an easy pop-fly or an easy grounder or missing the ball altogether). Yet "not too much. Not errant, arrant, wild"—the three adjectives are not redundant (like "hanker and long for") but are skillful variations of meaning; no pitch is "errant" (wandering or deviating from his intention), "arrant" (flagrantly and shamelessly wide of the mark), or "wild" (out of control). The pitcher does not want to walk the batter, cause his catcher to drop his pitch, or throw so wide of the plate that the catcher can't reach it (allowing baserunners, if any, to advance). Rather "every seeming aberration: is "willed" (intended, under perfect control). He wants "Not to . . . communicate" (not to hit the batter's bat squarely) yet (here is the paradox) he *wants* "to communicate." He wishes the batter to understand his intention but "too late" to make a base hit.

The poet exemplifies in his own verse the subtle skill he celebrates. He "varies the avoidance" of the obvious, not only in his choice of words ("errant, arrant, wild") but in the very form of his poem. It consists of five pentameter couplets, each different in its "riming." The first pairs "aim" with "aim at." The second couples two three-syllable words with only the hissing of a final sibilant to connect them in sound. The third pairs two four-syllable participles ending in -d, but throws things off a bit by shoving the subject of the second of the two parallel sentences up to the end of the first line. The fourth pairs "willed" and "wild" (alliteration and consonance). The fifth has perfect rime.

So—at the literal level alone—the first poem is clearly superior. But obviously (however, in this context, it won't be obvious at all to many students) the first poem is symbolical. The poet is speaking not only about pitcher and batter but about poet and reader. (The clues are words like "art," "passion," "technique," "comprehended," "communicate," and "understand"—words more often found in discussions of poetry than of baseball.) The poet wants to be understood by his reader—but not too easily. If he is too obvious (literal, or trite), the reader will find his work dull and uninteresting; if he is not, sometimes, "a moment misunderstood," the reader will not return for a second reading. The poet, after all, is not writing directions for how to assemble a piece of furniture. He wants to communicate with the whole reader. To do this he must throw a few sliders and curve balls—must use figurative language (like paradox and symbol) and other devices of indirection. As Emerson says of the poet, he "must mount to paradise / By the stairway of surprise." LP

Margaret Johnston Griffin **TO MY SON** (page 230)

James Joyce **ON THE BEACH AT FONTANA** (page 230)

The one virtue of "To My Son" is its structure. Stanza 1 shows that the speaker identifies with her son to such an extent that he is the principal source of pain or pleasure in her life. In stanza 2 she urges him not to hurt her by bringing disgrace on himself and thus on her. In stanza 3 she urges him to bring praise and pride to her by establishing a reputation for uprightness. The development is logical and orderly.

Beyond this, the poem is without merit. It has no specific dramatic situation. It contains nothing fresh or memorable in language, imagery, or figurative expression. The language constantly borders on triteness and occasionally achieves it, e.g., "proud world" (10). (The clichés "Like mother like son" and "She reaped as she sowed" are perhaps excusable because put into the mouth of "the world," but they do not bring distinction to the poem.) The meter—anapestic tetrameter—is too swift for the subject. The poem has glaring examples of padding—"Do you know that" (1), "seem to be" (2), "if task it shall be" (9).

Most objectionable, however, is the poem's content. The mother wishes her son to be upright and honorable, not for her son's sake, not for the world's sake, but for *her* sake. What she wants, moreover, is not simply the quiet self-satisfaction of having brought up a good son, but a *reputation* for having done so. She wants the world to "do homage" to her. She wants his behavior to reflect glory on herself. Her motivation is selfish.

This motivation would be acceptable if there were any hint of dramatic irony in the poem, any suggestion that the poet was judging the speaker. But there is none. The title identifies the speaker *as* the poet!

In the second poem deeply felt emotion is conveyed through the use of vivid imagery, vivid language, and imaginative figures of speech.

The speaker is a father, and his thoughts are occasioned by his being with his son on the beach as a menacing storm comes up. The poet, however, does not *tell* us that a storm is coming up; he creates it for us through our senses. In lines 1–2 we hear the wind whining among the pebbles of the beach, and the pierstakes groaning in the surge of the waves. "Whining" and "groan," both onomatopoetic words, reproduce the high-pitched sound of the wind and the low-pitched sound of wood rubbing against wood. The word "crazy" here primarily means filled with fine cracks; but, with the personification given the pierstakes by the verb "groans," it takes on also its more common meaning, and we visualize the pierstakes as a bunch of demented old men lurching against each other in the water. This image leads into the image of lines 3–4 where the sea is personified as a senile old man foolishly counting stones and slobbering over them. The literal image we see is that of waves coming higher and higher up the beach, their frothy edges seeming to touch and release each stone singly as they creep up and recede. In these lines with their remarkable alliteration of the *s*-sound (six times) and repetition of the *l*-sound (four times), we hear the hissing of the waves, and are reminded (see page 188) that *sl-* is frequently connected with words meaning *slippery-wet*. The phonetic intensive "slime" is here reinforced by the proximity of *s*'s and *l*'s in "senile," "single," and "silvered."* In stanza 2 we

---

*The first stanza of "To My Son" contains forty-three words, of which only four or five convey any sort of image: *fibre, cord pain, please, praise*. The first stanza of "On the Beach at Fontana" contains eighteen words, of which only five do not convey an image: *and, the, the, a, each*. Thus, 72 percent of the words in the latter stanza are image-bearing as against about 12 percent in the former. This leaves out of account that Joyce's words often carry more than one image ("slimesilvered" is both tactile and visual; the "crazy pierstakes" and "senile sea" participate in both literal and figurative images).

are given kinesthetic, thermal, and tactile as well as visual imagery. The boy is "trembling," chiefly from cold but perhaps also from fear, and the father touches his "fine-boned" (a beautifully particularizing adjective) shoulder and wraps him "warm" from the cold wind and colder sea. In stanza 3 the word "fear" is used twice, first as a metonymy for wind and sea (result substituted for cause), second as a metonymy for dark clouds and lowering sky. With this effective identification of the storm with fear, counterpointed against the father's "unending / Ache of love," the storm is transformed into a symbol. The father would like to protect his son not only against this particular storm but against all dangers that will threaten the boy in his future life. The "ache" comes from his intense desire to do so and his realization of the impossibility of doing so.

The meter is iambic $a^3 b^3 a^4 b^2$ with the a-rimes feminine and the b-rimes masculine. The iambic meter is slowed down further by spondees and heavy unstressed syllables. In the last line an unusually heavy stress is thrown on the word "Ache" by substitution of a monosyllabic foot for the expected iamb. LP

William Blake **A POISON TREE** (page 231)

Granfield Kleiser **THE MOST VITAL THING IN LIFE** (page 231)

One might almost judge these poems from their titles alone. The first title presents an image; the second is an abstract phrase, more suitable for an essay or sermon than for a poem.

The second poem is abstract from beginning to end. It has no dramatic situation. The poet addresses the reader directly. His message—that the most vital thing in life is to control one's feelings—is stated baldly and repeated over and over. The reader is told to "curb resentment," to "maintain a mental peace," to "learn to keep strict silence," to "keep [his] mental balance." The tone is preachy and didactic. There is no development: the good advice simply comes out in a string of platitudes. The poem is without imagery. Its one metaphor is the utterly trite one of a "battle" (13). The poet mixes formal diction ("defrauded") and colloquial diction ("peeved") without purpose and without any sense of impropriety. His meter (iambic-anapestic trimeter, with feminine endings in the odd-numbered lines) is much too swift and bouncy for so serious a theme. A number of words seem included simply to sustain the meter: "quite" (4), "mental" (6), "all" and "simply" (8), "Be assured" (23). This is didactic verse, not poetry; it conveys advice, not experience.

"A Poison Tree" also has a message, but it is conveyed through a parable or extended metaphor rather than explicitly stated. The poem has a beginning, middle, and end, and could not be rearranged in its presentation as could "The Most Vital Thing in Life."

The speaker (who is not the poet) sets up the basic contrast and theme of the poem in the first stanza. To tell one's wrath is to end it. To conceal one's wrath is to cause it to grow and become destructive. The speaker presents two episodes from

138

his life: one in which he was open and candid about his feelings, the other in which he suppressed his feelings. The first episode is presented briefly, for it ended quickly. The second occupies the rest of the poem, for it is of slow development. It is related in a sustained metaphor, which begins in the last phrase of the stanza. The speaker has buried his wrath like a seed, and like a seed it begins to "grow." In the second stanza the speaker nurses his anger. He waters it with fears of his foe and with tears of rage and frustration. He suns it with hypocritical, deceiving smiles. The seed has sprouted. In the third stanza the seed-become-tree bears an apple, poisonous because it is the fruit of wrath, but bright and shiny on the outside because the wrath has been concealed. The speaker's "foe" sees and covets it, and in the final stanza steals and eats it. The speaker finds his foe dead beneath the tree, and is "glad." Thus the consequences of concealed wrath are shown to be horrifyingly destructive, for they include not only the death of the "foe" but the moral perversion of the speaker. The most chilling aspect of the conclusion is released by the word "glad." It touches emotional centers never approached in "The Most Vital Things in Life." The speaker has destroyed not only his "foe" but himself. (It is here we see that the speaker is not the poet. Where the speaker is "glad" for the death of his foe, the poet is appalled, and makes us feel appalled. Dramatic irony is at work.)

Note should be taken of the simplicity and economy with which this tale is told. The seed-sprout-sapling-tree development does not need stating; it is implied in the verbs of the poem. The facts that the apple is poison (stanza 3) and that the foe has been killed by eating it (stanza 4) also need no statement; they are implied by the title and the sequence of events.

Blake's message has been embodied in a simple but powerful and moving poem; Kleiser's message remains a versified message.

And what about the messages themselves? Blake's poem advocates expressing one's wrath. Kleiser's recommends suppressing it. Which advice is more valid? One may wish to hedge a little here and to suggest that it depends on circumstances (the occasion for the anger, its intensity, and one's relationship to the person causing it). One can agree with Kleiser that it is unwise to express irritation over every petty annoyance or to tell every stranger exactly what one thinks of him. But Blake is talking about "wrath" and about wrath felt toward persons with whom one is in daily association. Kleiser's maxims are tepid, conventional, and often questionable. (Is controlling one's temper really "the most vital thing in life"? more important than love? more important than standing up for justice? Is it really true that "to win a worthwhile battle / Over selfishness and spite, / You must learn to keep strict silence / Though you know you're in the right?") Blake's advice is bold and unconventional and in fact anticipates by over a century some of the insights of Sigmund Freud. In short Blake's poem presents a poet who is both feeling and thinking deeply, Kleiser's presents a poet who is doing neither.

A further question remains about the interpretation of Blake's poem. Does the speaker *plan* the death of his "foe," or is he merely pleased when it occurs? Is this poem about revenge? The answer, certainly, is that the speaker does not plan the death from the beginning. The central issue of the poem is not between forgiveness

139

and revenge but between the expression and concealment of anger. Suppressed anger, the poet believes, festers and turns poisonous. At some point it turns into hate and the hate *possibly* into planned revenge. The question cannot be answered with certainty and is ultimately unimportant. The speaker's gladness at his foe's death fully reveals his moral perversion whether the death has been plotted or not. A good case can be made, indeed, for the contention that the speaker's "foe" is his foe *because* the speaker conceals his anger from him, rather than vice versa. If "friend" and "foe" were interchanged in the first stanza, would not the "foe" become a friend and the "friend" turn into a foe?   LP

Richard Middleton   **ON A DEAD CHILD** (page 232)

John Crowe Ransom   **BELLS FOR JOHN WHITESIDE'S DAUGHTER** (page 232)

A child's death is a dangerous subject for a poet. It invites sentimentality. Though the occasion is one for genuine grief, there is always a temptation to "hoke" it up a bit, to sweeten it, to picture the child as a little angel and to soften the harsher contours.

In both poems considered here, the speaker is an adult attending the funeral of a child, and in both the speaker finds it difficult to believe that the child is dead. In the first the speaker is possibly an older relative of the child or a close friend of the child's parents. In the second he is specifically a friend and neighbor of the child's father, named in the title. This title has a double meaning. The "Bells" refer to the chuch bells which ring for the funeral in the final stanza; they also suggest that the poem itself is a tribute, a chiming of rimes, composed in the dead girl's memory.

"On a Dead Child" suffers from lack of specificity. All we learn about the dead child is that he?/she? was "a little rose" and liked to play games. But in the poem it is the adult, not the child, who is playing a game. As if he did not know why he had come, he "wander[s]" up to the child's casket, pretending that the child is "no more dead" than the roses strewn about the grave. He tells himself that the child lies motionless only because it is "tired" from too much "straying" (suggesting a gentle kind of play). And though the child does not greet him, the adult pretends to believe that it is not dead: "Yet still I knew that you were only playing— / Playing at being dead." In stanza 3 the adult confesses that the child lay so still, its eyelids so quiet, that he "might have thought" it really dead; but he rejects this thought immediately, assuring himself that the child was "peeping" through its closed eyelids; and so he does not cry. Instead, he smiles, gently calls the child by name, adds his own rose to the "sweet heap of roses" around the grave, and leaves the child to its "game."

The first and last stanzas of the poem allude to a passage from the fifteenth-century work *Imitation of Christ* by Thomas à Kempis (written originally in Latin but translated into many languages): "Man proposes, but God disposes"—meaning roughly that, whatever plans a good man makes, God has the final disposition in human affairs. In the poem it is an additional method used by the adult to soften

140

the reality of the child's death. "Though God's ways are mysterious, He does nothing without good reason, and that reason is always for the best" might be a modern version.

"On a Dead Child" is a sentimental poem. It chooses its vocabulary from words designed to educe tender feeling: "God" (twice); "little" (twice); "roses" (four times); "childish feet"; "smiled"; "gently"; "sweet"; it avoids words of opposite feeling.* It never persuades us that the child—"A little rose among the roses"—is a real child; more seriously, it does not persuade us that the adult is a real adult. The adult is the childish figure in the poem. By pretending that the child is only pretending to be dead, he avoids confrontation with the harsh fact of death; yet the poem presents this avoidance not as a form of neurotic escapism but as acceptable adult behavior.

The poet-speaker in "Bells for John Whiteside's Daughter" also finds it difficult to believe that the child he knew is dead. She was so rapid in her movements, so fleet of foot, so loud and boisterous in her play, that her stillness now is almost beyond belief. Rather than pretend that she is merely playing, however, he speaks of her as being in a "brown study" (a state of somber, abstracted brooding). But such a state is so uncharacteristic of the child that it "astonishes" the speaker and the other adults gathered for her funeral.

The child in this poem is clearly not a "little rose" but a real child—active, noisy, and often vexatious in her play. Indeed, her games are metaphorically described as "wars," whose clamor reached the adults in their "high window," and whose tyrannies disturbed the geese whom she woke from their "noon apple-dreams" and "harried" into the pond. The term "little lady" applied to her is ironical rather than sentimental in intention and effect (her "rod" is both scepter and prod). The one long sentence comprising the three central stanzas has a freshness of imagery and imagination unmatched in the other poem and gives us a vivid impression of the child at her play. The geese—lazy, sleepy, proud—serve both as victims of the child's

---

*Except in the title, the poet carefully avoids using words like *casket, coffin,* or *grave,* because these would clash with the speaker's fantasy that the child is only playing dead. For the casket or coffin he substitutes the metaphor "bed" (6), which is momentarily confusing because it also suggests a garden bed and a deathbed—until we realize that strewing a bed of roses with cut roses would be senseless and that a deathbed would not be on display at a funeral. The metaphorical use of "sleeping" (9) for death also confuses the meaning. That it is meant metaphorically is shown by paraphrase:

> Though I knew that you were only playing at being dead, you lay so still I might have thought you were really dead; however, you were surely peeping between those eyelids, and so I did not cry. [It would not make sense to say: When I saw you peeping, I knew that you were not really asleep, and so I did not cry.]

This avoidance of funereal terms also confuses the setting. It seems clearly outdoors, as the child's eyelids lie quiet "to the sky"; yet the casket is open, for the speaker can see the child's face. But at most funerals the casket is open only at the church and is closed when brought to the graveside. One is at first tempted to read "bed" as referring to the grave rather than to the casket; but surely the body would not be lying uncoffined in an open grave.

play and as a character-contrast to the child herself; yet the poet's whimsy of having them speak "in goose" is appropriate to the kind of imaginative play that a child might engage in.

In the last stanza, however, the speaker is brought back to the present reality. The bells ring for the funeral service, and the adults who have been "sternly stopped" by the child's death are "vexed at her brown study, / Lying so primly propped." If they had been sometimes "vexed" by her play in life, they are more "vexed" to see her here, lying so "prim" (who was never prim in life), "propped" rigidly in her coffin (who had such "speed" in her body and such a "tireless heart" in life). "Vexed" is an inspired word here; while pointing up ironical contrasts, it expresses genuine grief through understatement. For additional comment on Ransom's poem, see Robert Heilman, in *The Pacific Spectator*, 5 (Aut. 1951), 458-60; Thornton H. Parsons, *John Crowe Ransom* (New York: Twayne, 1969), pp. 53-55; and Robert Penn Warren, "Pure and Impure Poetry," *Kenyon Review*, 5 (Spr. 1943), 237-40.
LP

Emily Dickinson **SOME KEEP THE SABBATH GOING TO CHURCH** (page 233)

Anonymous **MY CHURCH** (page 233)

In these poems of identical length, identical rime scheme, and similar meter,* both poets take nature for their church.

The difference between the poems is largely one of tone. In "My Church" the tone is earnest, solemn; the language and imagery tend toward the grandiloquent. The poet is making a universal pronouncement of his religious belief. His religion has just one temple, which, being wide as the world, set with stars, and without roof or walls or floors ("save the beautiful sod") is obviously the whole natural world. The poet's religion has no narrow creeds restricting membership by requiring acquiescence in abstruse theological doctrines. Its one article of faith is belief in a loving and illimitable God. The thought is noble, but the expression is not memorable. The poem is not notably bad; but neither is it notably good. It lacks freshness, particularized imagery, sense of occasion, striking orginality.

---

*The first poem alternates tetrameter with trimeter lines; the second is trimeter throughout. In both the iambic foot is prevalent; but the first mixes it freely with anapests (in accord with its more playful tone); the second uses anapests sparingly (in accord with its more solemn tone). Both poems introduce metrical unorthodoxies. In line 5 Dickinson omits the fourth stress in a tetrameter line—or perhaps we can explain it by saying she substitutes a metrical pause (in any case, this practice is customary in her metrics). In the second poem the last line ends with two four-syllable feet:

the LOVE / of the il- LIM- / it- a- ble GOD. /

A conventional prosodist would dismiss this as "incorrect." A more charitable interpretation might be that it graphically illustrates the impossibility of confining this God within limits.

The tone of "Some keep the Sabbath . . ." is playful, fanciful, and, though not unserious, not at all solemn. The reader senses a specific occasion: the poet is at home (as is her wont) on a beautiful Sunday morning while her family and friends are all at church. The poet makes a personal rather than a universal statement. While other people keep the Sabbath by going to formal services, she keeps hers by staying home. Her church also is nature, but instead of being "wide as the world" it is confined to the area around her house and has "an orchard for a dome." Her church has a bobolink for chorister and God for a preacher, and God's sermon "is never long"—never boring or uncomfortable to sit through. The "sexton"—who sings instead of tolling a bell—is presumably another small bird. Two of the metaphors are open-ended. The poet, instead of dressing in surplice, "just puts on her wings" (a joyful spirit? readiness for imaginative flight? angelic behavior?—any or all of these perhaps). God's sermon, likewise, may be any of a number of things— the joy He communicates through the beauty of nature, the sunshine streaming through the orchard branches—it would be unwise to be too specific. Whatever it is, it is pleasurable and gives a lift to the spirit. So also does the quiet humor of the poet's comparison (combining metaphor, metonymy, and understatement) of God to "a noted clergyman." Underlying all is possibly a more appropriate way of worship than attending formal services. Others attend formal services every Sunday out of duty and are sometimes bored. The poet attends her "church" out of pleasure and is never disappointed. The others hope to be rewarded for their dedicated worship by going to heaven "at last" (when they die). The poet is going to heaven "all along" (samples its pleasures every Sabbath).

"Some keep the Sabbath . . ." is the superior poem because of its continuous play of fancy, its humor, the originality of its metaphors, and its particularizing imagery. As a touchstone of the difference between the two poems, we might compare the two lines in them most nearly parallel in meaning—line 4 ("And an orchard for a dome") from the first, and line 10 ("Nor floors save the beautiful sod") from the second. In the first poem we might have expected (would have got from a more conventional poet) a substitution of "the heavens" or "blue skies" for the "dome" of her church; instead we are given "an orchard." Because it is unexpected, it comes with a small shock of surprise; at the same time it is seen to be appropriate, for it domesticates the poet's church (which she attends by staying at home), makes it more personal, and reduces it to manageable size (conformable with the bobolink and the "little sexton"). In the second poem, to substitute for the "floors" of the church we are given the "beautiful sod." The two words join with a "clunk" as in the coupling of boxcars. The adjective is abstract and overused in poetry (the first poem creates a sense of beauty without using the word); the noun seems to have been chosen largely to rime with "God," for its connotations do not go well with "beautiful." LP

Karl Shapiro **BOY-MAN** (page 234)

Henry Van Dyke **AMERICA FOR ME** (page 235)

The first three lines of Shapiro's poem evoke a picture of Eton schoolboys in their dress coats and top hats (*hats* is a metonymy for heads or minds). Line 6 is a metaphor in which America is pictured as a small boy or a dog and the green rug suggests England's heritage of tradition and the beautiful lawns of its public and historical monuments; the act itself shows the American's disrespect for, or lack of interest in, tradition, history, and culture. The paradox of line 26 expresses the American's ability to retain the energy and appearance of youth through middle age: at forty he seems younger in looks and manner than his oldest son (who is probably trying to act and to look "grown up"). The deliberately mixed metaphor of lines 28–29 works beautifully: time is simultaneously compared by simile to a panama hat and personified as smiling. The panama hat suggests informality, youth, confidence, and carefreeness, as do the rakish tilt at which it is worn, and the smile. The prayer in the last stanza is dramatic irony: it shows the American's confidence in physical energy, business efficiency, and material resources (vitamins, steel, motor oil), his complacent feeling of superiority to Europeans, and his unquestioning acceptance of American values as opposed to those of others. The poet himself regards these qualities with suspicion.

Shapiro's poem combines mockery and admiration in approximately equal quantities: he admires the American's youthfulness, energy, good looks, humor, and confidence in the future; he is appalled by the American's self-complacency, materialism, love of comfort, and scorn of the old, the foreign, the different, and all that does not have utilitarian value (such as literature, culture, dignity, liberal knowledge). Shapiro does not share the American's easy assumption of superiority to other peoples. His attitude is summed up in the thematic idea suggested by the title: the American has youthfulness (good), which is also immaturity (bad).

The poem itself is freshly conceived, brilliantly written, and balanced in judgment.

Van Dyke's poem exemplifies the self-complacency, the easy assumption of superiority, the trust in the future, and the scorn of the past that Shapiro attributes to the American. Its lilting dipodic meter is in itself appealing but does not dispose us to consider its subject matter deeply or seriously. Some of the imagery is also appealing, but much of it depends on stock appeals to sentiment—home, heart, the flag, youth, freedom, "oh, to take your hand, my dear," and so forth. The poem is rhetorically skillful, but the rhetoric is too often as shallow and as specious as that of a typical Fourth of July oration. For example, in line 4 the phrase "beyond the ocean bars" is an attractive one and lends attractiveness to the land that lies beyond them: the reader probably does not pause to consider that Europe is just as much "beyond the ocean bars" when viewed from America as America is when viewed from Europe. The following line (which is also the final line of the poem) is even more skillful. The opening phrase "the air is full of sunlight" causes us to supply an additional reading for the closing phrase: not only "the flag is full of stars" but also "the night is full of stars" (we unconsciously supply real stars to balance the real sunlight). This is skillful, but on critical reflection we realize that the air is no more full of sunlight nor the night sky more full of stars in America than in Europe and that the stars in the flag have absolutely no relevance to the comparison but constitute only a sentimental appeal—a bit of flag-waving. Finally, the third stanza confuses the whole comparison. In the song "Home, Sweet Home," from which the last six words of the stanza are taken (a sentimental piece itself), the idea is that other places may be more splendid, but, "be it ever so humble, there's no place like home." Van Dyke's third stanza seems to bear out this idea, but the rest of the poem suggests that America is more splendid too—more full of sunlight, stars, youth, freedom, room, friendly wild nature, and hope for the future. Is Van Dyke exalting America over Europe because of "what she is and what she is to be" (her superiority) or because, though inferior, "there's no place like home"? The opposed ideas are not balanced, as they are in Shapiro's poem, but merely confused—a confusion that the lilting rhythm and glittering rhetoric will disguise from most readers. (There can be little doubt that Van Dyke's poem has enjoyed a much wider audience and a greater popularity than Shapiro's poem has enjoyed or ever will enjoy.)   LP

Eugene Field   **LITTLE BOY BLUE** (page 236)

Coventry Patmore   **THE TOYS** (page 236)

"Little Boy Blue" is an appealing poem. Its melody is pleasing, and so are its rimes. The word order is natural and unforced, and so are the words themselves. The poem makes effective use of alliteration and other musical devices. The picture it presents of the loyal toy soldier and dog awaiting the return of their Little Boy Blue is touching. The poem is skillfully done, and it has been much beloved by the American public. It is nevertheless a sentimental poem, manipulating its materials to draw tears from the reader, subtly falsifying life by dimming the darker colors and brightening up the warmer ones. It aims at being sweetly sad.

Its title is sweet. The boy who died is not Bobby, or Peter, or Donald; he is "Little Boy Blue"—the name has nursery rime associations. And he has not only a sweet name but a sweet disposition. He played nicely with his toys on the evening of the night he died (though he must have been sick, and most children are short-tempered and hard to manage when sick), and then he toddled sweetly off to bed at the appointed time, without a single protest, quite contrary to ordinary boy-nature. If Boy Blue ever had fits of ill temper or disobedience, they are not mentioned; only his pretty actions, such as kissing his toys, are mentioned. In describing Boy Blue and his possessions, the poet uses the adjective "little" eleven times in twenty-four lines. Not only is Boy Blue "little," his hands are "little," his face is "little," his chair is "little," his toys are "little." Most of these "little's" are quite superfluous; the word is being used only to manipulate the reader's sympathies, to evoke a stock response. Also, instead of telling us that Little Boy Blue *died*, the poet says that he was "awakened by an angel song." It is a sweet way of describing death; the uglier features are avoided, and death becomes a gentle and sweetly sad experience, like a song. (Some students will have difficulty with the "angel song" metaphor and think that Little Boy Blue grew up—apparently rather suddenly—leaving his childish toys behind.) This death occurred many years ago, but the little toys are still true.

But now, three questions. First, how does the poet know that Little Boy Blue "dreamt of the pretty toys" if he died in his sleep? Second, in what sense are the toys "true"? Do they really wonder what has happened to Little Boy Blue "since he kissed them and put them there"? Or is this not an example of what Ruskin called "the pathetic fallacy"—the fallacy of attributing human emotions to inanimate objects? That is, has not the author sentimentalized not only the little boy but also even his toys? And third, why, after all these years, are the toys still where Little Boy Blue left them? (Here is a question which the poet did not intend us to ask. If the toys are still in the chair where Boy Blue left them, his parents must have closed up his room when he died and resolved to leave everything just as he left it. People do occasionally do such things, to be sure, but only very rarely; and we usually feel that such a reaction to death is excessively sentimental or even morbid, not healthy. Quite understandably, the poet glosses over this aspect of the situation and concentrates our attention instead on the supposed fidelity of the toy dog and the toy soldier, as though this quality was what really kept them there.) In short, the author is not treating death seriously; instead he is playing with us and with our emotions.

"The Toys," at first view, may seem a slightly crude poem beside "Little Boy Blue." The meter is not so lilting, the rime is not so regular, there is no stanza pattern, and even the syntax may at times seem slightly strained.* But the meter is such as to keep our attention focused constantly on the content; it does not set up a separate tune, or by a pretty lilt soften and sweeten a pathetic subject matter. Moreover, the treatment of the subject matter is honest. Having once described his son as "little," the poet drops the adjective and does not use it as a spurious means of attaching sympathy to his subject. He does not idealize the behavior of little boys. Though his son is grave, quiet, and thoughtful, he is also, like most boys, sometimes willful and disobedient. The father's behavior, too, as contrasted with that of the parents of Little Boy Blue, is normally human. He loses his temper, strikes the boy and scolds him, then later feels remorse and worries about what he has done. But the boy, though he has been sobbing, is not so grief-stricken that he cannot sleep, as a sentimentalist might have made him. He is deep in slumber, and beside his bed, to console himself, he has arranged his treasured collection of toys. These toys are enumerated and described: they include "a red-veined stone," "a piece of glass

---

*Actually, the syntax in lines 3–6 is skillfully arranged so that "dismissed" may take either "him" or "His Mother" as its object, both meanings being appropriate. By one construction "His Mother" is the subject of an absolute phrase; by the other it is the object of the verb.

abraded by the beach," and "two French copper coins." The imagery is fresh and precise. We are not told, moreover, that the boy kissed these toys before going to sleep, or that he is dreaming of them, or that they, on their part, are faithfully waiting for him to wake up. The incident is moving because it has been honestly treated. Moreover, the poet has effectively used the incident to communicate, by analogy, a larger truth about life. We are all children, ultimately, and have our childish ways. We grown-up children have our grown-up toys no less foolish really than the contents of a child's pocket. And we too disobey the Commandments of Our Father and stand equally in need of forgiveness.

In referring to his son's having disobeyed "the seventh time" (3), the poet enriches his meaning by a Biblical allusion to Matthew 18: 21–22. When Peter asked Jesus how often he should forgive his brother's sinning against him, Jesus answered, Not seven times, but "seventy times seven."

[This discussion is abridged from the essay "Are Tears Made of Sugar or of Salt" in Laurence Perrine, *The Art of Total Relevance: Papers on Poetry* (Rowley, Mass.: Newbury House, 1976), pp. 125–29.]

16. Good Poetry and Great

John Keats   **ODE TO A NIGHTINGALE** (page 240)

The most helpful single volume for study of this poem is *Twentieth Century Interpretations of Keats' Odes*, ed. by Jack Stillinger (Englewood Cliffs, N.J.: Prentice-Hall, 1968), presently (June, 1982) out of print. Besides Stillinger's excellent introductory essay, it contains the essays by Brooks and Fogle separately listed below, and a note by Anthony Hecht. Additional useful references include Harold Bloom, *The Visionary Company* (New York: Doubleday, 1961), pp. 427–32; Cleanth Brooks, *Understanding Poetry*, 3rd ed. (New York: Holt, 1960), pp. 44–47; Douglas Bush, *John Keats: His Life and Writing* (New York: Macmillan, 1966), pp. 132–38; Morris Dickstein, *Keats and His Poetry* (Chicago: Univ. of Chicago Press, 1971), pp. 205–21; Richard Harter Fogle, "Keats's Ode to a Nightingale," *PMLA*, 68 (1953), 211–22; F. R. Leavis, *Revaluation* (New York: Norton, 1963), pp. 244–52; H. M. McLuhan, "Aesthetic Pattern in Keats' Odes," *University of Toronto Quarterly*, 12 (Jan. 1943), 175–79; David Perkins, "The Ode to a Nightingale," in *Keats: A Collection of Critical Essays*, ed. Walter Jackson Bate (Englewood Cliffs, N.J.: Prentice-Hall, 1964), pp. 103–11, reprinted from David Perkins, *The Quest for Permanence* (Cambridge, Mass.: Harvard Univ. Press, 1959), pp. 244–57; Stuart M. Sperry, *Keats the Poet* (Princeton, N.J.: Princeton Univ. Press, 1973), pp. 262–67. LP

Robert Frost   **THE DEATH OF THE HIRED MAN** (page 243)

There are useful discussions of this poem in Reuben A. Brower, *The Poetry of Robert Frost: Constellations of Intention* (New York: Oxford Univ. Press, 1963), pp. 157–65; John Robert Doyle, Jr., *The Poetry of Robert Frost: An Analysis* (Johannesburg: Witwatersrand University, 1962), pp. 215–17; John F. Lynen, *The Pastoral Art of Robert Frost* (New Haven: Yale Univ. Press, 1960), pp. 112–13; Laurence Perrine and James M. Reid, *100 American Poems of the Twentieth Century* (New York: Harcourt Brace Jovanovich, 1966), pp. 31–33. Lawrance Thompson, *Fire and Ice: The Art and Thought of Robert Frost* (New York: Holt, 1942), pp. 112–14; Charles C. Walcutt, "Frost's 'Death of the Hired Man,'" *The Explicator* 3 (October 1944), item 7. LP

T. S. Eliot   **THE LOVE SONG OF J. ALFRED PRUFROCK** (page 247)

"Prufrock" is one of the most discussed poems of the twentieth century. Of the mass of commentary that has accumulated concerning it, some of the following may be particularly helpful: Roy P. Basler, *Sex, Symbolism, and Psychology in Literature* (New Brunswick, N.J.: Rutgers Univ. Press, 1948), pp. 203–21; Cleanth Brooks and Robert Penn Warren, *Understanding Poetry*, 3rd ed. (New York: Holt, 1960), pp. 386–99 (also in earlier editions); Elizabeth Drew, *T. S. Eliot, The Design of His Poetry* (New York: Charles Scribner's, 1949), pp. 34–36; Paul Engle and Warren Carrier, *Reading Modern Poetry*, rev. ed. (Glenview, Ill.: Scott, Foresman, 1968), pp. 148–55; Laurence Perrine and James M. Reid, *100 American Poems of the Twentieth Century* (New York: Harcourt Brace Jovanovich, 1966), pp. 110–12; Grover Smith, *T. S. Eliot's Poetry and Plays* (Chicago: Univ. of Chicago Press, 1956), and Morris Weitz, *Philosophy of the Arts* (Cambridge, Mass.: Harvard Univ. Press, 1950) pp. 94–107, 145. LP

PART TWO
POEMS FOR FURTHER READING

Leonard Adame **BLACK AND WHITE** (page 256)

Questions: 1. Who are the guerillas, the generals, the secretary? Describe the situation. 2. What different meanings are suggested by the title? 3. What other contrasts are important in the poem? 4. What is the speaker's attitude toward what he depicts?

Scene: the plaza of a small town in Rhodesia close to the jungle. The dead bodies of black guerilla fighters are laid out for display like a "catch" of fish or game, still damp, though the African heat has begun to swell their bodies. A sign has been placed near them declaring that they have been "put here as a [moral] lesson" (and, of course, as a warning against the evil of opposing the "legitimate" white government). The captured rifles of the guerillas are displayed as trophies on the ground above their heads. A circle of newsmen and photographers has gathered around the display snapping pictures. The press secretary for the government makes an official pronouncement in terms as impersonal and detached as if the bodies of the men lying there were indeed only a "catch" of fish.

The phrase "black and white" has at least three distinct meanings. It refers (1) to the conflict of black and white peoples, (2) to the black and white moral judgments made (certainly by the government and probably also by the guerillas) about the rights and wrongs involved in this conflict, (3) to the black-and-white photographs being taken of the scene. It refers possibly also to the black-and-white newsprint in which the event will be reported. The "keyboard" of rifles suggests the black and white of the typewriter keyboards on which the newsmen will compose their stories.

Besides the contrast of black and white, there are contrasts of silence and sound, of heat and cold. The dead men lie quietly (4) and the speaker reads quietly (3), but the photographers surround the dead taking their snapshots as the government forces must once have surrounded them shooting their rifles, and as the newsmen will soon be clicking their typewriter keyboards. Then both the news accounts and the photographs will be stored in "the silent world" of black and white. Does the phrase "the silent world" suggest also the apathy and lack of indignation with which the world at large will probably respond to this event? The bodies of the dead men lie "in the plaza sun," in "the African heat," but the snapshots of the photographers will "freeze" it all (again as if these bodies were only so much meat) for storage. (Though the word "freeze" is here used metaphorically to refer to stopped motion, its literal meaning cannot be kept from surfacing in this context.)

Leonard Adame, as a Chicano poet, must have a keen awareness of the racial conflict and social injustices involved in his poem. He reports it all, however, as quietly and objectively (but tellingly) as the poem's speaker, who designates himself with a lower-case "i." LP

Samuel Allen **TO SATCH** (page 256)

The image of "Satch" in heaven pitching stars is playful and original and his camaraderie with God delightful. Though the speaker in the poem is "Satch," the poem is entitled "*To* Satch." By thus gently reminding us that it is the poet who is putting the words in Satch's mouth, the discrepancy mutes any note of egotism that might otherwise be present. LP

Kingsley Amis **THE LAST WAR** (page 257)

"The Last War" is a seriocomic satirical allegory about the end of mankind in a final war brought on by the folly, greed, and mutual distrust of the nations of the world. In genre it resembles, at first, a familiar kind of English detective story in which one of the guests at a weekend house party in a large country home is suddenly found dead; foul play is suspected; all the guests have motives; and before the detective can solve the mystery, other murders are committed to keep evidence from being given. But it is quickly found out that at this house party there is no detective and finally that no one survives, not even an attractive pair of young lovers. Moreover, it is apparent from the first line that this poem differs from the usual detective story in being allegorical. The house guests represent the nations of the world, and the murders and killings represent war. In this "last war" the innocent (if any) and guilty, rich and poor, civilized and uncivilized, large and small are destroyed alike. None survive to provide a happy ending. When the servant comes in to tidy up on the morning of the third day, he finds nothing but corpses, some beginning to stink, and, feeling ill, he goes to bed at noon. But since the cleaning man allegorically represents the sun, the meaning is that when the sun arises on the third day (or week, month, year) of the war, it shines on a world in which no human being is left alive, and at noon it either goes into eclipse or hides itself behind clouds.

Very loosely metrical, the poem is written in stanzas in which the four long lines have roughly six beats each, and the short final line three beats. The third and fifth lines of each stanza rime, either perfectly or approximately, and each of the seven stanzas uses the same rime sound (ending in -*n*). LP

Matthew Arnold **DOVER BEACH** (page 258)

"Dover Beach" is Arnold's lament over the decline of religious faith in his time. "The Sea of Faith," he tells us, was once "at the full," but now he only hears "its melancholy, long, withdrawing roar," like the roar of waves receding or of the tide going out. Certainly, the mid-nineteenth century was a time of religious crisis—a time when vast numbers of thinking people were losing the simple Christian faith of their childhood teaching before the advance of scientific and rationalistic thought.

The conflict and the agony are recorded in work after work of literature. Arnold's poem, first published in 1867 but possibly composed some ten or twelve years earlier, is surely one of the most eloquent expressions of despair ever written, combining profound pessimism with imperishable beauty.

The speaker is in a room overlooking the cliffs of Dover. He is so situated—where the cliffs curve—that not only can he look out over the English Channel and occasionally glimpse the coast of France (twenty-two miles away at this point) as it catches a gleam of moonlight, but he can also see, across the way, the face of the cliffs themselves and the waves breaking on the shingle at their foot. In the room with him is a beloved woman (wife or sweetheart) to whom he unburdens his despair—not over any personal misfortune but about the state of the world.

The poem turns on a series of contrasts, of which the two most important are those (a) between the physical beauty of the world he sees outside his window and its actual spiritual darkness, and (b) between the full tide he sees outside the window and the ebbing "tide" of faith which he feels is responsible for the world's spiritual darkness.

Looking from his window, the speaker is first impressed by the beauty of the moonlit scene before him, and he summons his companion to the window to share its beauty with him. But then he becomes aware of the sound of the breakers crashing on the shingle, and this sound is a sad one. Being a person of broad intellectual culture, he is reminded by the sound of a passage in a Greek drama by Sophocles, who compared the ebb and flow of the sea to the ebb and flow of human misery. Then he thinks of his own time, and he is reminded by the sound of the ebbing of religious faith. This thought is so melancholy to him that he cries out to his beloved, "Ah, love, let us be true to one another!" for a loving human relationship seems the only value left in a world which has lost every other source of meaning—a world which, despite its illusory physical beauty, has "really neither joy, nor love, nor light, / Nor certitude, nor peace, nor help for pain"—surely two of the most pessimistic lines in English poetry. The simile ending the poem gives concrete embodiment to this abstract statement and is deservedly one of the most famous in English poetry. As an image for complete meaninglessness in human life, it can hardly be surpassed. Words of negative connotation pile up—*darkling, confused, alarms, struggle, flight, ignorant, clash, night*—to give a picture of utter confusion, blindness, cross-purposes, and uncertainty, in which warring armies cannot tell friend from foe and strike at both alike in the darkness. This uncertainty embodies the lack of "certitude" mentioned in line 34, which in turn stems from the ebbing Sea of Faith. The one remaining consolation—the possibility of a loyal personal relationship between two lovers, because of its positioning, seems a very frail one indeed. Instead of one person lost on a tiny raft at night in midocean, we are left with two people on the raft clinging to each other out of desperation. The poem begins with light and ends in darkness.

Students must be made to see that the image in the last three lines is the figurative, not the literal, term in a simile. This poem is not about war, nor was it written during time of war—it is a poem about the loss of a common religious faith that once linked men together in belief, hope, and some degree of brotherhood or community—a loss that has resulted in a world where men work only for self-advancement and at cross-purposes with each other.

It is also important to note that the poem was written, not by a believer blaming the rest of the world for its lack of belief, but by a poet who himself can no longer accept the stories and assumptions on which the old faith was based, and who regards its consolations and certainties no longer possible for thinking men. If he had been himself a believer, he would have cried out, "O Lord! bring these people back to a belief in your eternal truth and loving overlordship!" Instead, his cry is to a human companion, "Ah, love, let us be true / To one another!"

The syntax in lines 7–14 is somewhat involved. The noun "roar" (9) is not the direct object of "hear" but the subject of the infinitives "[To] "Begin," "cease," "begin," and "bring" (12–13). The direct object of "hear" is the whole infinitive phrase of which "roar" is the subject. In reading the poem one must reject the temptation to drop one's voice at the end of line 11. LP

Margaret Atwood **LANDCRAB** (page 259)

A land crab is one of a number of species which live mostly upon land, returning to the sea only for breeding—and thus violating expectations about the normal environment of crabs.

The reversal of sea and land in the habitat of this crab evokes thoughts of the origin of the land-dwelling human being, which according to one theory was the sea. Thus there may be a parallel: both crab and mankind have deserted their original environment.

The parallel is not an attractive one to the speaker, and she forthrightly denies the marine origin of people, preferring instead to infer some miraculous creation of humanity. However, the denial is rendered less forceful by the speaker's alluding to the fabulous Greek stories of Deucalion (who after the great flood was instructed to sow his mother's bones, and took that to mean the stones of the earth, which were transformed into men and women), and of Cadmus (who was instructed to sow dragon's teeth, which sprang up as armed warriors).

The speaker seems to be repulsed by the idea of kinship with the crab, since the descriptive details of lines 5–23, while accurate observations of appearance and behavior, are not humanly attractive. But there are vestiges of personification in these lines—"timid," "routine," and "dance"—which imply that despite her preference not to be identified with the crab, she does detect similarities. Lines 24–27 expressly attribute to the crab a human emotion, "contempt" for the comparative softness and vulnerability of mammals.

The speaker does concede that if she is more than a crab, it represents at least "a piece of what we are." It displays for us some of our characteristics which, at those moments when we acknowledge them, are the materials of our nightmares. If the crab seems like "the husk of a small demon" (line 13), there is also something terrifyingly demonic in us—the true link between the species. TRA

153

W. H. Auden **MUSÉE DES BEAUX ARTS** (page 260)

The poem descriptively alludes to three paintings by Pieter Brueghel the Elder (which might be shown to students): lines 5–8, *The Census* (or *The Numbering at Bethlehem*); lines 10–13, *The Massacre of the Innocents*; and lines 14–21, *Landscape with the Fall of Icarus.* The title of the poem may be derived from the name of the museum in Brussels where the Icarus painting hangs, the Musées Royaux des Beaux Arts, though it simply means "Fine Arts Museum," a title general enough to include all three "Old Master" paintings.

The poem is in free verse and has an irregular rime scheme. In the opening verse paragraph the following lines rime: 1/4, 2/8, 5/7, 6/13, 9/11, 10/12, and there is no rime for line 3. The concluding paragraph, while not regular, tightens up the rimes somewhat, in keeping with the single focus of the subject: 14/15, 16/20, 17/21, 18/19. The two sets of rimed couplets begin to suggest some more explicit closure of meaning for the poem, but the last two lines return to the more random pattern, reinforcing the understated meaning—that something as momentous as a boy falling out of the sky does not signal a definitive event, but only a momentary amazement to the men who continue on about their business. The apparently irrelevant or random riming may thus be seen as a reinforcement of the theme, that great events seem irrelevant or not personally significant to the mass of self-involved people.

The sequence of the pictured events may also be seen as reinforcing the theme: from the birth of Christ, to the slaughter by Herod of the first-born sons, to the mythical story of Icarus—events that would seem to the modern picture-viewer of decreasing personal significance, even if the last of them did originally symbolize a very human problem, the danger of rashly pursuing a superhuman aspiration. TRA

W. H. Auden **"O WHERE ARE YOU GOING?"** (page 260)

The central situation presents a man about to set forth on a dangerous mission alone—a journey to a mountain pass and beyond the mountain pass. This mission symbolically represents any dangerous or unpopular enterprise—one requiring lonely courage and endeavor.

The dialogue is between two types of men: (1) the fearful stay-at-home and armchair-sitter who seeks excuses to justify himself for inaction and to discourage others from dangerous adventure or high endeavor; (2) the man of action, the darer and doer. In each of the first three stanzas the first speaker asks questions and makes statements designed to deter the adventurer from his mission—he will have to go among foul poisons and maddening odors where even the strongest ("the tall") turn back; he will lose his way in the dark, not noticing when his footsteps leave the paved road; he will fall prey to horrible birds of prey or phantoms and bogies and will contract horrible diseases. In the last stanza the second speaker impatiently and scornfully answers the questions asked by the first, and flings out of the house to begin his mission. The poet's sympathies are obviously with the second speaker.

154

The number of persons involved in the dialogue may be figured as six (rider, farer, and hearer versus reader, fearer, and horror; or as four (see line 16); *he* (rider-farer-hearer) and *them* (reader, fearer, horror); or as two (the two types); or as one (in which case the speakers represent conflicting impulses within a single person). The important thing is that the speakers represent *two* conflicting attitudes toward life and living—the courageous and the timid, the participating and the merely observing, the involved and the detached. LP

D. C. Berry ON READING POEMS TO A SENIOR CLASS AT SOUTH HIGH (page 261)

The poet begins by assuming, from their orderly appearance in rows of chairs, that the students are "frozen" and incapable of a living response to his poetry. But as he reads, planning "to drown them" with his words, the power of poetry floods the room, and the surprised poet and the class metaphorically swim together until the ringing of the school bell, which breaks the enchantment. All of them, students and poet, then go on to other more normal pursuits, back to their ordinary lives. The experience, however, has transported the poet beyond himself, and it takes his domesticated, imaginatively named cat to bring *him* back to normal.

The poet's defensive condescension—his prejudice that these students are cold to poetry, his fear that his poetry may not move them—is washed away by the mutual experience, to the extent that he himself must be restored to his human form. The poem wittily converts the pejorative image of "frozen fish" into the vital image of "thirty tails whacking words," and his plan of drowning his audience converts into the water in which, for the time, the poet and students have a medium they can share. Both "frozen fish" and "drown" are used metaphorically, apparently as the poet's self-conscious device for asserting his superiority, but both come so vitally to life that even after the experience the poet feels fins at the ends of his arms. Ironically it is his cat who restores him from his fishy condition. TRA

Earle Birney TWENTY-THIRD FLIGHT (page 262)

The poem is a parody of Psalm 23, David's song of confidence and faith in the Lord which celebrates the gifts of comfort and security during life and of eternal rest after death. Birney's locale is Honolulu, its airport and one of its hotels; his shepherd is a nubile "shepherdess" who officially greets tourists and assures their comfort at a hotel. In contrast to David's confidence in the future, the speaker questions his lonely fate as the greeter deserts him, leaving him to wonder what will become of her and of himself.

The poem ironically presents both the "paradise" of the tropical tourist destination and the warmth of the welcome offered him by a professional greeter. With more humor than sobriety, it draws contrasts between the high solemnity of the Psalm and the trivial modern replacement for faith, a secular world where fulfillment seems to be the languor of a beach, the attractive attentions of a beautiful young woman.

"The waters of Waikiki" in the last line extends the reference of the poem to Psalm 137 ("By the rivers of Babylon, there we sat down, yea, we wept, when we remembered Zion"), a reference that Birney may have derived from T. S. Eliot's use of it in *The Waste Land*, III.182 ("By the waters of Leman I sat down and wept"). This allusion ends the poem on a slightly bitter note, equating the secular pleasures of Hawaii with pagan Babylon during the captivity of the Israelites, and perhaps forecasting as David does the destruction of the "daughter of Babylon." TRA

Elizabeth Bishop ONE ART (page 262)

With a forced tone of nonchalance, the speaker in this modified villanelle insists that all losses can be faced stoically. She begins with insignificant losses—keys, a little time, memories of places and names—and proceeds to those of greater emotional value—a prized keepsake, loved houses. Hyperbolically, she reports the loss of realms, rivers, and a continent. The climax of the poem occurs in the final stanza, the loss of a beloved person, which too can be mastered—almost. The last line, with its parenthetic command to herself, reveals that the mastery of this loss requires a great exertion of will, if indeed it can be mastered at all.

Whimsically, the poem is presented as a lesson to the reader: "Lose something every day," until practice in mastering the sense of loss will render future losses less disastrous in their effects. The first three stanzas, in the second person, present the lesson; in the last three the speaker offers her own experience as supporting evidence. But with the increasing sense of regret and even pain, the ironic stance of the speaker is made clear: mastering the sense of loss is not "one art" that can be learned through coping with lesser losses.

The word "loss" is used both metaphorically and literally, undercutting the statement that all losses are equal. The inequalities are manifest when one questions if the references to losing keys, losing time, and losing a beloved person employ the term "loss" in the same sense. What the poet achieves, in seeming to believe that the word is single in its meaning, is the statement that not all loss can be mastered. TRA

William Blake THE LAMB (page 263)

William Blake THE TIGER (page 264)

"The Lamb" was first published in *Songs of Innocence* (1789) and "The Tiger" in *Songs of Experience* (1794). Blake described the two volumes as "Showing Contrary States of the Human Soul." Though the poems in *Songs of Experience* are generally darker in tone than those in the earlier book, Blake is not necessarily suggesting that innocence is better than experience. Rather, each state shows the incompleteness or the inadequacy of the other.

In the "Introduction" to *Songs of Innocence* (page 178), Blake was bid by his muse to "Pipe a song about a Lamb." This is it. The central question asked in this poem is "Little Lamb, who made thee?" The central question asked in "The Tiger" is "Did he who made the Lamb make thee?" "The Tiger" was obviously written to complement "The Lamb." Together the two poems make a poetic diptych.

In "The Lamb" the speaker is a child, and the chief effect of the poem is a childlike simplicity, produced by the use of a simple vocabulary—mostly monosyllabic, end-stopped lines—one statement to a line, a song-like meter (six four-beat lines in each stanza, framed at beginning and end by a pair of three-beat lines), paired rimes, and frequent repetitions. The situation and content of the poem also express this childlike simplicity. The child talks to a lamb, asks it a question and answers the question himself, and in his answer shows his trustful unquestioning acceptance of the Christian story he has been taught. The lamb was created by Christ, who in the New Testament is called "the Lamb of God," and who through his incarnation became "a little child." The child and the lamb are thus one with Christ in name as well as in gentleness and love, and the poem appropriately ends, "Little Lamb, God bless thee."

In "The Tiger" the speaker is an adult, possibly the poet; he does not literally speak to the tiger, he apostrophizes it; and the central question of the poem is left unanswered.

The image in the first two lines is one of the most vivid in English poetry. Primarily we are meant to see two eyes glaring in the dark (see line 6); but if we think of the orange and black stripes of the tiger's body, we also have a flame-like image. The tiger is associated with images of fire throughout the poem. He is imagined to have been made in a cosmic smithy ("forged," "hammer," "chain," "furnace," "anvil"), and his creator is personified as a powerful smith. But is this smithy in "distant deeps or skies"—hell or heaven? And was the smith Satan or God? And, having created the tiger, did the smith "smile" to see what he had made? These are the questions urged on the reader, insistently, like the blows of a hammer on an anvil (the interrogative "what" is used thirteen times during the poem), and in a meter whose accents fall also with the force and regularity of hammer blows. The tiger is described as awesome—that is, as arousing both fear and admiration in the beholder. Its "fearful symmetry," the burning brightness of its eyes, its twisted sinewy heart, the "deadly terrors" of its brain—these qualities suggest beauty, strength, fierceness, and violence. But if the tiger is awesome, its creator is even more so. He is "immortal" (3, 23), daring (7, 8, 24), winged (7), strong (9–10), "dread" (12, 15), and an artist (9).

The difficult lines 17–18 have been explained in too many ways to go into here—in terms of astrology, as metaphor for dawn and dewfall, as symbolic of love and pity, as an allusion to the war in heaven between the good and the rebel angels depicted in Milton's *Paradise Lost*, as an allusion to symbols in Blake's private mythology, as an image for showers of sparks sent out from the cosmic forge and of the water used to temper the glowing metal, etc. Perhaps, in their broadest and simplest sense, they can be taken to suggest, "When even the stars wept, did the creator of the tiger smile?"

No answer to its central question is stated in the poem. Is one implied? A survey of Blake criticism produces no consensus. About half of the critics say that the question is rhetorical, intended by Blake to be answered Yes. The creator of the Lamb was also the creator of the Tiger, and He looked on his work and found it "good." The power of the poem is the power with which it expresses this mysterious paradox in the nature of God, creator of both the rainbow and the whirlwind. But another half say that the question is unanswerable, and was not intended to be answered by Blake one way or the other—that Blake's poem is about the mystery and ambiguity of the universe, which is ultimately beyond man's understanding. [And one lonely voice—Kathleen Raine, in *Encounter*, II (1935), 48—declares boldly: "The answer is beyond all possible doubt, 'No'; God, who created the lamb, did not create the tiger."]

A greater variety of answers is produced by the question, What do the lamb and the tiger symbolize? But here we welcome a variety of answers, for the symbolism is rich and permits a range of meanings. (The poems obviously call for symbolical reading. We are being asked much more than whether the same god created the aardvark and the camel.) Among the answers suggested are good and evil, God's love and God's wrath, gentle meekness and powerful energy, innocent purity and strong sexuality, peace and war, mercy and justice, pardon and punishment.

Textual note: The text of "The Tiger" used here differs in line 12 from that published by Blake in *Songs of Experience* ("What dread hand? And what dread feet?"). In the original manuscript this line is followed by a discarded stanza of which the first line is "Could fetch it from the furnace deep?" The cancellation of the stanza left line 12 syntactically incomplete, and Blake seems to have been dissatisfied with it, for in a copy later given to a friend he altered the line in ink to "What dread hand formed thy dread feet," and another friend, perhaps on Blake's authority, printed the poem in a book of memoirs with "forged" in the place of "formed." I have used the version which seems to me best, and which may have represented Blake's final intention.   LP

William Blake THE GARDEN OF LOVE (page 264)

The important words and images in this poem may be ranged in two columns. On one side are the Garden of Love (1, 7), play (4), the green (4), flowers (8, 10), joys and desires (12). On the other side are the Chapel (3, 5), shut gates (5), "Thou shalt not" (6), graves (9), tombstones (10), Priests in black gowns (11), binding with briars (12). The words and images in the first series have positive connotations: they represent the natural and are associated with joy. Those in the second series have mainly negative connotations: they represent institutionalized religion and are associated with death.

Blake was a deeply religious poet who had his own highly unorthodox version of Christianity. He believed strongly in individual liberty, he felt that man's natural impulses are good, and he despised the institutions of church and state for attempting to control man's behavior with repressive rules and laws. In this brief allegorical lyric the speaker relates what the institutionalized church has done to the natural state of man. It has replaced the green where the speaker used to play as a boy with a chapel, its gates shut, and "Thou shalt not" writ over the door. The garden beds around the chapel, where sweet flowers used to grow and ought to be growing now, are filled with graves. Black-gowned priests, following prescribed rounds, are binding the speaker's joys and desires with briars. Clearly "desires" and the "sweet flowers" in the "Garden of Love" are linked with the joys of what the speaker regards as an innocent sexuality, which the Church has forbidden or restricted by threats of punishment ("briars") and death ("tombstones") under a repressive and negative moral code ("Thou shalt not" . . . pick the flowers, fornicate, commit adultery, engage in natural pleasures). As is evident from "Soft Snow" (page 94), Blake believed in free love, just as he believed in political and religious freedom. (Ideas and opinions expressed on this program are not necessarily those of the management.) LP

Sterling Brown **SOUTHERN COP** (page 265)

Brown's poem is a stinging indictment against racial prejudice, showing how it reduces black men and women to the status of creatures who may be shot dead just because they are running. But it has enough compassion in it, and enough wisdom, to show that whites are also the victims of such prejudice. It proceeds chiefly by means of irony and understatement. Perhaps the most obviously ironical lines in the poem are 7–8 ("The Negro must have been dangerous, / Because he ran"); the most obvious understatement is lines 15–16 ("And all we can say for the Negro is / It was unfortunate").

The first lines of the four stanzas, though parallel in form, carry different degrees of irony. The most ironical is that beginning stanza 3. Ty's behavior is in no way to be condoned, let alone approved. The least ironical is that beginning stanza 2. This stanza examines the psychology behind the shooting, and though that psychology is irrational, it is understandable. Verbally, no irony at all may be intended in the first line of stanza 4, for Ty is surely to be pitied, both for his simple-mindedness and for the ordeal of having to suffer the consequences of his mistake; but the situation makes the line ironical, for the dying Negro and those who loved him are the ones most truly deserving of pity. There is also irony in the contrast between Ty's having all the power ("his big gun smoking") and his being psychologically defenseless ("rabbit-scared"). The irony of the opening line must be weighed in a delicate balance. It is Christian to forgive, and it has been said that "to understand all is to forgive all," but full forgiveness for the brutal exercise of power is humanly difficult (perhaps only God is capable of it), and one doubts that the speaker is in a wholly forgiving mood. His use of irony elsewhere argues against it.

Sterling Brown is a black poet. Whether the irony is verbal or dramatic depends on whether one takes the speaker to be the poet or someone quite different from the poet—say, a prejudiced white who truly believes what he says: that Ty's behavior should be condoned and perhaps even rewarded. The evidence supports the first supposition. No real sense of a separate speaker is created by the poem, and if we try to suppose one, we find ourselves involved in contradictions. A white bigot would refer to Ty's victim as a nigger, not a Negro; and the insensitivity of bigotry is difficult to reconcile with the speaker's obvious sensitivity to human behavior. These inconsistencies disappear if we take the speaker to be the poet himself, using verbal irony incisively and skillfully and with varying degrees of weight, able to see the situation both from the black man's point of view and the white man's, but clearly and justifiably angered over the black man's victimization by the racial attitudes that molded Ty Kendricks. LP

Janet Burroway **THE SCIENTIST** (page 265)

The speaker is a poet and a woman in love with (probably affianced to) a surgeon (or a medical student preparing to be a surgeon). She is going over in her mind and writing a poem about a recent visit to his laboratory, at which she had seen and asked him to tell her about a human skull. (The words in quotation marks throughout the poem are his, in answer to her question.) Although she suspects that he suspected that she had asked the question, not out of any real curiosity about the skull, but either because, as a poet, she hoped to learn some strange new words for her poetry, or because, as a woman in love with him, she wanted to show interest in his work, he complied with her request.

The tenor of his remarks was that "There's nothing mysterious" or even very interesting about the skull. It is formed of the commonest elements, worth in the aggregate about fourteen cents. It is necessary, for it supports the skin (the domain of beauty) and it protects the brain (the domain of thought), but in itself it is "nothing."

The speaker at first is inclined to agree with him that the skull is simply a dull intermediary between the miracles of thought and beauty, just as her hand is a dull intermediary between the conceiving mind and the poem being written on the page. (She considers poetry "miraculous" like the mind which inspires it, but, since she is referring specifically to her own poem, she speaks of it deprecatingly as the "posturing stanza.")

But the look on her lover's face, she realizes, contradicted everything that he had been saying and that she has momentarily assented to. The glow in his eyes had indicated deep interest in the skull that his fingers gently examined: there is mystery and miracle in the skull as well as in skin and brain. Lines 29–33 use words that combine the vocabularies of poetry, science, and religion. Her lover's eyes "rhymed" depth from the eye sockets of the skull he holds. His jawline "articulated" (both joined and spoke) with his "temple" (part of the skull and a place of worship). His fingers gently probing the bone of the skull "revealed" (made manifest, provided a "revelation" of) his "god" (truth) in "the praying of their plying" (for the scientist the search for truth is equivalent to prayer).

In the last three lines the speaker returns to the suspicion of her request which she had sensed in her lover's mind. Wonderfully, she is "justifying" that "doubt." As a poet she has been moved to write about this experience, using, in part, the vocabulary he has provided. As a woman she has been moved to deeper love "by the mystery of his denying." His denial of his belief in the miraculousness of the skull remains, like the skull itself, and like her poet's hand, both a mystery and the server of a function. The poem harmonizes science, poetry, love, and religion as forms of the same human impulse. LP

Constance Carrier **LISA** (page 266)

This portrait of a young girl mysteriously seeking privacy and solitude, without having a reason for her choice but consciously aware that she has chosen, evokes the duality of her world and the contrast between this present world and the one she will come to inhabit. This moment of awareness of the two worlds of childhood is presented as an introduction or rehearsal for that future time when she will step into that other world of womanhood, with its need for both privacy and a public life.

The poem moves through pairings and contrasts, emphasizing the dualities of both present and future. The paradoxical metaphors of line 2 introduce the strategy: the lilac shade is both "dome" and "cave," contrasting height with depth, soaring with sinking. Doubleness is mimicked in the frequency of compound adjectives in the first stanza, single words made of pairs. The second stanza defines the duality of the child's experience (noise and silence), and stanza three continues the pairing of contrasts, culminating in "alone and yet not lonely," a phrase that draws the clear distinction between physical fact and mental condition. The grammatical ambiguity of line 12 captures a central theme: this quarter hour belongs only to her, and for this time she belongs only to herself. TRA

Leonard Cohen **GIFT** (page 267)

1. In what sense is "silence . . . nearer to peace than poems"? What meanings of "peace" are relevant?
2. How can the speaker *bring* silence to the person being addressed?
3. What does the speaker reveal about himself by the statement "I know silence"?
4. In what sense of the word "poem" can silence be called "another poem"?
5. Can you infer the relationship between the speaker and the person being addressed? TRA

161

The first publication of this poem included a lengthy note by Coleridge attributing its inspiration to a combination of having taken a prescribed dose of opium, for an illness he was suffering, and then reading a seventeenth-century travel book about the Chinese ruler; he claims that in his "reverie" he had composed between two and three hundred lines of verse, but as he was beginning to write them down he was interrupted by a visitor, and returning to his work discovered that he had forgotten the rest. (The account is available in any collection of Coleridge's works, and need not be quoted here.) Whether this was literally true is less important than the effect Coleridge had in mind in reporting it; the account was written some fifteen years after the poem, and seems to have as its purpose emphasizing the air of magic and mystery of the poem itself, as well as promoting the Romantic ideal of poetry as spontaneous, impulsive, and free of narrowly rational thought.

But as many commentators have shown, the poem itself is highly crafted, not likely the product even of a practiced poet unless he is paying close attention to his effects. Elisabeth Schneider analyzes at length the assonance, consonance, alliteration, and internal and end rimes of just the first five lines, demonstrating the "half-caught echoes, correspondences of sound felt but too complex to be anticipated or to remain tabulated in the mind even after they have been analyzed."

Through line 36 the poet describes the site of Kubla Khan's pleasure-dome: it is a landscape of contrasts and opposites, with a river bursting forth with great force from a fountain in a "romantic chasm," meandering through a pleasant valley, then sinking once again into a cavern leading to the "sunless sea." The dome itself is built over "caves of ice," and the dome is surrounded by gardens and forests, bounded by walls and towers. The scene combines wildness with gentleness, heights with depths, explosive creative force with calm obliteration, warmth with coldness, holiness with demonism, tumult with lifelessness, artifice with nature, the momentary present with an ancestral past, light with dark, a peaceful scene with prophecies of war. It is, says Harold Bloom, a "vision of creation and destruction, each complete." It presents "the balance or reconciliation of opposites" which for Coleridge was "the mark of the creative imagination."

At line 37 the poem turns to a different scene, a "vision" the poet once had of another distant and exotic moment, of a singing maiden playing on an antique instrument whose song seems to him to have corresponded to Kubla Khan's pleasure-dome. If he could revive within himself the feelings aroused by this vision, he too would be able to create "in air" what Kubla did on earth—and his creation would mark him off from the multitudes who would see in him a holy man of magical powers.

His desire is to create poetically the totality that was expressed in Kubla Khan's achievement; as he phrases it, however, this is only a wish, something beyond his powers. Yet as Bloom points out, what the poem "Kubla Khan" does is precisely that.

This intriguing poem has excited much commentary, among the best of it the

162

following: Walter Jackson Bate, *Coleridge* (New York: Macmillan, 1968), pp. 75–84; Harold Bloom, *The Visionary Company* (Garden City, N.Y.: Anchor/Doubleday, 1963), pp. 229–33; G. Wilson Knight, *The Starlit Dome* (London: Methuen, 1968), pp. 90–97; Elisabeth Schneider, "Kubla Khan," from *Coleridge, Opium and Kubla Khan*, reprinted in *Coleridge: A Collection of Critical Essays*, ed. Kathleen Coburn (Englewood Cliffs, N.J.: Prentice-Hall, 1967), pp. 88–93. TRA

Walter de la Mare **THE LISTENERS** (page 269)

"The Listeners" is an atmospheric, not a symbolic, poem. Its purpose is to conjure up a sense of mystery, eeriness, and strangeness. It succeeds in doing so through its haunting description, its haunting rhythm, and its apparent presentation of one episode from a long narrative whose beginning and end are left unrecounted and unexplained. For an excellent refutation of misguided symbolic interpretations, see the note by Frederick L. Gwynn and Ralph W. Condee in *The Explicator* 12 (February 1954): 26. LP

James Dickey **THE BEE** (page 270)

The poem juxtaposes two contexts in the present (the still woods, and the screaming highway), with the father and son moving from the marginal roadside area first toward the highway, then into the woods. It similarly juxtaposes two time periods (the speaker's college football days in the past, and the threatened future life of the child), with the father's thoughts moving first backward, then forward, from the present time which separates them. The roadside in the present is the boundary in both space and time, and the father's physical action in saving his son is parallel to his mental motions in drawing strength from his personal past in order to insure his son's future.

There is also an implicit spiritual motion. Quoting his old coach, the poet blasphemously urges himself, "God damn / You, Dickey, *dig*"; he then seems to pray to the coach: "O backfield / Coach Shag Norton"; and finally identifies himself spiritually with the "savior," the dead coach who lives in the air, dedicating himself to his service in the final quotation. At the beginning of the poem, apparently self-confident and not consciously concerned about his ability to protect his son as they walk along a highway, he is called upon to perform an unexpected and painful act of heroism, and draws upon the guidance he received in youth. He then leads his son into the deep, quiet woods where the "tobacco- / mumbling voice" of the dead coach is invoked to teach the sleeping child the spiritual lesson: "Coach Norton, I am your boy."

Spiritually, the poem reveals the same juxtaposition of opposites viewed from a middle or marginal position: at one extreme, implicit in the blasphemy, is traditional Christianity; at the other, the exaltation of the coach as savior and spiritual father;

in the middle where the speaker must act out his life, is a spiritual self-reliance that can call up the necessary physical strength and sacrifice.

The unusual structuring of the lines provides a visual reinforcement of juxtaposition viewed from a middle position. The norm in poetry is a matching of phrase to line. But for the most part, the line ends here do not mark phrasal pauses; these come in the spaces within the lines, while line endings are vigorously run on, as are the closing and opening lines of the verse paragraphs. When the poem reaches its concluding statement, beginning in line 50, the mid-line pauses are virtually eliminated. One may see in this technical device a reference to the sense of the poem, which places the spatial, temporal, and spiritual moment in the middle of the continuum from nature to highway, from past to future, and from self-confidence to dependency. TRA

Emily Dickinson **BECAUSE I COULD NOT STOP FOR DEATH** (page 271)

Beyond doubt, this is the most discussed of Emily Dickinson's poems, and it has excited a wide array of interpretations. The literal content seems to offer few difficulties: a woman so busy with her life is called away from it by a kindly gentleman (Death), who takes her for a carriage ride past the living, pauses at what must be her grave, and proceeds through centuries toward the destination "eternity." There are many fine details characterizing the stages of life in stanza 3; stanza 4 emphasizes both the femininity of the speaker and the chilliness of her ride; stanza 5 mysteriously understates her burial; and the last stanza perpetuates the ride in Death's carriage beyond the human comprehension of time (the concept of eternity, as Keats says in the last stanza of "Ode on a Grecian Urn," teases us "out of thought").

There is little quarrel among the critics about these literal matters. The continuing question is what this little allegory *means*. Does it link death with sexuality (the gentleman come courting)? Does it pretend to render a judgment on posthumous experience? Does it define the values of life as they are discovered in the moment of dying? Does it celebrate the soul's entry into heaven? These suggestions, and several others, have been made by eminent critics and scholars. Furthermore, there is little agreement about the tone of the poem—is it confident? whimsical? terrified? triumphant? uninvolved?

What follows, then, is *one* interpretation which is both plausible and consistent with the poet's ideas. The teacher may wish to use this poem, and the references below, as an introduction to discriminating between critical approaches and interpretations.

Death is remarkably, and surprisingly, characterized in this personification as "kindly," a word which so violates normal expectations as to signal the need for interpretation. Death has traditionally been thought of as "kind" to the extent that it releases a person from a life of suffering or from the limitations imposed by mortality. Such a meaning might be implied by the fact that "Immortality" is included as a personified fellow-passenger in the carriage, but the images of life in the poem do not suggest a life of pain—it contains both labor and leisure, nonchalantly linked by alliteration, which are as easily put away as a basket of sewing; and it is represented by the playing children and the maturing grain. In fact, life and death seem equally attractive, and the speaker, pleased with Death's "civility," apparently accepts his invitation with pleasure. The poem presents Death's visit not as an inevitable and unavoidable event, but as a polite invitation which the speaker finds attractive—an interpretation which divides the speaker from ordinary people.

The tone of the poem is governed by the speaker's willingness to accept Death's kind offer, and the key to the speaker's choice lies in the final stanza. Until then, the poem has been a retrospective recollection of events, reported from the speaker's present situation and colored by her perceptions and attitudes "centuries" later. Although in real terms (calendar terms, sun terms) hundreds of years have passed since the beginning of the ride with Death, to the speaker this whole span of time "*Feels* shorter than the day" she died. Now being dead, the speaker no longer shares the feelings or the ideas of the living. The word "surmised" (line 23) underscores this, for in mid-nineteenth century America, and in several other poems by Emily Dickinson, the word had decidedly negative connotations; it meant to guess in error, or to guess without personal experience as a basis. The speaker guessed at the destination of her ride—eternity—but has not reached what the living suppose that implies, heaven. Instead, what she is now experiencing is an endless, cool, and detached journey toward an unknown destination. The speaker retains the power to remember her life, and retains her consciousness, but her present situation is undefinable. In this interpretation, the poem presents an allegorical dramatization of posthumous experience: it is neither hellish nor blissful, but only eternally conscious and emotionless.

Among the important critical readings of the poem, the following offer much variety: Richard Chase, *Emily Dickinson* (New York: William Sloane Assoc., 1951), pp. 249–51; Theodore C. Hoepfner, "'Because I Could Not Stop for Death,'" *American Literature*, XXIX (1957), 96; Charles R. Anderson, *Emily Dickinson's Poetry: Stairway of Surprise* (New York: Holt, 1960), pp. 241–46; Clark Griffith, *The Long Shadow: Emily Dickinson's Tragic Poetry* (Princeton, N.J.: Princeton Univ. Press, 1964), pp. 127–34; Richard B. Sewall, *The Life of Emily Dickinson* (New York: Farrar, Straus, 1974), pp. 571–72, 717; Robert Weisbuch, *Emily Dickinson's Poetry* (Chicago: Univ. of Chicago Press, 1975), pp. 113–17.   TRA

Emily Dickinson **I TASTE A LIQUOR NEVER BREWED** (page 272)

The poet's delight in nature is expressed through an extended metaphor in which ecstasy is likened to intoxication. The liquor on which the poet gets drunk is air and dew and all the beauty of summer. This liquor is natural: it has not been brewed; and "not all the vats upon the Rhine" (famous for its breweries) yield a comparable liquor. She drinks it from "tankards scooped in pearl" (cumulus clouds in summer skies by my interpretation, but other interpretations are possible). The "inns of molten blue" are summer skies, and "endless" is an overstatement modifying "days" or "summer" or both. Bees and butterflies (both of which take nectar from flowers) are her drinking companions, but the poet declares she will outdrink both—drink them under the table! Indeed she will make such a spectacle of herself and raise such a hullabaloo that seraphs and saints will run to the windows of heaven to investigate, and, looking out, will see the poet leaning drunkenly against the celestial lamppost!

The fancifulness of the poem's metaphors keeps the poem bubbling with high-spirited fun. The alliteration of "debauchee of dew" (6) follows the vowel-alliter-ation of line 5 (all vowels alliterate with each other), in which *every* syllable except one (*-bri-*) begins with a vowel, so that reading it is like taking continuous small sips of air. The trochaic substitution in the first foot of line 7 not only emphasizes the word "Reeling" but introduces a reeling movement into the line. (The basic met-rical and rime pattern is iambic $x^4a^3x^4a^3$, but in line 15 a metrical pause replaces the last beat, giving emphasis to the delightful assonantal phrase "little tippler" by which the poet characterizes herself.)   LP

John Donne SONG: GO AND CATCH A FALLING STAR (page 272)

In content this poem expresses an extremely disillusioned and cynical view of human life and particularly of feminine virtue. The speaker, addressing an unidenti-fied interlocutor, bids him in the first six lines to perform a series of tasks which have the common characteristic of being impossible. The implication is that the task he commands in the last three lines of the stanza is equally impossible: to find any condition of life that favors the advancement of "an honest mind." (In modern idiom, "Nice guys finish last.")

In the second stanza the speaker zeroes in on his true target—feminine virtue. If, he tells his companion, you are a person with a gift for seeing miraculous events or things invisible to the ordinary eye, go on a journey, ride "ten thousand days and nights," do not return until you are old; no matter how wide or long your search, even with your gift for seeing wondrous things, you will be unable to find a woman who is both beautiful and faithful in love. (He may perhaps find some faithful ugly ones, but those women with opportunities to be unfaithful will take them.)

In the third stanza the speaker seemingly retreats half a step from this extreme conclusion. *If* you find one, he tells his companion, let me know, for it would be sweet to make a "pilgrimage" to see such a saint. But then he retracts this injunc-tion, showing that he has not really retreated at all. Do not tell me, he says, for even were she still true when I received your letter, still, by the time I could complete my journey, were it only next door, she would have proved unfaithful to two or three lovers. His "pilgrimage," he is convinced, would turn out to be a fool's errand. It is as impossible to find a woman both "true and fair" as to catch a falling star.

How seriously are we to take this poem? Should we imagine the speaker or poet as a man extremely embittered from a series of personal betrayals? Possibly. But it is called a "Song," and was indeed written to an "air" already in existence. Its meter is songlike (tetrameter, except for two monometer lines in each stanza). Its riming is copious (alternating in the first four lines, then a couplet of feminine rimes, then three rimes on one sound). Moreover, its images and overstatements are so extreme, or so witty and charming, and its progress so amusing, that it is hard to take the poem gravely. It seems more playful than disenchanted, more entertaining than sad. The poet, one feels, has adopted a fashionably cynical pose and tried to see how ingeniously and entertainingly he could deal with it. In short, the poem—and its speaker—are too lively to be lugubrious. LP

John Donne THE FLEA (page 273)

"The Flea" is a poem not to be taken too seriously as a reflection of human life, but to be enjoyed for what it is—a virtuoso display of ingenuity and wit. Resembling a kind of miniature play, the poem has two characters, dramatic conflict, stage action, and dialogue (though we hear only one speaker). The action is indicated by the speaker, and takes place before and between the stanzas. The situation is one in which a young man is attempting to seduce a young woman by the use of highly ingenious but highly sophistical reasoning. Basically, his argument is that losing her virginity will be no more damaging to her than a flea bite.

Before the first stanza, a flea has bitten the young man and then has jumped to the young woman and begun to bite her. The young man sees an opportunity and seizes it. He points to the flea and remarks that it has innocently mingled their two bloods within itself, which is no more than sexual intercourse does (according to a traditional belief), and yet is more than she will allow to him. (When he says that the flea has done "more than we would do," he means, of course, more than *she* would do, for he is eager enough himself.) His remark that the flea's action cannot be called a "sin" or "shame" or "loss of maidenhead" indicates that she is a virgin and wishes to preserve her virginity until she can surrender it without sin.

Between the first and second stanzas the young lady raises her finger to squash the flea. The young man protests, urging her to spare the flea, in which, because of their commingled bloods, they "almost, yea more than married are." With dazzling sleight-of-wit he has parlayed his claim that the commingling of their bloods within the flea is tantamount to a sinless act of sexual intercourse into a claim that it is tantamount to marriage. The flea is their "marriage-bed" and "marriage-temple." If she kills it, he claims, she will be destroying three lives—his, hers, and its—and committing three sins—murder, suicide, and sacrilege. (The line "Though use [habit] make you apt [habitually disposed] to kill me" indicates that the speaker has already attempted many times to seduce the young woman and has failed. He is metaphorically playing with the poetic lover's traditional complaint that he is "dying" of his unrequited love and therefore that the lady is "killing" him by withholding her favors.)

But the young lady pays no attention to the speaker's protest. Between the second and third stanzas she has cruelly (according to the young man) killed the flea—

has "purpled [crimsoned]" her nail with "blood of innocence" (the flea's only guilt, the speaker claims, was contained in the drop of blood it sucked from its murderess); and now she declares triumphantly to the young man that neither he nor she has been injured (let alone "killed") by the flea's death. With one quick stroke of her finger she has indeed thoroughly discredited the young man's "logic." But the young man is not for a moment discountenanced. Nimbly, he turns his defeat into a further argument for his original design. Because his fears proved false, he contends, all fears are false, including hers that she will lose honor in yielding to him. She will lose no more honor in submitting to his desires, he claims, than she lost life in killing the flea. This argument (a generalization from a single instance) is, of course, as specious as those that have gone before, yet we can hardly fail to admire the young man's mental agility in turning the tables and putting the young woman on the defensive once again.   LP

John Donne   **THE GOOD-MORROW** (page 274)

As the title announces, this poem is a morning greeting addressed by the speaker to his love. The questions in the opening lines colloquially declare a parallel between this morning's awakening and an awakening to life that took place when they began to love. All time before then was like infancy, or like a miraculous two-century sleep. The conversational quality of these lines continues throughout the poem, producing the kind of syntactical and elliptical problems found in line 5: "but this, all pleasures fancies be" means "with the exception of this (our love), all pleasures are merely imagined ones." The mock innocence of the first three lines is elaborated on in lines 6-7: the speaker has in the past had his share of sexual experiences, but to his innocent sleeping soul they were only prophetic dreams of the love he now shares.

Pursuing his reference to other love exploits, the speaker assures his lady that there can be no cause of jealousy between them. He puns on the words "watch" and "wake," synonyms in Donne's time, to insist that the alertness to each other which this morning has brought is not for fear of loss, because (he logically says) our mutual love rules out the possibility of loving others. Each of them is the whole of the other's society, just as the room they share is equivalent to all other places. The elliptical syntax of lines 11-12 extends this spatial reference. "Let" in these lines means both "let us concede" and "let us ignore." For other people whose sense of the spaciousness of the world derives from traveling, explorers and mapmakers are necessary; but these two lovers in themselves contain all worlds. (Line 14 alludes to the Renaissance theory that each individual human being is a microcosm, a little world that parallels the greater universe and contains all its elements. Each of the lovers is thus a world, and being joined by their love, each *has* a world.)

The third stanza further extends the geographical metaphor, but it begins with a Renaissance commonplace, that the face of the lover is mutually mirrored in the eye of the partner, both of them being simultaneously a mirror and the image in the other's mirror. Line 16 momentarily returns to the theme of jealousy, as the speaker assures his love that their mirrored faces reveal the honesty in their hearts. They are themselves like the hemispheres of the newly explored and mapped earth—but better, since they do not have the sharp coldness of the north, nor the sinking sunset of the west. Lines 19–21 employ another Renaissance notion, that mortality and decay are the result of the mixture of unequal or dissimilar elements in the body. Donne concludes that since the two of them are not dissimilar (being "one" in their love), or, at least, since they are completely "alike" in the intensity of their feelings, they need not fear death.

The rich allusiveness of the poem, with its hyperbolic declarations balanced against recurrent denials of any need for jealousy or the fear of infidelity, make this a more complicated poem than its declarative statements suggest. The speaker insists on the perfection and permanence of their mutual love, but this idealism is presented in a context that acknowledges the probability of change. The references to new geographical discoveries attest to the temporal nature of human knowledge, just as the opening stanza shows that individual human beings develop and change. Despite the insistence in the last three lines, death is a certainty for these perfect lovers; and if the real hemispheres of the earth contain "sharp north" and "declining west," the microcosm of the lovers' united being will ultimately be subjected to the same vicissitudes. At the same time that the poem declares the permanence of this love, it alludes to the actual impossibility of it.

The fullest analysis of this poem is by Clay Hunt, in *Donne's Poetry: Essays in Literary Analysis* (Hamden, Conn.: Archon Books, 1969), pp. 53–69, a reprint of the Yale University Press edition, 1954. Other valuable comments may be found in Wilbur Sanders, *John Donne's Poetry* (Cambridge: Cambridge Univ. Press, 1971), pp. 64–68, and Judah Stampfer, *John Donne and the Metaphysical Gesture* (New York: Simon and Schuster, 1970), pp. 142–46. TRA

John Donne   **THE SUN RISING** (page 275)

Like other Donne poems in this text, this presents the dramatic situation of a speaker addressing a second party (in this case, the personified sun) from an easily identified place and time: he is in bed, with his love, at break of day. As in "Batter My Heart, Three-Personed God" (page 106), "The Flea" (page 273), and "Song: Go and Catch a Falling Star" (page 272), the poem has a sense of immediacy arising from the speaker's apparent change of heart or mind as he is speaking, so that these poems have the effect of motivating their own conclusions out of the ideas with which they begin.

In the impertinent and colloquial opening lines, the speaker angrily chides the busybody sun for interrupting the lovers. Let him go elsewhere, remind other people for whom punctuality is a necessity (schoolboys, apprentices, courtiers, farmers) that it is time for them to be up and busy. Lovers, he says, are not governed by the sun with his "rags of time," seasons, hours, days, months; his peeping through their curtains is improper and rude (as rude as is the speaker in addressing the interloper).

169

While the first stanza insists that this is neither the time nor the place for the sun to intrude, it does acknowledge the sun's power in keeping the world on time. But in the second stanza the speaker denies that the sun's beams do have the power to control mankind: he can shut them out merely by blinking, though he won't do so because that would mean not looking at his love. With a traditional overstated metaphor, he suggests that his love's eyes are so bright that they might blind the sun himself; but if they have not, then the sun should go off on his daily inspection of the world, and return—tomorrow (as he inevitably will)—to report whether the East and West Indies, sources of spices and gold, haven't left their accustomed places to gather into the person of his love, here in the bed. And if the sun in his journey should ask for all the kings of the world, he will be told that they too have left their kingdoms, and are gathered into the person of the speaker.

The third stanza extends the metaphor of the world contracted into the one bedchamber. The woman is all the nations, the speaker all their rulers—and there is nothing left out there for the sun to shine upon. All those who call themselves princes are imitations, as is their honor and their wealth. Having reduced the world to that point, the speaker then pityingly tells the weary old sun that he can do his job of warming the world merely by shining on the two lovers, as he invites him to do.

Thus the initial attitude, chasing away the powerful sun, changes to welcoming his warmth and attention. What does the speaker really want, then? (And does he, literally, have any choice in the matter?) Most of all he wants his lady to overhear the extravagance of his praise for her and his claims of the importance of their love. The changes in attitude, from chiding the sun to denigrating his power to welcoming him into the chamber, while they are inconsistent, have in common the one theme, that he and his love are superior to the whole world, to the sun itself. The intellectual playfulness of his dialogue, the wide-ranging references, even the inconsistencies, mean "this woman means more to me than the whole world." The sprightliness of this "overheard" speech may have his lady laughing at his outrageousness, but she could not help being flattered by it.   TRA

Keith Douglas   **VERGISSMEINICHT** (page 275)

The setting is probably the North African desert where British forces under General Montgomery fought a prolonged and bitter campaign against German forces under General Rommel ("The Desert Fox") during World War II. The speaker, a British soldier, accompanied by one or more fellow-soldiers, has returned, three weeks afterwards, to the site of a particularly fierce engagement. They find, still sprawled under the barrel of his antitank gun, the body of a German soldier who had made a direct hit on the speaker's tank before being killed. In the gunpit spoil the speaker finds a photograph of the dead German's sweetheart, signed with her name and the German word for "Forget me not." The poem is based on a series of ironies: the inscription "Forget me not" addressed to a soldier incapable now of memory; the fact that the dead soldier's war equipment is still "hard and good" while its user is "decayed"; the horrible contrast between the living man loved by the girl and the corpse with its burst stomach and dusty eyes; the dual nature of man which makes him capable of both love and killing; the fact that the shot aimed at the soldier "has done the lover mortal hurt" (an ironic understatement). What the speaker discovers in the dead German is a man once much like himself. His tone expresses neither enmity, hate, nor triumph, but only pity and shared humanity. The poem may be usefully compared with Hardy's "The Man He Killed" (page 19).   LP

Paul Laurence Dunbar   **THE DEBT** (page 276)

1. The "debt" or, at least, the "interest" the speaker has had to pay on it is explicitly identified. So (in broad terms) is what the speaker bought. What are they?
2. What the speaker was loaned to make the purchase is left to the reader's imagination. Can you think of circumstances that would fulfill the poem's metaphors?
3. What figures of speech occur in lines 6–8? Can the phrase "my friend" be construed in more than one way?   LP

Ray Durem   **AWARD** (page 277)

The poem sardonically presents a retirement award to an FBI investigator who has wasted twenty-five years in surveillance of a man, presumably because he was suspected of being a black "troublemaker." The speaker does confess to two "crimes," but both of them are indictments of social and political systems which permit the bribing of the police and enact laws prohibiting racial minorities from using public facilities—the systems, not the speaker, have been criminal.

The speaker contrasts the waste of time and of the taxpayers' money on such a pointless investigation with what he considers some of the real social and moral crimes perpetrated over the preceding quarter century. They include political and corporate corruption (the bribery not only of the police but of an assistant to the President of the United States, probably a reference to President Eisenhower's assistant Sherman Adams, and such corporate crimes as price rigging); racist laws and acts of terrorism (legally segregated schools and public facilities, and the murder of black school-children in the South); and national policies of military intervention and the suppression of freedom (the nation's support of a Caribbean dictator, the Korean War, the intervention of the Marines in Guatemala, and the arming of the French forces trying to suppress the independence movement in Algeria). The poem bitterly asks how a country that permits such vicious acts can pretend that it is protecting the nation by eavesdropping on an ordinary middle-class citizen whose only illegal actions have been the result of the nation's own immorality.   TRA

171

Russell Edson **THE MOUSE DINNERS** (page 277)

To argue over whether or not this is a "poem" is futile. No conclusion can be reached unless agreement is first reached on a definition of "poem." But two things are certain. It is *not* verse. It *is* prose. The contention of this book has been that *poetry* may be written in verse *or* prose (see pages 166–67) and that some prose contains much more poetry than much verse. And the fact is that many contemporary poets are writing short prose pieces like this and calling them "poems." But the question of whether this is better called a "poem" or, say a "prose fable" (a kind of cross between Aesop and Kafka) is really an uninteresting one. The significant questions are, Is it worth reading? Does it have literary merit?

On first reading, "The Mouse Dinners" seems perhaps bizarre, somewhat wacky, yet amusing. On repeated reading it comes more and more to have a resemblance to actual life, and even by its very wackiness to illuminate life. Part of the strangeness comes from ambiguities in its mode of narration. It excludes quotation marks, sometimes omits clear signals as to whose voice we are hearing and whether we are hearing or overhearing it, shifts back and forth between past, future, and present tenses, and at one point so blurs time, place, thought, and speech that the whole work has the effect of a dream-collage, an effect fitting the fantastic elements of its content. The following account clarifies but oversimplifies its structure, losing some of the richness of its ambiguities.

The story is told by an omniscient narrator, one who "knows all," is able to enter the minds of his characters at will, and can report to us not only what they do and say but also what they think. In the first paragraph we hear the pure, unmixed voice of this narrator: "A woman was cooking a mouse for her husband's dinner, . . ." We will hear this "unmixed" voice twice again, in "cried the husband" and "cried the wife" in paragraphs 5 and 6. But, in fact, the storyteller is present throughout, reporting what the characters are thinking or saying. Paragraphs 2, 3, and part of 4 report what the woman is thinking while she is cooking the mouse. Her thoughts are mediated through the narrator; we know this because paragraph 4 begins "Then she'll say" rather than "Then I'll say," as it would if her thoughts were presented to us directly. But in paragraph 4, a strange thing happens. Instead of continuing "he says that every night" it suddenly shifts to "you say that every night." Somewhere in this paragraph, perhaps at this point, the scene shifts from kitchen to dining room, the time shifts from preprandial cooking to postprandial conversation, and meditation changes to speech. As in a dream, the scenes blend into each other almost imperceptibly. We know for certain, however, that at least the last word—"Hypocrite!"—is spoken aloud, by wife to husband, for the husband responds to it. In paragraphs 5 and 6 the narrator reports the spoken words of husband and wife. In the last paragraph we are given the thoughts of the husband as mediated by the narrator ("Ah yes, he is a mouse," it begins, not "Ah yes, I am a mouse").

The story recounts a crisis in a marriage based on twenty years of misunderstanding. The husband (perhaps then a suitor), mistakenly thinking that the woman

172

liked mouse, had himself pretended to like mouse so that she'd like him. After marriage the wife, to please her husband, has made herself an expert in preparing mouse dinners in a rich and innovative variety of ways (the enumeration of these ways provides much of the poem's imaginative verve). The husband, to please his wife, has developed a ritual to show his appreciation for her culinary feats. In eating his dinner, he employs a jeweler's loupe and a dentist's pick to get every last delicious morsel of meat off the tiny bones. Afterwards, he belches, pats his stomach, and tells her it's the best mouse he's ever had, then adds, "One less vermin in the world" (not only has it been a delicious meal, but they have performed a useful service in ridding the world of an undesirable creature). But after "Twenty years of this . . ." (her unspoken thought in the second paragraph), the wife has probably tired of thinking up new ways of preparing a dish she doesn't like, and has clearly become fed up with his unvarying ritual and suspicious of his unvarying compliment (How can each mouse dinner she has prepared always surpass the one before it?). The whole thing has become a crashing bore. In paragraph 3 she is on the point of rebellion; in paragraph 4 she rebels, calling her husband "Hypocrite!" Her husband denies the charge while admitting its truth ("Hypocrite? No, no, I never liked mouse"). A hypocrite is one who pretends to be something he is not (in this case, a mouse-lover); the husband, however, is shocked by the word: he would have preferred to have his hypocrisy called by a nicer name—evidence of love for his wife, perhaps, or courtesy extended to please her. But he is, in fact, not only a hypocrite but (as she next calls him) a mouse. Either from eating mouse for twenty years and/or from behaving like one, he has turned into a mouse. The metamorphosis is symbolical: it can be read both literally and metaphorically. His denial of his own truth to gain her love has led to his wife's twenty-year ordeal of preparing dinners she doesn't like, to his twenty-year ordeal of eating dinners he doesn't like, and to the loss of his wife's love and respect, for which the pretense was adopted in the first place.   LP

Robert Frost **ACQUAINTED WITH THE NIGHT** (page 278)

At a purely literal level this poem says merely that the poet has taken many walks at night through the city and is thoroughly familiar with its nighttime aspects. But clearly the poem is meant to be read symbolically. The chief symbol is the night, which suggests the darker aspects of existence. But to grasp anything like its full significance, we must examine the details of the poem. The following discussion does not pretend to exhaust their implications.

That the poet has walked out and back in rain indicates that he has endured physical discomfort. That he has walked beyond the furthest city light—beyond the city limits—may suggest that he has "transgressed"—gone beyond legal or moral limits. His having looked down "the saddest city lane" indicates that he has seen the poverty and misery of the city's slum areas. His unwillingness to explain to the watchman what he is doing out so late at night suggests feelings of guilt or embarrassment.

The "interrupted cry" across houses from another street—possibly a scream of terror cut short by strangulation—suggests violence and evil. That the cry is not directed toward him suggests his loneliness. The illuminated clock which seems detached from the earth and at "an unearthly height" (because its tower is blotted out by darkness) may at first seem like something supernatural, but is really only a man-made instrument which can "proclaim the time" but cannot judge it. It thus suggests a universe without moral or divine oversight—a universe indifferent to man.

The night in Frost's poem is thus a remarkably subtle and evocative symbol for hardship, guilt, sorrow, loneliness, evil, desolation, and isolation at the personal, social, and cosmic levels. The clock against the sky, man-made but "at an unearthly height," strikingly proclaims the absence of authoritative moral direction, human or superhuman, in an indifferent universe.

And how does the poet respond to this dark perception of the universe? The calm, matter-of-fact tone of voice in the first and final lines counters the dark experience of the intervening lines with a quiet refusal to be daunted. The final line is indeed an understatement. The poet has been more than "acquainted" with the night—he has explored it thoroughly; but his tone of voice says, in effect, "I can take it."

Though the poem resembles a sonnet in containing fourteen lines of iambic pentameter, its rime scheme is that of *terza rima,* made famous by Dante's use of it in *The Divine Comedy,* of which the "Inferno" is the best-known section.

Some critics have read the "luminary clock" as a metaphor for the moon. But (a) one cannot easily tell time by the moon as one can by the sun; it rises at a different hour every day and is often observable in full daylight; (b) this is a city poem, and its imagery is city imagery; (c) if the clock *were* the moon, then the phrase "at an unearthly height" would be literal, obvious, and uninteresting; (d) Frost has himself identified the clock as a tower clock in Ann Arbor [see *Frost: Centennial Essays* (Jackson: Univ. Press of Mississippi, 1974), p. 521; and *Frost: Centennial Essays III* (1978), p. 296].

There are excellent discussions of this poem in Reginald L. Cook, *The Dimensions of Robert Frost* (New York: Rinehart, 1958), pp. 107–08; and in Reuben A. Brower, *The Poetry of Robert Frost* (New York: Oxford Univ. Press, 1963), pp. 126–29. LP

Robert Frost **MENDING WALL** (page 278)

At first reading this poem will seem to be about walls and about two New England farmers who have opposite philosophies concerning them. Each philosophy is stated twice: the speaker's in the first line and in line 35: "Something there is that doesn't love a wall"; the neighboring farmer's in line 27 and in the final line: "Good fences make good neighbors." But as we dig into the poem a little deeper we may conclude that the poem is less about walls and opposed philosophies concerning them than it is about opposed kinds of mental habit. The neighboring farmer's philosophy is clear and definite, and we know exactly where he got it. He got it from his father, who got it from his father, who got it . . . . In short, it is a traditional piece of folk wisdom, a proverbial saying which he has accepted as dogma without questioning its meaning or validity. The speaker, on the other hand, states his philosophy more tentatively: *"Something there is* that doesn't love a wall." He seems not quite certain what that "Something" is, though, as a matter of fact, he knows exactly what "spills the upper boulders in the sun" over the winter months. It is "the frozen-ground-swell" underneath the wall: the expansion of the earth caused by the freezing of the moisture always present in the ground. Nature causes the wall to crumble. But he inclines to think there may be more to it than that: not just nature but something *in* nature or in the-nature-of-things "doesn't love" a wall. He hasn't put a label on it. But not only is he more tentative in his thinking than his neighbor, he is also more reflective, thoughtful, and flexible. He has a questioning habit of mind. Of his neighbor's proverbial saying he asks, *"Why* do they make good neighbors? Isn't it / *Where* there are cows?" (*"Why"* is the kind of question his neighbor has never asked.) But in asking this question, or rather these two questions, he confesses that there is some truth in his neighbor's position, and he identifies exactly the source of that truth. When one or both neighbors own livestock, the wall prevents contention between them by keeping the livestock in their proper fields and keeping one farmer's cows from eating the other's crops. (A "good neighbor," as defined by the proverb, is one whom you can live next to without friction.) The neighbor's attitude toward walls, like most proverbial wisdom, contains a half-truth. ("Look before you leap" and "He who hesitates is lost," though contradictory, both state half-truths; that is, each is true in some situations, neither is true in all situations.) It is now apparent that the speaker's attitude toward walls is not so diametrically opposed to his neighbor's as at first appeared. He recognizes the necessity, the desirability, of *some* walls. Indeed he has all by himself on occasion gone out and "made repair" after hunters have completely torn down part of a wall. Still, the desirability of a wall depends upon the situation, and "here there are no cows." Before *he* built a wall he'd ask what he "was walling in or walling out." He continues to think that there is "Something" that "doesn't love a wall, / That wants it down," but he is not himself opposed to all walls, just unnecessary ones, and especially those that wall in or wall out something that ought not to be walled in or out. However, he is flexible. *He* is the one who contacts his neighbor "at spring mending-time" to let him know when he is available. He knows what his neighbor's attitude toward walls is, and he knows that to stay on neighborly terms with him, he must honor that attitude even while trying to argue him out of it.

But there is much more to the contrast between these two farmers than simply their attitudes toward walls. The speaker is observant: he can tell the difference between the gaps made by the frozen-ground-swell in winter and those made by hunters in other seasons. He knows how handling rocks all day can wear one's fingers "rough." He has imagination, a playful, whimsical turn of mind, and a sense of humor. Some boulders, he observes, are so round that they "have to use a spell to make them balance: / 'Stay where you are until our backs are turned.'" He compares the process of mending wall to "just another game, / One on a side." He anticipates his point about the cows by saying: "My apple trees will never get across / And eat the cones under [your] pines." His perceptiveness is apparent when he thinks about how to explain what the "Something" is that doesn't love a wall. Whatever it is (Love perhaps? Some principle of community or brotherhood?), the speaker knows that, to reach his neighbor's understanding, he must communicate the idea in concrete terms, not in abstractions. He fleetingly thinks of "elves" because his fancy has a fondness for elves and because elves (if one actually believes in them, as the speaker almost surely doesn't) are a physical agency which the neighbor's mind could grasp—and might accept if he were an Irish peasant rather than a New England farmer. But the speaker immediately realizes the absurdity of this explanation and casts it aside, for "it's not elves exactly, and I'd rather / He said it for himself." This last remark shows the speaker's grasp of an important principle of education: that the learner will be much more likely to grasp and accept a concept that he has figured out for himself than one he has merely had *explained* to him (if you want a fancy name for this method of teaching, it's *heuristic*). Thus we find in the speaker a mind that is probing, perceptive, and critical, but also imaginative, whimsical, and playful, though possibly a little indefinite in its inability to define that "Something" even to itself. In the neighbor we see a matter-of-fact, uncritical mind which accepts traditional wisdom unquestioningly and holds on to it dogmatically. It is this contrast of minds that provides the central interest of the poem. In the speaker's perception his neighbor "moves in darkness"—the darkness of ignorance and uncritical acceptance. He sees his neighbor there, "Bringing a stone grasped firmly by the top / In each hand, like an old-stone savage armed." The implications of the simile are two: first, that an unquestioning habit of mind is primitive, like that of paleolithic man; second, that there is something potentially menacing about such a habit of mind. No doubt the speaker and his neighbor will continue to get on amicably enough, and not start throwing rocks at each other: the neighbor is conscientious and hard-working, and both men want to be "good neighbors" in some sense of the term. Nevertheless, it is people shouting slogans, clinging to half-truths dogmatically, that rush into wars against each other and go on "holy crusades." It is this kind of mental set that creates unnecessary "walls" between men, and which "Something" (Love? Reason? Brotherhood?) "wants down."

Such, at least, is my reading (a fairly old-fashioned one) of what has become one of Frost's most controversial poems. On one axis, the range of opinion goes from Robert Graves' statement "If anyone asks: 'But what *is* the something that doesn't love a wall?' the answer is, of course, 'frost'—also its open-hearted namesake, Robert Frost," to Elizabeth Jennings' assertion that "Good fences make good neighbors" is the moral of the poem. On another axis, opinion ranges from Carson Gibbs's assessment of the speaker as "witty, tolerant, and reasonable" to Donald Cunningham's that he is "hollow, vain, and foolish." For varying viewpoints, see Elaine Barry, *Robert Frost* (New York: Ungar, 1973), pp. 109–12; Marie Boroff, *Language and the Poet* (Chicago: Univ. of Chicago Press, 1979), pp. 24–30; Donald Cunningham, "Mending a Wall," in *Gone Into If Not Explained*, ed. Greg Kuzma (Crete, Nebraska: Best Cellar Press, 1976), pp. 65–73; Carson Gibbs, "Mending Wall," *The*

Explicator, 20 (Feb. 1962), item 48; Robert Graves, "Introduction," *Selected Poems of Robert Frost* (New York: Holt, 1963), p. xiii; Elizabeth Jennings, *Frost* (New York: Barnes & Noble, 1966), p. 24; John C. Kemp, *Robert Frost and New England* (Princeton, N.J.: Princeton Univ. Press, 1979), pp. 13–26; Frank Lentricchia, *Robert Frost* (Durham, N.C.: Duke Univ. Press, 1973), pp. 104–07; John F. Lynen, *The Pastoral Art of Robert Frost* (New Haven: Yale Univ. Press, 1960), pp. 27–31; Marion Montgomery, "Robert Frost and His Use of Barriers," *South Atlantic Quarterly*, 57 (Sum. 1958), 349–50; Richard Poirier, *Robert Frost* (New York: Oxford Univ. Press, 1977), pp. 104–06; Charles N. Watson, "Frost's Wall: The View from the Other Side," *New England Quarterly*, 44 (Dec. 1971), 653–56. LP

The other editor speaks

"Good fences make good neighbors" may be the most famous phrase in all of Frost's poetry; and like many famous quotations, it is misleading when quoted out of context, or when it is offered as Frost's "philosophy."

The poem is a narrative, restricting itself to the speaker's attitudes. It poses the narrator against his neighbor, as men of two opposing philosophies, and as can be the case when we report our experiences, the narrator is given the privilege of considering his position the correct one. The neighbor is only permitted to speak his famous line, twice; what *he* thinks of the speaker is altogether missing from the poem. It can be instructive to ask a class to imagine exactly what the neighbor might be thinking about the speaker—what a man who "will not go behind his father's saying" (or so the speaker claims) thinks about a man who first informs him it is time to mend the wall, and then wants to ask what walls are for, and who seems to believe in some vague "something . . . that doesn't love a wall."

A proper reading of the poem requires taking into account the limitation and the implicit prejudice that results from one participant's report of a debate, and which naturally renders the resolution suspect: the speaker clearly thinks he has "won" because he is a thinking man who wants "to go behind" rural lore, while his neighbor "moves in darkness" of the mind. And the reader needs also to understand the dialectic opposition of the two points of view. The speaker is a man who wants to know the reasons for his actions, who investigates and meditates, who likes to believe (probably thinking himself only whimsical) in the vague "something," in using spells to balance the stones, even—almost—in elves. That is, he is a compound of rationality and a desire to find something beyond rationality. He is also a man of apple orchards, of domestication, of playing games according to equitable rules, who takes pride in being civil and civilized.

Stripped of the prejudiced reporting of the speaker, the neighbor is a man who accepts traditional teachings, who shares in the responsibility of maintaining private property, and whose land is in its natural state, a pine forest. He also believes in neighborliness, and in the soundness of workmanship. What the speaker's attitude contributes to the portrait of the neighbor reveals more about the speaker than about his opponent in the game of wall-mending. Because of the neighbor's taciturnity, the speaker thinks him shallow-minded, ignorant, primitive, unable to think or investigate. That is, he interprets the neighbor's attitude as further evidence of his own superiority. The man who is different from him is the man who is inferior to him. Does the neighbor go so far in interpreting the speaker's difference?

John F. Lynen points out that the poem presents an unresolved question: "Should man tear down the barriers which isolate individuals from one another, or should he recognize that distinctions and limitations are necessary to human life?" Attempting to answer this question, many readers have tried to pin the poem down to a simple set of paired opposites—liberal and conservative, rational and instinctive, civilized and primitive, and many more. But although the terms of the poem teasingly invite the search for an easy symbolic reading, and also tease the reader into supposing that the speaker is "right," no easy symbols or easy solutions are available. The poem is memorable for the irresolution that keeps us searching.   TRA

Thomas Hardy **CHANNEL FIRING** (page 280)

Hardy's dating of this poem may make it seem prophetic, since World War I broke out in August, 1914; but it was a prophecy almost anyone could have made, for the event referred to in line 1 was well known: the Royal Navy was conducting gunnery practice in the English Channel, and the guns could be heard many miles inland. (Hardy is reported to have been surprised, in fact, that the war began only a few months afterward.)

The speaker in the poem is one of the dead, presumably a clergyman buried within the chancel of his church where the clergy were usually interred; he is familiar with the altar, chancel windows, and "glebe cow," and seems to be in the habit of having chats with others buried nearby, including "Parson Thirdly." The folklike simplicity of the poem, achieved through its tetrameter quatrains and simple diction, makes the whole experience seem rustic and unsophisticated, the material of a ballad. The dead have been awakened by the great guns ("loud enough to wake the dead," we might say), and at first they suppose that "Judgment-day" has come. The noise has even terrified the hounds, the churchmouse, the worms, and the cow —not because they anticipate the apocalypse, of course, but because they instinctively fear loud sounds.

God, however, sardonic but comforting, tells the dead to return to their sleep: it's only men threatening men, not a divine event. Although many men *deserve* to go to hell, God has not destroyed the world, nor does he seem to want to anytime soon, for he takes pity on mankind's need for "rest eternal."

Parson Thirdly's reaction to this news in the penultimate stanza is pragmatic: if God is not going to separate the sheep from the goats, it might have been more pleasant to have "stuck to pipes and beer" instead of depriving himself for the sake of piety.

The tone of the poem shifts markedly in the last stanza. Instead of the folk narrative of the speaker and the paternal chattiness of God, the last stanza turns to brooding lyricism. Alliteration, consonance, and assonance (*roaring/readiness; again/guns; hour/roaring; readiness/avenge*) pack the first two lines. The last two abound in *st* and *t* sounds: *Stourton Tower, Camelot, starlit Stonehenge*; and the last two feet in this iambic poem are trochees, mysteriously trailing off in the mournful music that the theme demands. The bulk of the poem has been whimsical, folksy, and not particularly alarming—ironically, since the subjects have included naval bombardment, skeletons, damnation and piety, and God's potential wrath; but the theme is the persistence among men of aggression, violence, and the recurrence of military conquest to establish and maintain civilization. God (who tends to speak in clichés, the rustic father of his rustic flock) puts it directly: "The world is as it used to be."

A "glebe cow" is pastured in the parcel of land allotted to a clergyman as part of his benefice; like the land and the parsonage, it is provided for his use but is not his private property. The name "Parson Thirdly" may allude to the Holy Trinity; a Parson Thirdly is a character in Hardy's novel *Far from the Madding Crowd*. The spelling "Christès" (line 15) is archaic, in keeping with the ballad style and the time references implicit in the last stanza.

For further discussion see: Babette Deutsch, *Poetry in Our Time* (Garden City, N.Y.: Anchor/Doubleday, 1963), pp. 9–10; John Crowe Ransom, "Introduction" to *Selected Poems of Thomas Hardy* (New York: Macmillan, 1961), pp. x–xii; Cleanth Brooks and Robert Penn Warren, *Understanding Poetry* (New York: Holt, 1976), pp. 45–48; J. O. Bailey, *The Poetry of Thomas Hardy: A Handbook and Commentary* (Chapel Hill, N.C.: Univ. of North Carolina Press, 1970), pp. 262–64. TRA

Thomas Hardy **THE DARKLING THRUSH** (page 281)

The end of the day, the end of the year, and the end of the century symbolically unite with the bleakness of the imagery in the first two stanzas of this poem to evoke a mood of utter desolation and hopelessness. The contrast between this desolation and the apparently unlimited joy of the thrush's song is the pivot on which the poem turns, and the contrast is so striking that it leads many students to read into this poem an optimism that is in fact not there. Conditioned by earlier experience with more cheerful poets and with sentimental clichés, they see in this poem the dark cloud with a silver lining, the tale of woe with a happy ending, darkness giving way to light, despair overcome by hope.

What the poem actually presents is subtler and less cheerful. The speaker is overcome with wonderment at the joy of the thrush's song, and momentarily—but only momentarily—he is prompted to wonder whether the bird may not know of some "blessed Hope." But, notice, he does not say that the thrush knew of some blessed Hope. He does not even say, "I thought [did think] . . . he knew," but only, "I *could* think . . . ." That is, it's *as if* the bird sang out of some blessed Hope. The speaker *could*—but didn't—think so. The thought has crossed his mind, but transiently, too swiftly to take up residence there. The speaker, after all, sees no cause for joy or hope "written" on the world around him. In the last line he flatly states that he is unaware of any hope. The bird sings, really, out of instinct, not out of knowledge, and at the bottom of his mind the speaker knows this. The poem concludes, then, not with hope, but only with the wistful wish that there *were* some reason for hope, and with wonderment at the mystery of the bird's joyous song. The conclusion of "The Oxen" (page 150) evokes a similar mood and presents a similar interpretive problem.

Image and mood blend perfectly in this poem. The simile of the "tangled bine-stems" that score the sky like "strings of broken lyres" is marvelously effective, both visually and emotionally exact, giving a sense of music destroyed, of something else come to an end—like the day, the year, the century. LP

Anthony Hecht **"MORE LIGHT! MORE LIGHT!"** (page 282)

The poem juxtaposes two scenes: in stanzas 1–3 the burning of a religious "heretic" in England in the sixteenth century; in stanzas 4–8 the execution of two Jews and a Pole by a Nazi officer in Germany in the twentieth century. The first scene is a composite, though based largely on the death of Bishop Nicholas Ridley, burned at Oxford in 1553. The second is an accurate account of an incident that occurred at Buchenwald in 1944.

A good account of Bishop Ridley's death may be found in *Nicholas Ridley: A Biography*, by J. G. Ridley (London: Longmans, Green, 1957), pp. 416–19. Hecht does not mention Ridley's name because he is not writing specifically about Ridley's execution but about all executions in the Tower (or elsewhere), using Ridley's as a typical example. Ridley, indeed, was not executed in the Tower but at Oxford. He did not compose verses before his death (but Sir Walter Raleigh and Sir Thomas More both did). The omission of the pronoun *he* at the beginning of the poem permits a swifter entry into the poem and also allows us to read "composed" (1) not only as a verb but also (at least temporarily) as an adjective. As adjective it relates to his maintenance of courage (5) and to "his soul's tranquility" (12).

A prose account of the incident described in stanzas 4–8 may be found in chapter 8 of Eugen Kogen's *The Theory and Practice of Hell: The German Concentration Camps and the System Behind Them*, translated from the German by Heinz Norden (originally published by Farrar, Straus and Cudahy in 1950; republished in paperback by Berkley Publishing in 1958). The two executions are alike in being horrible and in being perpetrated on persons who "have made no crime." Perhaps the most important differences are these: In the first executions the victims are permitted to maintain a "pitiful dignity"; they are allowed to say some last words or to pray and are condemned to death by at least a semblance of legal process. In the second execution the last vestige of human dignity has disappeared. Related to this, the first executions are of persons condemned and executed individually. The deaths in the second incident are related to the mass executions in the Nazi concentration camps. The "ovens" are adjacent to the gas chambers where those executions took place. The smoke from these ovens is like ghostly wraiths in appearance, and horribly, it contains actual matter from the bodies that were burned there. The "soul" referred to in the first incident (12) is replaced simply by "black soot" in the second.

According to legendary report, "More light! More light!" were the last words uttered by the German poet and scientist Goethe (1749-1832), who died at Weimar (17), where for many years he had been the center of a brilliant intellectual circle. "Lead, Kindly Light" (8) are the opening words of a famous hymn ("The Pillar of Cloud") by Cardinal Newman (1801-1890). The word "light" is used in the title and in lines 8, 17, 18, and 25 to suggest a variety of meanings: literal light, intellectual enlightenment, divine mercy, human compassion, civlized values. In line 27 the word is used, ironically, in its adverbial form and with a different meaning. The final line suggests the extinction of all light with the black soot settling upon the eyes.

Hecht's poem is about "man's inhumanity to man." His use of two incidents separated in time suggests the continuance of his inhumanity throughout history, and the difference between the two incidents suggests that, if anything, it has gotten worse. Goethe's dying cry has gone unanswered—horribly unanswered.

Anthony Hecht is an American poet and is himself a Jew.   LP

A. E. Housman **BREDON HILL** (page 283)

The poem is dominated by the imagery of bells, their chiming partly conveyed by the three rimes in each stanza. But the bells have a different meaning for the speaker at different times in the poem, and in this difference the drama of the poem lies.

In stanzas 1–4 the speaker recalls summer Sunday mornings spent with his sweetheart on Bredon Hill. They heard the bells ringing for church service in "steeples far and near." Though heedless of the summons, they found the ringing a "happy noise," for it formed a background to their delight in each other. That she preferred his company over going to church probably made the bells even sweeter to the speaker, and he would call back to them, "Oh, peal upon our wedding" and we will come "in time."

In stanzas 5–6, however, we learn that the girl went to church that winter, not for a wedding but for a funeral service—her own. "Unbeknown" to her lover, she had died and gone to church (was carried there in her coffin) without him. Only one bell was tolled—a bell in only one church, and only one bell of its set of bells—the funeral bell.

In the final stanza the lover again hears the bells ringing on Bredon as he had that summer. But they no longer make a "happy noise"; they only remind him more keenly of his lost happiness. In accents of extreme bitterness he cries out (futilely) to bid them "Be dumb," and with almost surly resignation adds, "I hear you, I will come." He will come when he is ready, either to mourn at his sweetheart's grave or to be buried himself.

Bredon Hill is in Worcestershire close to the Shropshire border: these are the two shires mentioned in line 3. From the top of Bredon on a clear day one can see three additional counties—Herefordshire, Warwickshire, and Gloucestershire. The image of "colored counties" (8) conflates that of farmland laid out in plots of different-colored crops with a map showing the counties in different colors.   LP

A. E. Housman **TO AN ATHLETE DYING YOUNG** (page 284)

The speaker is a fellow townsman of the dead athlete, possibly (though not necessarily) one of the pallbearers carrying his coffin to the cemetery for burial. The athlete had died within months of winning the annual race for his town. The poem is an extended apostrophe addressed by the speaker to the athlete.

The parallelism of action and language between the first two stanzas beautifully underscores the ironic contrast in situation. After his victory in the race, the townspeople had "chaired" him (borne him in triumph on their shoulders) through the market-place to his home. Now, less than a year later, they bring him "home" again, again "shoulder-high." But the meaning of "home" has changed between the two stanzas. In the second it is a metaphor for the grave. The "road all runners come" is death, and the youth is being borne "shoulder-high" in his coffin. The "town" to which he now belongs ("stiller"—an understatement—than that which noisily "cheered" just a few months ago) is the cemetery or necropolis (*city of the dead*).

The chief ironic shock of the poem, however, comes in the third stanza. Most people would consider the death of a young athlete at the peak of his ability an occasion for lamentation; the speaker considers it one for congratulation. "Smart lad," he says (not *Poor lad*), and proceeds to praise the young athlete for dying "betimes." Except for his hyperbolic use of the word "Smart" when he literally means *fortunate* (the athlete did not commit suicide), the speaker is perfectly serious, and speaks for the poet; that is, the irony involved here is neither verbal nor dramatic but situational. Both speaker and poet regard the athlete as fortunate; the irony lies in the discrepancy between our expectation (initiated by the title and sustained through the first two stanzas) that the athlete's death will be regarded by the poet as pathetic or "tragic" and our discovery that it is regarded quite otherwise.

In the rest of the poem the speaker supports this attitude and is not undercut by the poet. The athlete has "slipped away" from "fields where glory does not stay." It is better, the speaker feels, to die when everyone is singing your praises than to die in obscurity years later (as so many once celebrated athletes do). The "fields where glory does not stay" are literally athletic fields, symbolically earth or life in general; the "glory" is fame and the pride of triumph. The "laurel" is the symbol, not just of victory (the ancient Greeks awarded a laurel wreath or "crown" to victors in the Pythian games) but of fame. The "rose" is traditionally a symbol for a girl's beauty. Though athletic fame is won by young men at an early age, the speaker declares, its duration is even shorter than a young woman's beauty. This runner, who set a new record for the course he ran, will not be alive to see his record broken; the silence that would have greeted his future athletic decline will sound "no worse than cheers" (an ironical understatement: he will be aware of neither) now that he is dead. In stanza 5 the speaker praises the athlete for having won (metaphorically) one more race: he has raced his fame to the grave and has arrived there first (has died while his name is still unforgotten). In stanza 6 the speaker again speaks to the athlete as if he had some choice in the matter, and urges him to set his "fleet foot on the sill of shade / And hold to the low lintel up / The still-defended challenge-cup." The "sill of shade" is the threshold of the door to the tomb, the "low lintel" is the crosspiece over it. The "still-defended challenge cup" (his trophy) is the kind that has the winner's name inscribed on it each year and which the winner is allowed to keep until he is defeated, when it passes into the hands of the new winner. This athlete has died with the challenge-cup still in his possession.

The last stanza contains a sophisticated literary allusion that supports some identification of the speaker with the poet (Housman was a celebrated classical scholar). In Book XI of the *Odyssey*, when Odysseus visits the Greek underworld (Hades), he is surrounded by shades of the "strengthless" dead. Since these shades are depicted as peculiarly impotent—strengthless and senseless—Housman is not predicting here some kind of immortality for the dead athlete, but simply making one more contrast between what he was in life and what he will become in death, "strengthless" and senseless. Nevertheless, these shades will find "unwithered" on his head the laurel garland (fame) "briefer than a girl's" rose garland (beauty). The last two lines of the poem allude to the symbols of stanza 3.

Housman in this poem dwells on the transience of youth, fame, and beauty, and on the desirability of dying while one still has them rather than after they are lost. It is a theme that appears elsewhere in his poetry (see especially *A Shropshire Lad*, XXIII and XLIV—"The lads in their hundreds" and "Shot? so quick, so clean an ending?"). It reflects one part of Housman's mind but not the whole of it, as can be seen from "Terence, this is stupid stuff" (page 14) and "Loveliest of trees" (page 73). LP

Ted Hughes **PIKE** (page 285)

Through the first four stanzas, the three-inch-long juvenile pike are observed in their natural habitat, "killers from the egg" yet combining both "delicacy and horror" in their beauty and in their ominous voracity. Their vicious jaws are "not to be changed at this date," neither in the individual lives of the young fish nor in the inbred characteristics of the species. Line 15 summarizes the defining quality of the pike: the killing teeth and jaws, its "instrument," are in fact its controlling characteristic, to which the fish's grace and "delicacy" are subservient.

In stanza 6 and the first half of 7 the speaker reports on the surprising cannibalism of similar small pike in an aquarium, for though they are well fed, they destroy one another as well as any other fish. "The grin it was born with" (line 21) suggests that the killing is not merely for food, but for sport or pleasure as well, and the incident described in lines 23–28, the fatal attempt of a fully grown fish to swallow another of its own size, is a chilling example of limitless voracity.

In the final four stanzas the speaker places himself in juxtaposition to the world of the pike, as a fisherman. The scene is a pond with lilies and carp (tench) that have survived more than 400 years, outlasting the men who had built the pond and even their own stone buildings; in its depth it seems an image of the age of England itself. The fisherman is terrified at the thought of the monstrous pike beneath the surface, not because he literally fears the fish but because they represent to him a dark dream released in the darkness of the depths, a dream of slowly rising horrors. The final image unifies the various observations of the behavior and nature of the pike, for it suggests that this perfectly adapted, voracious creature may lead people to discover depths of darkness in themselves. TRA

Randall Jarrell **THE DEATH OF THE BALL TURRET GUNNER** (page 286)

The poem captures both the terror and the ironic humor of its subject in the phrase "washed me out," which takes literally the euphemism for the failure to qualify for military duty. Rather than failing to measure up to training standards, the speaker has been so mutilated that his body must be flushed from his turret by a water hose.

The poem refers explicitly to the U.S. Army Air Corps in World War II. The B-17 "Flying Fortress" bombers had a gunner's glass turret on the belly of the fuselage, and airmen wore fur-lined leather jackets; anti-aircraft shells were called "flak" as an acronym for the German word "fliegerabwehrkanone," though the shorter word sounds like an onomatopoetic imitation of the noise of the explosion; and the bombers were attacked by squadrons of fighter planes.

The first three lines of the poem abound with musical devices, chiefly alliteration (*sleep, state; loosed, life; fell, fur, froze*) and assonance (*mother's, hunched; fell, belly, wet; sleep, dream*). These culminate in the internal rime "black flak," whose flat *a* and harsh *k* sharply bring to a halt such devices. After this rime, the only musical device is the concluding and horrifying rime "froze / hose." This pattern of sounds reinforces the irony of the poem's conclusion.

The metaphors of the first two lines create a parallel between the position of the unborn child in his mother's womb and the man's position in the "belly" of the bomber. The movement from one to the other is ominously referred to as falling, and the animal processes of generation and birth are obliquely implied in "my wet fur." The speaker seems to pass directly from the moment of birth to his place in the gun turret, and his existence is governed by the dreams of his mother (for her child's success, happiness, and safety) and the subsequent dream of the "State" (for its own safety and its national ideals). These dreams are both shattered when, flying above 30,000 feet, he is shocked by the shells of anti-aircraft guns to the opposite kind of dream, the nightmare of attacking fighter planes. He awakens from idealistic dreams to discover that reality is a nightmare, but his wakefulness lasts only a moment. TRA

Ellen Kay **PATHEDY OF MANNERS** (page 286)

Though it wittily satirizes certain modes of social behavior, this poem does not quite fit the literary category of "comedy of manners," for it has no happy ending; nor does it fit the category of "tragedy," for it does not dramatize the sudden "fall" from high to low estate of a protagonist of heroic stature. It is accurately labeled a "Pathedy of Manners," for it concerns the pathetic waste of life and talent by a woman whose false values made her prefer appearance to substance and choose manners over merit. Inasmuch as her false values are also those of a class, the poem presents a form of social pathology.

Brilliant, beautiful, and wealthy, the woman of the poem wasted her gifts on inauthentic goals. She might have made some great and useful contribution to humanity; instead she chose to shine in fashionable society, and expended herself in acquiring the superficial graces to make her successful there. She learned to distinguish authentic pearls from paste (in necklaces or cufflinks) and to tell real Wedgwood from a fraud, but she let fashionable opinion ("cultured jargon") govern her artistic tastes rather than a truly formed and independent judgment. Back home from the obligatory trip abroad, she made an "ideal" marriage (that is, she married a man with impeccable social credentials) and had "ideal" (well-behaved, well-dressed, clean) but lonely children, in an "ideal" (fashionably situated and well-appointed) house. (The thrice-repeated adjective exemplifies verbal irony.)

Now at forty-three, her husband dead and her children grown, she is going through a middle-age crisis, reevaluating her life and regretting that it has not been more meaningful. She "toys" with the idea of taking a new direction, but it is too late. The phrase "kill time" (19) has a double meaning. She would like to destroy the time lost since her college years, but she can only waste time by dreaming of doing so. Her dreams of taking up that lost opportunity are only an illusion; and she can only "re-wed" (another double meaning) these illusions. Unable to pursue an independent course of action, she can only fend off "doubts" (about the value of her present life) with "nimble talk." Though a hundred socially elite acquaintances call her, she is without a single intimate friend. The poem ends with a brilliant combination of pun and paradox. "Her meanings lost in manners, she will walk / Alone in brilliant circles to the end." In terms of true intimacy she will be alone, although she will move in brilliant social circles to the end of her life; in terms of meaningful living she will walk in circles till the end of her life, not advance along a line of significant purpose.

The speaker is probably a college classmate of the protagonist, who has seen her the day before, roughly a quarter-century after their first acquaintance. This meeting has caused the narrator to reflect on the protagonist's life.   LP

John Keats   **LA BELLE DAME SANS MERCI** (page 287)

Vocabulary: *sedge* (3), *haggard* (6), *meads* (13), *zone* (18), *manna* (26), *grot* (29), *thrall* (40), *starved* (41), *gloam* (41).

Even with full explication, this literary ballad retains its air of melancholy mystery, because the meaning of the encounter between the knight and the faery lady is never made explicit. This sense of an unresolved riddle is characteristic of many folk ballads, and it may be that Keats was after no more in the poem than a narration of fairyland and dream omens. When the knight concludes "this is why I sojourn here," the reader might very well reiterate the narrator's opening question, for the events reported by the knight don't seem to account for his despair, his physical debility and suffering, and those are what the narrator has asked about.

The three opening stanzas ask the question—"what can ail thee?"—and describe the landscape and the knight. Both are incongruous, the speaker reports: knights should be hearty, purposeful, strong, not pale and feverish; they should be in quest of adventure, not "loitering" beside the dried marsh grass at a lakeside; it is early winter, and the natural creatures have withdrawn either to more congenial climates or to their stored-up winter hoards. This is no place for a knight, nor despite his armor does this man seem heroic.

The tale of the knight's encounter with the faery connects her with the fullness of nature: like an animal, light-footed and wild-eyed, she is met in a meadow, and the knight bedecks her with nature's flowers, and as if rescuing a lost maiden sets her on his horse, rapt with her beauty and her song. (But lines 19–20 ambiguously report her initial response to him: does "as" mean "while," or does it mean "as if"?) Like a goddess of nature, the lady repays his adoration with nature's plenty, and speaks to him an unknown language; surely, he supposes, she is saying she loves him. Strangely, once she has taken him to her cave, her "sweet moan" becomes weeping and sighing, and he must tame her by kissing her "wild wild eyes"; again, as if in repayment, she lulls him to sleep, but that sleep turns to nightmare with a dream that began in the cave and continues to be repeated here on the "cold hill side" where he awakens and the narrator finds him. The dream is apparently of his precursors, vigorous kings, princes and knights, now in the paleness of death as he will be, warning him that he has been enslaved by "La Belle Dame Sans Merci."

Obviously, what a reader whats to know is "who *is* this beautiful woman without mercy, and why has she done this to the man?" Does what happened to the knight have any relevance to our lives? Does the poem do more than warn us against sexual indulgence? One plausible (but by no means the only or inevitable) interpretation links the poem with the processes of nature and human attitudes toward them. The first three stanzas establish a sense of appropriate behavior as the seasons change, and of appropriate actions for people: in winter, squirrels, birds, even grasses retreat before the coldness and dryness, and wandering knights with their manly strength should be leading their active lives where they can perform their heroic deeds. But this man has fallen in love with the beauty and wildness of nature, and supposes that she loves him, and that he can tame her and live with her. What his horrid dream discloses is that this is illusion, and that by loving her he has become her thrall. His fate is the fate of all men—death—but he must also languish in despair because he has set his heart on what must always be changing.   TRA

John Keats   **ODE ON A GRECIAN URN** (page 289)

Like other poems by Keats (e.g., "Ode to a Nightingale"), this ode explores the human desire to escape the inevitable effects of living in a temporal world, expressing this desire in response to the permanence of an art object. The poem is a meditation on the continuing beauty of a painted vase from classical Greece, and what it seems to communicate to a man who knows his time on earth is brief by comparison. The structure is a dramatic enactment of the stages of the speaker's emotion and imaginative projection.

The poem opens with the speaker praising the urn's calm stillness and its freedom from the ravages of time. Punning on the word "still," Keats encapsulates his attitude: the urn is both silent and unmoving, and it still exists in time. Like the maidens painted on its surface, it has retained its virginal beauty as well as the freshness of a bride. In the paintings on the vase he sees a similarly tantalizing doubleness: they seem to have narrative meaning, displaying figures (human or divine) in a state of motion, yet as paintings they cannot move. He asks, in the last six lines of the first stanza, a sequence of increasingly insistent questions: what narrative events do the paintings refer to?

In the second stanza, however, he changes his attitude, presumably in the light of his not receiving answers to his questions. (In Keats's odes there is a skillful manipulation of psychological transitions that occur *between* the stanzas, where changes of thought and feeling are only implied by what precedes and follows the break.) The speaker moves from the excited forcefulness of his questions to a calm denial of the validity of answers. He now prefers *not* to hear the narrative facts that the urn will not reveal, and relishes instead the "unheard melodies" of feelings without explicit meanings. In lines 15–20, he turns to one of the scenes on the urn: a pastoral scene in which one youth makes music, a tune played on pipes, while another, a "bold lover," is about to capture a maiden he pursues. The speaker celebrates the fact that this amorous pursuit will never end—neither in "winning" the woman nor in losing her. Since they are permanently frozen in a painting, the youth will continue to exist in his state of anticipation just as her beauty will never fade.

The third stanza extends the speaker's delight in the image of time stopped at the height of anticipated bliss: the pictured trees will never be subject to seasonal change, the piper will never tire of playing, and the unfulfilled lover will be forever young and forever in the excitement of desire. This is contrasted with the state of "breathing human passion," which is subject not only to the debility of time but also, more emphatically, to the certainty that continued intensity of feeling would finally exhaust and sicken a mortal human being. Human passion such as the speaker is capable of feeling would ultimately become cloying or feverish, a fact previously implied in the excessiveness of the line the speaker devised to describe the permanence of bliss: "More happy love! more happy, happy love!"

Perhaps because he has exhausted his own capacity to respond to the scene of the piper and the lover, or perhaps because he recognizes that his ecstatic description has become "cloyed," or perhaps because his celebration of the lover's happiness has led him to think of the reality of the human condition—that is, for a number of psychological reasons implied between the stanzas—the speaker in stanza four turns to a second scene, on the other side of the urn. A priest ("mysterious," because he is an initiate in secret rituals, and because he is himself a mystery to the speaker) is leading a heifer bedecked for ritual sacrifice, and a crowd of worshippers follows. Like the end of the first stanza, the beginning of the fourth presents the speaker asking for information: who are the people? what or where is the altar? The priest's mystery extends beyond his religious rites to envelop the whole scene. Imaginatively stepping beyond the pictured scene, the speaker asks further: if these people are here, what has happened to the place they have come from? Line 38 is a turning point in the poem, for the speaker for the first time projects his imagination to a place not actually portrayed on the urn—he tries to create an image to answer his question, the image of an empty, abandoned town.

The psychological space between the fourth and fifth stanzas is the most striking in the poem. In his desire to penetrate beyond the pictured events, the speaker had created an image of desolation, an emotional contrast to the permanent anticipation of the lover or of the priest and worshippers. He discovers that such permanence as he has been praising implies other "still" moments of opposite emotional meanings. While some people are frozen in their state of desire (both lover and worshipper), he can imagine other scenes of permanent desolation.

In the fifth stanza the speaker recoils from what his imagination has produced. The urn is no longer a "sylvan historian," a source of feeling and meaning—it is now, as he willfully distances himself from his projected feelings, a "shape," covered with "marble men and maidens," a "silent form." It has tantalized him into expressing his own desires for permanence (ideas that "thought" could not support, any more than thought can encompass "eternity"). He has been tempted in the course of his meditation to celebrate a pastoral world of idealized love and perfection, but he now recognizes that it is not the warm, sunny world he wanted, but a world gone cold with the realization that the stoppage of time necessary for its perfection implies the permanence not only of love's anticipation but also of loneliness and desolation.

The last five lines, with their famous simplifying tautology that "beauty is truth, truth beauty," comment ironically on the value of the urn as a source of wisdom or feeling. It will outlive the generations of man, and will retain its beauty while human beauty fades. Though its beauty makes it seem friendly, its philosophical advice can never satisfy someone in quest of the meaning of change and transience. The urn can only say "is," not "will be," and thus though it will outlast the life of a human being, it cannot give any information that will make his passage through a lifetime any more meaningful. The urn beautifully exists beyond time (as the speaker had said in the first stanza), and cannot teach the meaning of living *in* time. TRA

A. M. Klein **FOR THE SISTERS OF THE HOTEL DIEU** (page 290)

"Hotel Dieu," which means House of God, is presumably a Catholic hospital, with an order of nuns as nurses. The simile in line 7 compares the nuns to birds because of a physical resemblance—to "safe domestic fowl," most likely chickens. The apostrophe in line 7 extends the simile to metaphor, and the verb "fluttered" (8) functions both metaphorically and literally. The domestic comparison is transformed into a mythical metaphor, the chickens having become "biblic" in their attentions.

The metonymy of "wing" for birds is the pivotal point in the poem, for it also functions as a metonymy for "angels": simile becomes metaphor, metaphor becomes symbol, the angels symbolizing the comforting care of a benevolent heaven as the poem moves from the observed appearance of nuns to the moral meaning of their nursing. TRA

Robert Lowell **MR. EDWARDS AND THE SPIDER** (page 290)

In the remarkable three-thousand word scientific essay that Jonathan Edwards wrote as a precocious boy of eleven, he described, from personal observation, how spiders floated from tree to tree, borne by the wind, at the end of a lighter-than-air strand of web, and how the wind always bore them in one direction, toward the seas, where they died. Later Edwards became a notable preacher and the greatest Puritan theologian of his time, the author of books on sin and predestination and the freedom of the will. In fiery sermons like "Sinners in the Hands of an Angry God" and "The Future Punishment of the Wicked" he used spiders as images in discussing death and damnation and the torments of hell. The greatest crisis in Edwards' personal life came when he was dismissed after twenty-four years from his pastorate in Northampton, Massachusetts, as a result of a controversy with his congregation. The leader of the anti-Edwards faction was his cousin Joseph (or Josiah) Hawley.

In this poem Robert Lowell images Jonathan Edwards as meditating, or preaching a sermon, on the subject of spiders. Actually, the poem is closely modeled on passages from the two sermons and the scientific treatise above referred to, and both the images and the language are more Edwards' than Lowell's. Lowell has given them coherent order, however, and has cast them into an intricate stanza pattern, of which the basic meter is iambic 5-5-4-4-3-5-5-5-6, and of which the rime scheme is similar, though not identical, in all five stanzas.

The real subject of Edwards' discourse is death and damnation. In stanzas 1 and 4, spiders are pictured as the victims of death; in stanza 3, as an agent of death; in stanza 5 (the Black Widow), as a metaphor for death. Death is inevitable for all men, Edwards argues, and for all but a few it is followed by a damnation of inconceivable torment and of infinite duration. Edwards' Calvinistic theology—his belief in original sin, in predestination, in the littleness of man, and in the absolute sovereignty of God—is clearly seen in this poem. In the first stanza the light lives and deaths of spiders suggest symbolically the inevitable destiny and destruction of men. Stanza 2 points out the powerlessness of man to combat his inherent sinfulness—which foredooms him to damnation—by any effort of the will. He plays against "a sickness" past his cure—"the fire / And treason crackling" in his blood. Stanza 3 reemphasizes the powerlessness of man to prevent death. Stanza 4 describes the casting of the sinful soul into the eternal fire, from which no struggle or strength can save it. Stanza 5, addressed particularly to Josiah Hawley, describes the torment and the duration of eternal punishment. To be punished thus, is "To die and know it"—to die yet not lose consciousness—to die and yet suffer, indescribably, forever.

[This discussion is slightly adapted from Laurence Perrine and James M. Reid, *100 American Poems of the Twentieth Century* (New York: Harcourt Brace Jovanovich, 1966), pp. 243–44.]

George MacBeth BEDTIME STORY (page 292)

"Bedtime Story" is science fiction in poetic form.

The speaker is a parent (mother or father) telling a "bedtime story" to a child of its species; but this story is supposed to be true—a chapter from history (19), not a "fairy tale." It concerns the accidental killing of the last man, "the penultimate primate" (the ultimate primate being the monkey or ape the man was stalking), the extinction of the human race as a species. The time of the telling of this story is, from our point of view, in a far far distant future; and the time of the incident which it concerns is, from our point of view, still in a distant future; but from the teller's point of view it is in a remote past—not "Once upon a time," but "Long long ago when the world was a wild place . . . ."

The speaker is a huge ant, evolved in size and intelligence from presently existing species. Because of the Queen and the sting, students may suggest a bee. But ants too have queens and stings, and these insects "march" rather than fly through the forest; they are organized in a military fashion (in "brigades"); they forage for greenfly (a kind of aphid that some ants keep like cows and "milk"); and their jaws cut through bark. Ants, moreover, have developed a high degree of social organization and cooperation and are thought by many to be the nearest competitors to man in the struggle for existence. In the poem they have become the dominant species, are larger than men, have developed a language and a recorded history, and have an ethical sense superior to man's.

Although this "bedtime story" tells how the last man was inadvertently killed by a soldier ant, the point of the poem is that man has destroyed himself—or, since the

190

poem is set in the future, may destroy himself. Two facts are stated about man: that he exterminates other species of animals "for pleasure," and that he kills his own kind in wars that "extinguished the cities." The poem is thus an indictment of man's passion for killing and a prediction that unless he acquires the power to govern himself by peaceable methods and becomes as "humane" to other species as the ants in the poem, he will be replaced by another form of life.

The conclusion of the poem links the fate of man with that of the dodo. Dodos are a presently extinct species with a reputation for foolishness. "Dumb as a dodo" is a familiar expression.

The poem is written in dactylic lines of four feet in the first three lines of each stanza and two feet in the last. The phrasing and run-on lines make it difficult to read trippingly, however, and it should not be read so.   LP

Marianne Moore   **NEVERTHELESS** (page 293)

As the title implies, the subject of the poem is persistence and pertinacity, both physical and moral. The various examples of plant life "overcome" apparent obstacles, from which the poet derives the moral lesson for human beings: "Victory won't come to me unless I go to it . . . The weak overcomes its menace, the strong overcomes itself. What is there like fortitude!"

What looks like random diversity, mingling bizarre examples, has its order, from seed to root to tendril to fruit, an upward growth representing the cycle of vegetable nature. It commences with the "multitude of seeds" on the surface of a crushed strawberry (transformed, by its "struggle" to maintain its integrity, into the semblance of animal forms); it proceeds to the protected internal seeds of an apple, doubly enclosed in the core. Whether vulnerably superficial or protectively enclosed, these seeds are designed to reach fertile soil and give birth to new growth.

Parallels exist in the root references: there is growth both in the rigid enclosure of frozen soil and in exposed air, and some plants' roots undergo such twisting that they seem to transform themselves into the shapes of animal forms. Even the fragility of grape tendrils and the stems of cherries possess transforming potency, the frail tendril capable of binding what has supported it, the "thread" transmitting the ripening coloration of the cherry. And the poem ends its plant references where it began, with sweet fruits that carry the source of new growth.

Thus what may seem a random collection of "oddities" in nature has a direction, drawing comparisons between the seemingly disconnected examples. The whole plant world illustrates the power of life to maintain and propagate itself—and so the human world should learn to persist, employing its inner moral virtues as well as its outward physical powers. To paraphrase the moral statements: "Real bravery, and true victory, are seen not only in overcoming external dangers but also in self-control."

The poem is written in syllabic verse (only the number of syllables in a line is counted, not accents) rimed xaa. The form, which appears like free verse, thus echoes the meaning, since random rhythms (like bizarre subjects) are "locked in" by syllable-count and rime. TRA

Howard Nemerov **GRACE TO BE SAID AT THE SUPERMARKET** (page 294)

Superficially the butt of Nemerov's satire seems to be the application of technology to the presentation of food, the complaint of a man who is disturbed by standardized, hygienic market methods. But this commonplace of modern social critics is given a sharper edge when the speaker pretends to be praying not to technology, but to geometry. His target is more ancient and more universal, the very source of these modern effects: our intellectualizing tendencies that we express not merely in the uniform packaging of meats but in the packaging of ideas in language.

The diction of this seriously witty, ironic poem is highly varied, ranging from plain colloquialism to scientific and mathematical terms, from the language of religion to that of literary criticism. Such wide linguistic reference punctures the pretensions of all these mis-users of language: advertisers ("streamlined . . . for greater speed," "like a philosopher should"), casual conversationalists ("if you want to put it that way," "maybe"), literary critics ("aesthetic distance," "significant form"), philosophers ("the greatest good"), preachers and theologians ("our birthright," "the mystical body"), and—the metaphorical center of the poem—mathematicians ("cubes," "cylinder," "ellipsoid," and the rest).

All of these display what Nemerov regards as a linguistic replacement of the honest, natural expression of human nature with inflated—or deflated—terminology. The subject of the poem is the human being as a carnivore, and the variety of dodges we employ to avoid acknowledging the fact. Line 15 represents the only honest expression of it: both we and the "brutes" we consume lead "bulging and blood-swollen lives," though we would prefer to think and speak otherwise. TRA

Mary Oliver **THE TRURO BEAR** (page 295)

Truro is a seaport in central Nova Scotia. As the poem presents it, the town is located amidst heavy woods and ponds, with hills, fields, and marshland in the vicinity. The landscape thus includes primitive forest, domesticated crop lands, stretches of wild fruit lands, and a seaport—a range from the wild to the urban—yet all of the wilderness has been tamed by "roads and houses." The speaker is familiar with this variety of sites, but is herself associated with the town, and thus finds the report of a bear highly unlikely. Despite the fact that it is probably only legendary (no eye-witness can be produced, though the speaker seems to have tried to find one), the bear begins to grow in the speaker's imagination, to the point that she imagines shadows growing shoulders.

Rationally she tries to account for the bear ("somebody's runaway dog"), but the seeds of doubt have begun to sprout in her mind. With the concluding question she defines her attitude: while common sense and rational investigation deny any "evidence," the imaginative possibility of wildness in this unlikely place is like the seed of a naturally sprouting happiness—even if the wildness is manifested in the shape of a beast that moves quietly through the "serious woods around the dark" ponds. TRA

P. K. Page **THE LANDLADY** (page 295)

Through line 10 this portrait generalizes the landlady's attitudes and motives, and includes the attitudes of her boarders. Although they seem "impersonal," her hovering, curious presence causes them to alter their behavior: they become secretive, punctual, and reticent to display their feelings. The second line initiates the syntactical pattern of the poem: the subject "boarders" is omitted from the two clauses of the second sentence. This device becomes the controlling pattern from line 11 ("She peers"), after which "she," or more properly the title "The Landlady" is the subject of the sentence fragments that constitute the remainder of the poem.

The portrait is of a woman whose curiosity about the lives of her boarders is obsessive. She achieves no contentment simply from knowing all there is to know about their habits, their actions, or even their health. "Like a lover," but without love, she is consumed with the details of their lives, and "must know all, all, all." Even "all" is insufficient for her hunger for knowledge, for what she seeks is the most secret meaning of their lives, "hoping the worst" will be revealed to her at last.

Without real malevolence but with an insatiable desire to know everything about them, the landlady becomes at the end of the poem a kind of monster of curiosity. But is this really the woman, or is it the speaker's invention? As the poem focuses ever more narrowly on the landlady as the speaker sees her, attributing to her an insane attachment to the lives of her boarders, a reader might legitimately wonder whether the portrait does not represent an equally obsessive hunger for privacy on the part of a boarder. TRA

Ezra Pound **SESTINA: ALTAFORTE** (page 296)

Ezra Pound, himself a vigorous, lusty-souled, and often quarrelsome personality as well as a poet and lover of poetry, clearly recognized a kindred spirit in Sir Bertran de Born, the twelfth-century nobleman and poet, "quarreled" with Dante for placing him in hell, and in this poem attempts to restore him to vigorous life and perhaps justify a higher place for him. He does so by letting Bertran speak for himself, in a dramatic monologue cast in the form of a sestina (see page 217). The spiritual kinship of Bertran and Pound is evidenced in the kindred vigor of Bertran's language in the poem and of Pound's in his headnote ("Eccovi! Judge ye! Have I dug him up again?").

Poems exalting war above peace are a rarity in post-World War I poetry. Rudyard Kipling was perhaps the last poet of standing to glorify deeds of heroism in battle; the tone of more recent war poetry is more likely to follow the example of Siegfried Sassoon in "Base Details" (page 44) and Wilfred Owen in "Dulce et Decorum Est" (page 7). It should be noted, however, that Pound's poem, first published in 1909 (five years before the outbreak of World War I) is based on a poem by Bertran, usually called "The Praise of War" (of which Pound gives a fairly literal translation in *The Spirit of Romance* [New York: New Directions, 1929], pp. 47-48), and that Bertran lived in a time before the introduction of gunpowder, when battles were fought with swords and spears and dominated by knights on war horses clad in spiked armor. Victory in such battles often went to the strongest, the bravest, and the most athletically proficient. For a close parallel to the tone of this poem, especially lines 13-15, one may turn to the Book of Job (page 16). Pound said of his poem, "Technically it is one of my best, though a poem on such a theme could never be very important" [Peter Brooker, *A Student's Guide to the Selected Poems of Ezra Pound* (London: Faber and Faber, 1979), pp. 44-46].

Briefly, Bertran is characterized as a man who rejoices in battle and who scorns "womanish peace." He compares his delight in battle with his delight in summer storms when, in lightning and thunder, "God's swords clash" (stanza 2), and to his joy in the sun rising "blood crimson," its rays ("spears") opposing the darkness (stanza 4). He feels that war is "where worth's won" (28).

Whether or not he justifies Bertran against Dante, Pound certainly succeeds, through the vigor of his language, in restoring Bertran to vigorous life.

Pound omits two of his end-words from the envoi, departing in this respect from the technical requirements of the sestina.   LP

Dudley Randall   **AFTER THE KILLING** (page 298)

Both the basic statement of the poem and its repetitiousness are obvious: that killing leads to more killing, which in turn and infinitely leads to more. Irony results from the alternation of quoted and narrative statements, the narration denying the quotation. But the poem ends with quotation, perhaps implying that once the last blood-thirster has killed, there are none left to die, nor is there a narrator left to report any further events.

Despite the repetitiveness of the poem, there are in fact no two identical lines (1 and 15, 3 and 16, 4 and 17, and 7 and 11 repeat the words, but capitalization, punctuation, and spacing differ). The implication may be that although killing as an abstraction is always the same, the individual persons and circumstances will always differ somewhat.

In a poem as spare and as repetitive as this, small details take on more significance than they ordinarily might. For example, the concluding quatrain *almost* repeats the first, but the differences loom large: not "the blood-thirster," as if this were a unique person, but "a blood-thirster," one of a type. The most striking difference between these quatrains is not verbal, but a matter of spacing, a resource for poetry explored by other free-verse poets. The extended space in "there will be   peace," its silence echoing the hesitant pauses represented by the line spacing from line 11 to 14, reinforces the finality of the last word.

It is ironic that the advocate of killing claims peace as his motive, by which he is presumed to mean a cessation of hostilities between people. However, the final "peace" in the poem does not suggest love or friendship, but the peace of death. In this satire against the idea that peace can be achieved by killing, the poet implies that it is the nature of man to desire peace, and it is his nature to believe that war achieves it. TRA

Edwin Arlington Robinson THE MILL (page 298)

"The Mill" was first published in 1920. Its setting is earlier, sometime during the industrial revolution, probably late in the nineteenth century. The miller's remark (5) means that individual millers are no longer able to make a living: they are being replaced by industrialization.

This poem furnishes a good opportunity for taking up the issue of clarity and obscurity. Clarity is a supreme virtue in expository prose: we want our students to be perfectly lucid in their own writing. In poetry and fiction clarity is still a virtue, but not a supreme one. It takes second place to power and richness of meaning. A poem should be as clear as it may be without sacrificing something more important.

Certainly, Robinson has not been at pains to be perfectly clear about what happens in this poem. The miller's remark (5) is cryptic. We are not told "what else there was" (13) in the mill, or "what was hanging from a beam" (15), or where the miller's wife went (16), or what kind of "way" she is thinking of (19), or what ruffles the water (23). But surely this story of a double suicide gains in power exactly *because* it is not at first perfectly clear. The reader feels a growing horror as its meaning gradually dawns on him, as bewilderment shifts to suspicion and suspicion to certainty. If we change "what was hanging from a beam" to "his body hanging from a beam," the poem is made clearer, but its effect is greatly weakened. We no longer experience the terror of the half-seen.

Obscurity in a poem may arise from various causes, including the poet's ineptitude. It is not always as integral a part of meaning as it is here. But it can be. The point can be driven home by analogy to the person who spoils a joke by explaining it. A joke, too, is a small work of art. It must not be made so clear that its effect is destroyed.

This poem is briefly discussed by Wallace L. Anderson in *Edwin Arlington Robinson: A Critical Introduction* (Boston: Houghton Mifflin, 1967), pp. 103–04. LP

Edwin Arlington Robinson **MR. FLOOD'S PARTY** (page 299)

Few poems balance so precisely on the point between comedy and pathos, tears and laughter, as "Mr. Flood's Party." For the poet to have poised it so was a triumph in the management of tone.

The drunk has always been a figure of comedy, and Mr. Flood, as he drinks and sings with himself, "with only two moons listening," is richly comic. The similes enhance the humor. Mr. Flood with a jug at his lips and the ghost of a warrior with a horn at his lips may be visually similar, but the discrepancy between their emotional contexts makes the comparison ludicrous. Mr. Flood setting his jug down may resemble a mother laying down her sleeping child, but the incongruity between the drunk's solicitude for his jug and a mother's solicitude for her baby again is ludicrous. But the fun is not supplied entirely by the poet; it is supplied also by Mr. Flood himself. The grave solemnity, the punctilious courtesy, with which Mr. Flood goes through the social ritual of greeting himself, inviting himself to drink, welcoming himself home, and cautioning himself against a refill ("No more, sir; that will do")—all show a rich vein of humor which makes us laugh with Mr. Flood as well as at him. This is a lovable drunk—though he is not loved. With two Mr. Floods, and two moons, we are almost prepared ourselves to believe that "the whole harmonious landscape rang" (it takes two people to create harmony) until we realize that this is only the heightened sense of appreciation that every drunk has for the beauty of his own singing.

But the things that make Mr. Flood ludicrous also make him pathetic. The allusion to Roland winding his horn calls up one of the most famous and moving episodes in all literature, in *The Song of Roland*, and the comparison, though ludicrous, is also plangent and moves us with emotions more profound than comedy. Roland was sending out a call for help, and Mr. Flood needs help too; but we know that no help came for Roland in time to save him. The comparison to the mother and her sleeping child, in much the same way, reminds us of the familial relationships and gentleness and love which are missing from Mr. Flood's life. These two images, with the help of the silver moon, lay a veil of tenderness and soft emotion over the poem, which moves us to compassion as well as laughter. Mr. Flood, after all, is not a mere ne'er-do-well. He has a delightful sense of humor and an old-fashioned courtesy. He was once honored in the town below and had many friends there. He has an educated man's acquaintance with literature: in speaking of the fleetingness of time, he can quote from "The Rubáiyát of Omar Kháyám" ("The Bird of Time has but a little way / To flutter—and the Bird is on the Wing"), and then use the quotation wittily and gracefully to propose a toast. The reference to *The Song of Roland*, though made by the poet, reinforces our sense of Mr. Flood as a sensitive and educated man. The song he sings—"For auld lang syne"—has added force because Mr. Flood can look only backward for better times; he can't look for them in the present or the future. Mr. Flood is old: the husky voice that wavers out, and the trembling care with which he sets down the jug are signs of age as well as of drink. His loneliness is stressed throughout the poem: he climbs the hill "alone" (line 1), there is "not a native near" (line 6), he speaks "For no man else in Tilbury Town to hear" (line 8), he must drink with himself (line 9), he stands "alone" (line 17), the moonlight makes a "silver loneliness" (line 45), he is "again alone" (line 52), he has no friends in the town below (lines 54-56). A ghost in the moonlight, Mr. Flood sends out his call for help, and is answered only by other ghosts—"A phantom salutation of the dead"—old memories.

We are not told why Mr. Flood has been cast out from the town below, why he is no longer honored, for what social sin or error he has lost his place in society. We know only that he is old, alone, friendless, dishonored, deserving of compassion but getting none. The "strangers" who would have shut their doors to him in the town below are probably many of them literal strangers, but some are former friends from whom he has been estranged. The final note of the poem is not one of laughter, but of heartbreak. [Reprinted from Laurence Perrine and James M. Reid, *100 American Poems of the Twentieth Century* (New York: Harcourt Brace Jovanovich, 1966), pp. 7-8.] LP

Theodore Roethke I KNEW A WOMAN (page 300)

This poem is a tribute of praise and gratitude from a middle-aged poet to a younger woman whose eager sexual genius taught him in fullest measure the delights of sensual love. The verb in the title may be understood in both its ordinary and its Biblical sense. The imagery of the poem throughout emphasizes physical movement and the attractions of the body. The woman was "lovely in her bones," and "when she moved, she moved more ways than one." The "bright container" (4) is her skin. The tribute paid in lines 6-7 is both humorous and deeply meant, for "English poets who grew up on Greek" would include such favorites of Roethke's as Sir John Davies, Ben Jonson, and Andrew Marvell. In stanza 2 the terms "Turn," "Counter-turn," and "Stand" are the English equivalents of the Greek words *strophe, antistrophe,* and *epode,* indicating the movements of the chorus in Greek drama while chanting a choral ode. The metaphor in lines 12-14 compares the woman to the curving sickle that cuts the grass in harvesting and the speaker to the straight rake which gathers it up. Moving in synchronism they produce a "prodigious mowing." Although the metaphor hardly needs further explanation, it is not irrelevant that the verb "to mow," in Scottish dialect, means to have sexual intercourse, and that the noun "rake" refers not only to the harvesting tool but to a sexually-oriented male. Stanza 3 continues the poem's tribute to the sexual talents of the woman. The "mobile nose" in the whimsical mixed metaphor of line 20 suggests that of a rabbit (or other animal) sniffing the air.

Stanza 4 is difficult, for the poet here turns philosophical, and his transitions are abrupt. But if the precise meanings are puzzling, the tone is not. Clearly the poet sees no contradiction between "eternity" and enjoyment of the sensual life. He swears his lady cast a "white" shadow, not a dark one. Perhaps such pleasure as she afforded him is a foretaste of eternity. If he is "martyr to a motion not his own [hers]," he has been a willing martyr, and his old bones still "live to learn her wanton ways." "To know eternity" is the important thing, "But who would count eternity

197

in days?" The question is rhetorical; the answer is, No one but a fool; eternity may be tasted in a minute. The poet himself measures time "by how a body sways." The first line of the stanza seems to refer to the natural process of the human life-cycle from conception to death while also to glance back at the sexual metaphor in lines 12-14. The simile "white as stone" calls up the image of a white marble gravestone, a marker separating life from eternity. The use of the past tense in the first three stanzas, and the switch to present in the fourth, may indicate that the woman is dead (and the poet himself is certainly older). But the last two lines indicate that he has not forgotten the lessons she taught him. The poem ends, as it began, as a celebration of sensual love.

For additional suggestions, see discussions in *The Explicator* by Virginia L. Peck, 22 (Apr. 1964), item 66; Helen T. Buttel, 24 (May 1966), item 78; Nat Henry, 27 (Jan. 1969), item 31; and Jenijoy La Belle, 32 (Oct. 1973), item 15. LP

Theodore Roethke THE WAKING (page 301)

In form "The Waking" is a villanelle. A villanelle is a nineteen-line fixed form using only two rimes and having two refrains (on the same rime) in the following arrangement (where A represents the first refrain, and *A* the second): Ab*A* abA ab*A* abA ab*A* abA*A*.

In "The Waking" the poet joyfully affirms his acceptance of a life in which the only constant is change. Though its tone is clear, the details of its meanings are not, and the following suggestions are made diffidently. Line 1: "I wake to sleep." Literally, this means, I wake in the morning only to have to sleep again at night. Symbolically it means, I am born to die—death is the inevitable concomitant of life. Nevertheless, the tone indicates a full acceptance of life on these terms. The speaker takes his waking "slow": he wishes to savor it fully. Line 2: The speaker feels his "fate" (change and death) in what he cannot fear (the life process). Line 3: He learns about life only through experiencing it. Line 4: "We think by feeling." Our deepest understandings come through intuition and emotion rather than through reasoning.
Line 5: The speaker hears his being "dance from ear to ear": he is joyfully conscious of his existence. Line 7: He is conscious of other people, and wishes to know about them. Line 8: He blesses the earth, which is the "Ground" of his existence and will be his place of burial. Line 10: Life is a mystery. The ultimate secret of how sunlight nourishes the tree, of how Light illuminates the "Tree of Life," or of how spirit enters matter, cannot be intellectually known. Line 11: Life is process. The worm climbs up the evolutionary scale of being; death constantly recurs in this evolutionary life cycle. Lines 13-15: Great Nature holds death and dissolution in store for all of us, so let us enjoy each moment while we may. "Lovely" may be construed as an adjective (paralleling "lively"), as an adverb (modifying "learn"), or as a noun of direct address to the "you" of lines 7 and 14. Line 16 (the most difficult of the poem's several paradoxes): Physical decay and the speaker's knowledge of constant change (degeneration and regeneration) in life's processes keep him resolved to make

the most of life and to trust the goodness of the cycle. Line 17: The present falls away from us eternally; what falls away from us is permanence. Change and death are constantly "near" to us. Line 20: Take all the above suggestions with two pinches of salt. At best (like all paraphrase) they are reductive, and some may be flat wrong. For additional discussion, see Richard A. Blessing, in the *Ball State University Forum*, 12 (Aut. 1971), 17–19, and Karl Malkoff, *Theodore Roethke* (New York: Columbia Univ. Press, 1966), pp. 121-22. LP

Christina Rossetti **SONG: WHEN I AM DEAD, MY DEAREST** (page 302)

Thematically, this lyric may be compared to Shakespeare's Sonnet 71 ("No longer mourn for me when I am dead"), for both poems take the occasion of imagining the poet's death to advise a beloved person to avoid grief and mourning. Rossetti's first phrase even quotes from the first line of the sonnet, though the phrase is common enough not to be a direct allusion. In both poems, the beloved is told in language appropriate to the times to avoid the customary mourning duties, and in both the effect of prohibiting these actions is to bring them forcefully to mind. By saying that she wants "no sad songs," "no roses" nor "cypress tree," Rossetti puts such symbolic responses in the hearer's mind. And by saying, gently as she does, that it will be memorial enough if the grass grows over her, wet with showers and dewdrops, she implies that her dearest need not even weep. But the reference to the flourishing of the grass inevitably calls up graveyard sentiments (as Shakespeare says, more robustly in keeping with his century, that he will be going to dwell "with vilest worms").

Rossetti's first stanza says, simply, "I need no memorials as expressions of your love—you may remember me or not, according to your will." The second justifies this attitude by saying that she will not, after all, be aware of any earthly events, neither cypress shade nor the pains of love expressed by the nightingale: she will be living in a twilit dream, not seeing sunrise nor sunset. Perhaps in that limbo, she will remember her love—and perhaps not.

The psychological situation presented in both poems is not altogether admirable. Most obviously in the Shakespeare sonnet, the motivation for the advice is in fact to draw the beloved closer, while life still lasts. Rossetti is less obvious, and more sentimental (a higher incidence of "graveyard" imagery, for example, calling for automatic emotions from the listener), and, unlike Shakespeare, she wishes to seem not to care one way or the other. But it is difficult to avoid feeling that the living speaker is attempting to manipulate the beloved into an intense expression of love, now.

The structure of Rossetti's poem is beautifully adapted to this purpose, ironically posing its structure against its emotional effects. The poem is written in iambic trimeter, with the pattern of extra-metrical unstressed syllables at the ends of lines 1, 5, and 7 repeated in the same positions in the second stanza; of the sixteen polysyllabic words, only three end on stressed syllables ("above," 5; "forget," 8 and 16;

and "nightingale," 11). The combination of these effects creates a falling feeling, as if the poem though technically iambic is emotionally trochaic, a rhythmic device echoing the sense of a poem in which the speaker *says* "take heart, don't mourn" but *means* "show how much you care."

The rime scheme is that of a double ballad stanza, each of the two stanzas consisting of quatrains rimed xaxa. But this "unsophisticated" riming is complicated by the rime of lines 4–5, and by the modified refrain of the last two lines of each stanza. What seems a natural, simple folk form is in fact highly crafted. TRA

Carl Sandburg FOG (page 302)

"Fog" is an imagistic poem—purely impressionistic and descriptive—without symbolical meanings. The charm lies in its unifying metaphor, established by "little cat feet," "sits looking," and "haunches." Although there is a visual image here, the chief effect is paradoxically auditory: one of perfect silence. The fog "comes," "sits," and "moves on" without making a sound.

This is probably to be classified as a free-verse poem, though it moves around a two-beat line, supplely, like a cat. LP

Anne Sexton PAIN FOR A DAUGHTER (page 302)

The two incidents described in the poem illustrate two stages in the growth from childhood to womanhood. In the first, the girl overcomes her own squeamishness in her love for her pony, inflicting the necessary pain to cure the animal. In the second, her love for horses results in a ghastly injury, and her father performs a similarly loving act of painful cleansing. Standing by, the mother witnesses the girl's ordeal and sees in it the precursor to the pains of childbirth and of death. Hearing herself replaced in the girl's cries, she recognizes that her child's experience has taken her out of the realm of childhood into the potentiality of full womanhood, with all its pains.

The poem is more tightly structured than may at first be apparent. The four verse paragraphs, reiterating the phrase "blind with . . . ," emphasize the power of emotion to block out competing feelings, culminating in the final scene. Blinded by fear to her earlier reliance on her mother for emotional support, the child reaches out not to "Mama" but to God. The first incident, in which her love for her pony supersedes her squeamishness, is evidence of growth; the last, structurally parallel, seems to suggest that in crying out for God's help she has grown out of her childish need for her mother's comforting.

But the parallelism reveals to the mother more than growth: for her, it is the beginning of loss, just as the child's development is both a gain and a loss. The title ambiguously points in this direction, referring both to the pain the child must suffer, and the pain suffered by the mother on the child's behalf and on her own. Both mother and daughter have been, and will be, "blinded with love . . . with loss . . . with pain . . . with fear," four stages in the progression of a woman's life. TRA

William Shakespeare FEAR NO MORE (page 304)

Both the tone of this dirge from the fourth act of *Cymbeline* and the dramatic situation which is its occasion are characteristic of the late romances of Shakespeare. This is sung or spoken by two young men who suppose their adopted stepbrother is dead; but not only is the stepbrother only in a drugged sleep, "he" is really a princess who has had to flee the tyranny of the court—and the two singers who have been raised as Welsh shepherds are in actuality her long-lost princely brothers. These plot details contribute little to interpreting this song as a poem, but they make it in its place in the play a reinforcement of the mysterious powers of goodness that defeat the malevolent plotting of the villains in Shakespeare's last plays. Since all does work out for the best, despite all odds, a funeral lament like this emphasizes escaping life's pains and fears, not the grief of the mourners. Their love is expressed not in joy that the dead person has gone to heavenly bliss (the play is set in pre-Christian Britain), but in the consolation that he is now safe from danger and is sharing in a universal fate.

The "fears" that beset the living are of two kinds: natural (summer heat, winter cold, lightning and thunder) and social, with the greater emphasis on the latter. Although they personally know nothing of court life, these young men describe the conditions of a capital city, where ordinary people have to work for food and clothing, and where social disparities (chimney-sweepers with their gruelling and miserable lives contrasted to "golden lads and girls") subject people to the frowns of their superiors and the cruelty of tyrants as well as to slander and rash censure. There is some "joy" in such a life, however slight: there is love, momentarily alluded to in line 17. But the preponderance of experience has been "moan," and death's release is to that extent to be welcomed.

The universality of death, encapsulated in the repeated rime "must . . . come to dust," contrasts the equality of the dead to the social hierarchies and injustices that govern the living. Rich and poor, mighty and weak, learned and ignorant, all "must . . . come to dust," and the inequities of society will be obliterated. Death is the great deliverer and equalizer. TRA

William Shakespeare LET ME NOT TO THE MARRIAGE OF TRUE MINDS (page 304)

This sonnet makes an interesting contrast to the one which follows, "My Mistress' Eyes Are Nothing Like the Sun." The subject here is a union of minds, while the other is a poem about physical attraction; and this sonnet is idealistic, the other realistic. The opening sentence refers to the marriage ceremony in the Anglican *Book of Common Prayer*: ". . . if either of you do know any impediment why ye may not be lawfully joined together in matrimony . . . confess it." This reference is made emphatic by the extreme metrical irregularity of the first line, and made more vivid by the regularity of the first three feet of the second line.

The first quatrain proceeds negatively: I do not admit impediments; love is not love if it alters or bends. The second quatrain reverses the rhetoric, insisting that love is permanent and fixed; and the third returns to the negative, "Love's not Time's fool" and again, "Love alters not." In effect, the three quatrains describe what intellectual love is not, what it is, and again what it is not. (One scholar discovers in this, and in other details of the poem, that this sonnet is "protesting too much," and that it must be seen as ironic overstatement. While the poem may seem too hyperbolic when laid beside "My Mistress' Eyes," there really is little within this poem to suggest less than sincerity.)

The examination of the three quatrains as rhetorical parallels reveals a frequent pattern of Shakespeare's sonnets: they are repetitive, offering three different contexts to make the same statement. In the first quatrain, the context resembles a courtroom or public debate, as the echo from the marriage ceremony implies question and response. Here, the response is suitably intellectualized, a matter of defining terms which is appropriate to the subject of "minds." The diction reinforces the effect, being rational and legalistic ("Let me not," "Admit impediments," "alters . . . alterations," "remover to remove").

The second quatrain develops two two-line images, the "ever-fixèd mark" of a beacon or lighthouse unshaken by storms, and the pole star by which navigators steer, both images sharing the context of nautical travel, its dangers and its safeguards. Line 8 states our inability to know the exact value of the star, even though we can make use of our instruments to steer by its steadfastness, and it contrasts the "wandering" of human life with the star's immobility. True intellectual love preserves us in danger, and guides us when we wander.

The third quatrain continues to develop single images in two-line statements linked together in a common context. "Time's fool" is the toy or plaything of personified time, having no value to him. This is "Father Time," who dispassionately destroys the "rosy lips and cheeks" of the young (this is the only reference to physical beauty in the poem—it *is* "Time's fool"). Time with his sickle is linked to the "grim reaper" who at the day of "doom" will finally destroy all life, and only then will the "marriage of true minds" be dissolved.

The couplet returns the poem to the courtroom of the opening quatrain. The poet invites disproof of his testimony, and employs as his witnesses two incontrovertible facts: since I have written (this poem proves that), and since certainly at least one man has loved, then my statements must be true. The couplet seems irrefutable, except that its conclusion is not necessarily valid: while it claims that these self-evident facts prove that the argument of his sonnet is also self-evident, there is no real connection. The "proof" is rhetorical rather than logical (and like the opening quatrain, couched in negative rhetoric).

This justly popular poem has been much analyzed. Among the most interesting commentaries are the following: Edward Hubler, *The Sense of Shakespeare's Sonnets* (Princeton, N.J.: Princeton Univ. Press, 1952), pp. 92-93; Kenneth Muir,

Shakespeare's Sonnets (London: Allen & Unwin, 1979), pp. 107–08; Paul Ramsey, *The Fickle Glass: A Study of Shakespeare's Sonnets* (New York: AMS Press, 1979), pp. 157–58; Katharine M. Wilson, *Shakespeare's Sugared Sonnets* (London: Allen & Unwin, 1974), pp. 301–03. TRA

William Shakespeare **MY MISTRESS' EYES ARE NOTHING LIKE THE SUN** (page 305)

This witty sonnet might serve as a model of courtship, if a lady were to be won by realistic honesty. The speaker at length rejects the customary (lying) praise of hyperbolic lovers, insisting that his lady is only a woman, not a "goddess," and yet she is "as rare" as any woman who has been praised with overstated comparisons. In other words, he loves her for what she is, and does not think she wishes to be lied to about qualities she does not possess. It is a different kind of praise he offers, a high estimate of her common sense and her delight in wit.

The object of his satire is the "false compare" of the Petrarchan sonnet tradition. The formalities of the tradition required that the poet begin by praising the lady's hair (usually as fine and bright as spun golden wire), proceed to her ivory or alabaster forehead, her eyebrows arched like Cupid's bow, her pearly teeth, cherry-red lips, and so on, moving down the various parts of her body (generally rather coyly below the waist) to her delicate light feet. But Shakespeare seems realistically to present the order in which a man might look at a woman whose inner worth is also important to him, moving from eyes to lips to breasts, then to hair, cheeks, breath, voice, and gait, and at each stop he realistically claims her to be less than ideal. To the modern ear, the least complimentary word in the poem is "reeks," but the word was not used to mean "stinks" until the eighteenth century, and Shakespeare's meaning is much less offensive—it means "exhales." His tactic throughout the poem is not to substitute some other quality for the traditional overstatement, but just to say "she is not like *that.*" What she *is* like is a woman, and for that he loves her. TRA

Wole Soyinka **TELEPHONE CONVERSATION** (page 305)

This poem was originally published in the British periodical *Encounter.* Its setting is probably London. The red booth (13) is the public telephone from which the speaker is calling. The red pillar box is a mailbox. The red double-tiered omnibus is the principal form of public transportation on London streets. The poet is from Nigeria. LP

Wallace Stevens **THE SNOW MAN** (page 306)

The single sentence constituting this poem is ambiguously framed, either offering advice or a definition: in its barest statement, it can be paraphrased, "only a person as cold-minded as a snow man would not think such a cold place implies misery." Is the speaker advocating such emotionlessness, as appropriate to the surroundings and as a defense against despair? Or is he lamenting the inhumanity that would be necessary to escape such emotions? The last two lines provide a partial answer: the reality of the situation is that this observable landscape contains "the nothing that is," and that it has no further dimensions of meaning beyond its mere physical existence. To "think of misery" therefore is to add a false meaning, one derived not from reality but from an observer's emotional reaction.

These last two lines may echo *Hamlet*, III.iv when the Ghost appears to Hamlet in Gertrude's closet but remains invisible to her. Hamlet asks his mother, "Do you see nothing there?" and she replies "Nothing at all; yet all that is I see" (lines 131–32). Stevens' snow man is an unemotional, practical realist, unable to see anything but actuality, and able to see that the actuality implies nothing beyond itself. Neither ghosts nor implications of meaning are available to him.

The only way a person can avoid thinking of misery in such a barren place is to be, like the snow man, "nothing himself," a person without feeling. The first three stanzas create the visual scene, in details that seem quite forbidding. The trees have been subjected to wintry transformations, "crusted" and "shagged" and made "rough" in appearance by the weakness of the distant sun. Stanzas 4 and 5 add the effect of the "sound of the wind," which to an emotional observer would imply misery. The defense against such feeling is "a mind of winter," coldly unemotional and in total harmony with the surroundings.

While this is the overt statement of the poem, there remains a third alternative to either misery or emotional coldness: the visual imagery implies the possibility of perceiving beauty in the chiaroscura of shapes and textures. The three types of evergreen trees have distinctly different shapes, and the winter has given them three distinct textures. The crusted pines tower above with their foliage at the tops of their tall trunks; the shaggy junipers sprawl flat and disorderly in their low branching; and the conical Christmas-tree-shaped spruces are roughened but glittering. Although the scene is not inviting, it nevertheless possesses stark beauty. The snow man's coldly analytical philosophy is a defense against misery and a definition of reality, but it does not comprehend esthetic responses.

For two slightly different interpretations of this much-discussed poem, see A. Walton Litz, *Introspective Voyager: The Poetic Development of Wallace Stevens* (New York: Oxford, 1972), pp. 99–100, and Daniel Fuchs, *The Comic Spirit of Wallace Stevens* (Durham, N.C.: Duke, 1963), pp. 69–70. TRA

May Swenson LION (page 307)

Despite its direct, forceful tone, the poem rests on ambiguity of feeling: the lion is dangerously powerful, and has the beauty of restraint. While part of the restraint derives from its condition as a caged force, part of it is an innate quality of the beast itself. Swenson captures this double source in the phrase "the ordained air /

of chosen loneliness" (lines 4–5), coupling external necessity with inner choice. The lion is alone, because by nature he's a loner, and because (as we subsequently learn) he is caged. (In nature, male lions tend to remain on the periphery of their family groupings, and in fact to leave predation to their females.)

Much of the forcefulness of the poem is achieved by the absence of punctuation and (until line 32) of finite forms of the verb "to be"; the portrait is impressionistically immediate, and despite many complete but unpunctuated sentences, the controlling phrases "lion is" or "lion has" are omitted.

The first four groups of lines, through line 15, describe the natural lion, as if he were free and at large in his own habitat. Details are sharply visualized, achieving feelings of power, magnificence, and sublimity through metaphors and similes; in the details of lines 10–11, the lion has delicacy and beauty ("frilled," "sinuously," "suede"), but for the most part the emphasis is on superiority and power. The fullest descriptive passage is in lines 12–15, referring to the lion's genitals. It reinforces the ambiguous feeling through a simple verbal ambiguity: "quiver" implies the two sides to the lion's nature, potency and force (as a container for unshot arrows) and delicacy (as a vibration). Line 15 also provides the transition from the description of the lion as he seems in nature to the lion in captivity, which explains his "never-used malehood."

The next two line-groupings (16–24) place the lion in a zoo and explicitly present the reactions of human observers. "Awestruck children" draw a comparison between the lion's animality and the "frightening" evidence of a similar animal nature in the growth of hair in their fathers' ears. Slightly older girls are reminded, by contrast with the lion, of the timidity of "lovers" who have not yet achieved their animal maturity. And the speaker, presumably a mature woman, recalls her childhood and its games of playing lion.

Her own memories, and her assumptions about the reactions of the other human observers, lead her to imagined projections about the lion. The intense presence of the lion "burns the brain" of the spectator, who therefore presumes that the lion is purposefully ignoring the fetid stench of its surroundings, and that it regards the bars of the cage as illusory. Such an attitude is a symptom of "heroic paranoia" (again coupling power with weakness), since the lion must be imagining itself in its jungle surroundings at dawn, and must be thinking of the deliciousness of the prey he will catch that day. The speaker's imagination, on behalf of the lion, leads finally to the creation of a sentence with "is" as the finite verb, for the only time in the poem. The vivid presence of the lion does not require this grammatical nicety; but as the lion (like the humans who look at him) is allowed to remember and to anticipate, he is allowed to fill out his sentence. TRA

Jonathan Swift **A DESCRIPTION OF THE MORNING** (page 308)

There is a long tradition, stretching back to ancient Greece, of poetic descriptions of morning, idealized and romantic treatments of the joys of the beginning of a new day. One of the most famous in English is Romeo's description of dawn in III.5:

> Look, love, what envious streaks
> Do lace the severing clouds in yonder east.
> Night's candles are burnt out, and jocund day
> Stands tiptoe on the misty mountain tops.

Swift's poem plays with the tradition in two witty ways: it is a city morning, not a rustic or natural one; and it presents details of realistic ugliness rather than idealized beauty. One critic compares the poem to a drawing by Swift's younger contemporary William Hogarth, whose "Morning" shows such social types as "the Begging Crone, the Loose Girl, the Persistent Rake, the Shivering Page, and the Old Maid" in a snowy street scene with dark buildings and a darker sky (Johnson, p. 11, cited below).

The first two lines of this poem are parodic, indicating their literary target in the "poetic" phrase "showed the ruddy morn's approach." What signals this morning, however, is not sunlight on a misty mountain top, but the beginning of urban bustle as the traffic begins to appear. Lines 3–4 lead us to anticipate a satire on sexual behavior between the upper and lower classes, as the servant girl sneaks back to her bedroom from her master's, to muss up her own bed to make it look slept in. But Swift is not really in one of his satiric moods in this poem; the only other direct references to the injustice of social rank occur at line 13 (the nobility can live in debt, and must be pestered by bill collectors) and lines 15–16 (the prison system requires the convicts to pay for their keep, and thus they are permitted to roam the streets at night to "steal for fees").

What the poem mostly catalogues are ordinary working-class people energetically starting their daily pursuits. They are not particularly attractive, but they are not grotesques: the apprentice in his worn-out shoes cleans the grimy shop front and sprinkles water on the floor to keep down the dust; Moll (a lower-class nickname for Mary), ruddier than the morn with her flaming face (perhaps from drink), flourishes her mop ostentatiously as she prepares to scrub; the scavenger pokes in the gutters for objects to sell; the dealer in "small-coal" (either charcoal, or small lumps of coal, for domestic heating) boomingly announces his wares, while his counterpart the truly small boy who cleans chimneys chimes in with his shrill soprano voice. The town is busy, and most of the business of these people is concerned with putting the street back into some semblance of cleanliness (the "small-coal man" is by contrast a source of grime, both from the smoky fires he supplies and from the coal dust that must coat his clothes and trail behind him as he walks). Whatever has gone awry in the night must be put to right, the removal of dirt and of thieves, so along with the cleaners come the turnkey and the "watchful bailiffs."

The last two couplets put an end to the busy activities—the prison doors are locked up, the bailiffs stand silently, and finally (late?) some schoolboys shuffle slowly to *their* form of imprisonment. The scene subsides into a relatively calm day.

Useful analyses of the poem are F. W. Bateson, *English Poetry: A Critical Introduction* (London: Longmans, 1950), pp. 175–80, and Maurice Johnson, *The Sin of Wit: Jonathan Swift as a Poet* (Syracuse, N.Y.: Syracuse Univ. Press, 1950), pp. 10–15. TRA

Dylan Thomas   DO NOT GO GENTLE INTO THAT GOOD NIGHT (page 308)

In form this poem is a villanelle. Its nineteen lines utilize only two rime sounds (based on "night" and "day"); its alternating refrains rime "night" and "light." Most villanelles are charming, graceful, light poems, characteristic of society verse. Thomas here gives the villanelle a force and intensity it had never had before— though many poets have tried to match it since. ("Do not go gentle . . ." is perhaps a turning point in the history of the villanelle.)

As shown by the concluding section, the poem is addressed to the poet's father. In some respects a fierce militant most of his life, the elder Thomas in his 80s went blind, became ill, and showed a tendency to turn soft and gentle. The son was dismayed by this change. He wanted his father to die as he had lived, to maintain his salty individuality to the last. Though the poet was something of a pantheist in his religious belief and felt that death was "good," he still considered it right and natural that men should resist death, put up a struggle against it, not die placidly. "Wise men . . . Good men . . . Wild men . . . Grave men," he tells his father in separate stanzas (punning on the word "Grave"), have all for good reasons raged against their approaching deaths. In the last section (where his tenderness toward his father is manifest), he prays his father (paradoxically) to "Curse" and "bless" him with his fierce tears" and to "not go gentle into that good night." ("Good night" is both a metaphor for death and a pun for farewell.)   LP

Dylan Thomas   FERN HILL (page 309)

"Fern Hill" is Dylan Thomas's evocation of the delight, the wonder, the long carefree rapture of boyhood summers spent on a farm in Wales. The reader is made to share his pleasure in the barns and fields and orchards, in the farmhouse itself, in the animals both wild and domestic, in afternoon and night and morning. In the fourth stanza the poet compares this boyhood experience to the experience of Adam and Eve in Eden. Like theirs, its chief characteristics were joy and innocence and a feeling of timelessness. Like theirs, his experience came at the beginning of life, and, like them, he felt it would last forever. But the theme of the poem is the transience of youthful joy and carefree innocence. All the time that he is heedless of time, he is bound by its chains, which hold him "green and dying." Just as Adam and Eve were thrust out of Eden, so the boy is to be thrust out of the garden of childhood.

The boy is the protagonist of the poem. Time is the antagonist—unseen, unfelt, and unheeded by the boy, but comprehended clearly by the mature poet looking back. The boy, "happy as the grass was green," feels that he has forever. But, inexorably, in its alternation of afternoon and night and morning, Time is carrying him out of the enchanted realm, "out of grace," toward age and death. The boy who is "prince of the apple towns" (6)—and described with such aristocratically connotative adjectives as "golden" (5), "honored" (6), "lordly" (7), and "famous" (10), who feels himself master of all he surveys—is at the same time, though unaware of it, a slave, held by Time in "chains" (54).

Thomas has a talent for refurbishing clichés and getting new or double meaning out of them, both the old and the new. "Happy as the grass was green" (2) and "Happy as the heart was long" (38) both remind us of the commoner expression "Happy as the day is long" and gather its meaning into fresher expressions. "Once below a time" (7) gathers up the meaning of "Once upon a time" and bends it to the use of the poem's theme—that the boy is really a slave of time, not master of it. In "All the sun long" (19) and "All the moon long" (25) the poet freshens the familiar phrases by substituting metonymies for the expected "day" and "night." In "Adam and maiden" (30) Thomas substitutes for "Eve" a noun which represents her in her innocence and at the same time sounds like "Eden," thus tripling its significance.

If you have to beg, borrow, or steal, get a tape or record of Thomas reading this poem and play it for your class. Thomas's voice is as "golden" as his poetry.
Mary C. Davidow in the *English Journal*, 58 (Jan. 1969), 78–81, and Sister M. Laurentia, in *The Explicator*, 14 (Oct. 1955), item 1, offer further interesting and useful observations about this poem. LP

Edward Thomas THE OWL (page 310)

The poet-speaker has been walking over the hills all day and takes shelter for the night at an inn nestled at a hill's foot. He arrives at the inn hungry, cold, and tired; yet (as he tells us), if hungry, not starved; if cold, not frozen; if tired, not so fatigued that he would willingly sleep out in the open. At the inn he finds food to satisfy his hunger, a fire to warm him, and a bed to provide for his rest; and his pleasure in each of these things is heightened by his previous discomforts. He also finds shelter at the inn. The North wind and the outside night are quite barred out except for the melancholy cry of an owl, shaken out "long and clear" upon the hill, reminding him of all that he has escaped by finding lodging at the inn, and reminding him also of the many people in the world who are not so lucky—poor people and soldiers (the poem was written during World War I) who must lie out under the stars, hungry, cold, weary, "unable to rejoice."

The owl's cry has a paradoxical effect upon the speaker. His food is "salted" (given savor) by the thought that others must go without such pleasure, and so is his repose; but they are also "sobered." He simultaneously feels gratitude that he is not one of those that must lie out under the stars, and sorrow for those who must. "Poetry," said W. H. Auden, "is the clear expression of mixed feelings"; this is it. The final stanza begins on a note of increased pleasure but ends on the note of compassion.

Lines 13–14 exhibit a curious and telling example of how context affects meaning, and of how the poet can make use of this fact to achieve poetic economy. The poet writes, "Salted was my food, and my repose, / Salted and sobered, too." In ordinary prose we should write that the speaker's food was salted, that his repose was sweetened, and that his thoughts or feelings were sobered; but the poet's grammar, literally construed, makes "Salted and sobered" modify "food" *and* "repose." Yet it works, and works well! We automatically interpret "salted" as meaning *given savor* or *made more pleasurable*, and notice no discrepancy therefore when the same adjective is extended to "repose" (though *salted* and *sweetened* in a narrow sense are opposite in meaning); and because we know that the real subject of discourse is the speaker's pleasure in his food and repose, we accept without question the attachment of the adjective "sobered" to the nouns named. Poetic magic? At least, poetic sleight-of-hand! To get the full force of the paradox involved here, we should perhaps say that the speaker simultaneously takes increased and decreased pleasure in his food and repose. It is a situational rather than a verbal paradox. Human beings do have ambivalent feelings. The paradox cannot be "resolved" by verbal analysis.   LP

Derek Walcott   **THE VIRGINS** (page 311)

Derek Walcott, a native Caribbean poet, is disturbed by what American commercial exploitation (the "American dream" of a better life for all achieved through abundant material goods) has done to the once simple life and unspoiled natural beauty of the American Virgin Islands. He expresses his distress through his observation of (and observations on) Fredericksted, the chief seaport of one of these islands, while walking through its streets. His observations are sharpened by his skillful use of irony and of words and phrases of double meaning.

The irony begins with the title, for clearly these islands (originally named after Elizabeth, the virgin queen) are no longer virgins. They have been prostituted to, or raped by, American materialism. The "dead" (deserted) streets down which the poet walks are deserted probably because of the midday heat, but the adjective leads the poet to the reflection that the town is "dead" in another sense, having lost its soul to tourism. (The phrase "the first free port to die for tourism" ironically reverses a more familiar pattern of words often found on local monuments: the first citizen of this town to die for freedom.) Continuing his metaphor, the poet describes himself as walking at a "funeral" pace (slowly). One suspects a pun in the adjective "sun-stoned" (built of stones heated by the sun; drunk or drugged by the sun's heat). There is a complex verbal irony in the poet's use of "civilized" and "the good life" and a situational irony in the conjoining of "the good life" and "the American dream" with a rising crime rate. The empty condominium (paradoxically drowning in vacancy) gives evidence of a building boom in which the developers' eager anticipations miscalculated the actual demand. The roulettes spinning "rustily to the wind" evidence the same kind of overdevelopment at the same time that they testify to what "tourism," "the American dream," and "the good life" actually substitute for the speaker's "small-islander's simplicities": not only a rising crime rate, but cheap dreams of quick wealth made at the gambling casinos. In line 16 "trade" has the double meaning of trade wind and commerce. The spinning of the roulette wheels is related both by circular motion and monetary motivation to the "revving up" of motorboats and yachts headed for the "banks" (fishing banks and money banks) of "silver" (silver-sided fish and silver coins). And if "silver" is related to coinage, perhaps "green" is associated with dollar bills. LP

Robert Penn Warren **BOY WANDERING IN SIMMS' VALLEY** (page 311)

The poem begins with exploration, it ends with a revelation.

The speaker, whom we may not unfairly identify with the poet (who grew up in rural Kentucky), is an adult recalling an incident from his boyhood. There are several time levels in the poem, and it is important to get them straight. First, there was a time (barely implied in the poem) when Simms brought his wife to live in the isolated valley farm, and together they were able to keep the place "trim" (she the house, and he the fields). Then the wife fell sick and became bedridden, and "for long years" Simms had to bear the burden of working the fields and nursing her, while the place went gradually "to wrack." When the wife died, Simms let out his "spindly" livestock to forage at will, lay down beside his wife, and shot himself. So isolated was the farm that their bodies were not discovered till two years later, and then only by accident. A hunter, sitting down to rest on the porch-edge, was disturbed by the smell, began to "prowl," found two bodies in an advanced state of decomposition in the upstairs bedroom, and "high-tailed" to town. The town officials (we assume) gave the bodies a decent burial but were unable to find a purchaser even at auction ("tax-sale") for the rundown, isolated farm. The time of the boy's visit is many years later, and the property has continued to deteriorate. There has been time for maples about eighteen inches thick to grow in the remoter fields. The barn is down, the house itself is "ready to fall," the "place" is being reclaimed by the wilderness. "Lonely and forgotten," it has had few if any visitors since the burial of the farmer and his wife. Its furnishings are undisturbed by human pillage; nature has been the destructive agent.

In stanza 1 the speaker, describing his entry into the valley, gives some idea of its inaccessibility (though there must have been easier access somewhere, some road by which Simms took produce to market and fetched supplies from town). He also subtly foreshadows, with his mention in the first line of "love-vine" and the fact that he was "well blooded" (deeply scratched by thorns), the two questions that will be raised in the final line of the poem concerning "love" and "life" (for which

210

"blood" is a metonymy). In stanzas 2–3 he relates what he knew (had been told) about the suicide of Simms and the finding of the bodies. Stanza 4 opens with a generalization—"A dirt farmer needs a good wife to keep a place trim"—as the boy reflects about the delapidation of the farm and the hardships of Simms' life after his wife became ill. Stanza 6 finds him standing in the upstairs bedroom, noticing further deterioration, and reflecting on the events that had taken place there. In stanza 7 the sinking sun brings him out of his near-trance, and he prepares to leave. But casting a last glance around, he suddenly sees "the old enameled bedpan, high on a shelf," and is brought again to a halt. In a final line, set off by itself and breaking the stanza pattern, we are told the questions that arose in his mind.

It is the bedpan which furnishes, in the full Joycean sense, the "epiphany" of the tale. It takes the boy deeper into the meanings of the events than his reflections had yet gone; it makes him ask and partially realize "what life is, and love, and what they may be"—what they are in essence, and what they may become in extreme cases, such as the Simmses'. Though the poem leaves us with a question, not an answer, it provides some of the materials needed for an answer. It tells us at once how terrible life can be, and how great human devotion can be. For Simms the latter part of life had been struggling, without help, to keep a poor farm going, the fields plowed and planted, the stock fed, and the crops harvested; and love had been emptying bedpans for a sick wife—as revolting and filthy a task as one can imagine (and certainly no part of "love's sweet dream"). Yet life was worth living for Simms only so long as he could carry those bedpans for his wife. When she died, he took his life, not in the fields or in the barn but by her side, not because the burdens of life had become too much for him (they could only be eased by her death) but because, when he had no one to care for, he had nothing to live for. He did it deliberately, taking thought first to let the livestock free to forage.

The poem is written in stanzas riming *abab*. Though there is no sharply definable meter, the rhythm flows loosely through five-beat lines—except for the last, which has six. The language (but not always the syntax) keeps close to the colloquial— ".12 gauge" (8), "to jaw" (9), "high-tailed" (12), "his old lady" (14). LP

Walt Whitman **A NOISELESS PATIENT SPIDER** (page 312)

The situation of a man accepting the energies of a spinning spider as an example to himself should recall the famous story of the fourteenth-century Scottish king Robert the Bruce (Robert I), who in apparent defeat retired into a cave for refuge. There he watched the tireless effort of a spider which despite repeated failure refused to give up spinning; the king resolved to continue in battle—and was victorious. By the nineteenth century this anecdote had become a moral exemplum of the virtue of pertinacity (a narrative version of "If at first you don't succeed, try, try again!").

In its earliest unprinted version this poem had as its theme the poet's sense of loneliness as he searches for love in a world of "fathomless latent souls of love." [See Gay Wilson Allen, *The Solitary Singer* (New York Univ. Press, 1967), p. 342.]

The present version transforms both the moral tale and the earlier unprinted poem, changing the subject to the soul's yearning for spiritual truth. "In measureless oceans of space," the soul seeks security, an "anchor." Despite the traditional symbolism of an anchor as Christ or as the hope for salvation (see Hebrews 6:19), the poem does not openly suggest that Christianity is the answer to the speaker's problem. In fact, a "ductile anchor" attached to a "gossamer thread" suggests fragility and plasticity, rather than security of a defined, systematic religion.

In Whitman's image, the spider resembles a fisherman, unreeling his lines as he launches them forth. The vocabulary of the poem tends to corroborate an implicit nautical or fishing context: *promontory, launched, unreeling, oceans, bridge, anchor.* Though the speaker seems not to be consciously aware of it, the imagery itself suggests a Christian solution to his problem—the anchor of Christian salvation, with the speaker's search evoking the church's role as a "fisher of men."

While the poem draws an explicit comparison between the spider's activity and that of the spiritually questing man, there are clearly implied contrasts as well: the contrast of size and perspective (a spider's promontory is indeed "little," and the area of exploration may seem to it to be a "vacant vast surrounding," but the range of "measureless oceans of space" inhabited by man is considerably grander); the spider's patience is in contrast to the "musing, venturing, throwing, seeking" of the man; the noiselessness of the spider may be contrasted to this verbal outpouring from the human being; and of course the spider's actions must be read literally, the man's metaphorically.

The poem should be examined for examples of alliteration, assonance and consonance, as poetic devices providing a replacement for regular rhythm and rime. Overstatement, particularly in the spatial references, emphasizes the need to recognize contrasts within the overt comparison.   TRA

Walt Whitman **THERE WAS A CHILD WENT FORTH** (page 313)

If students have studied Tennyson's "Ulysses" (page 87), they might be asked to consider the difference between Ulysses' claim that "I am a part of all that I have met" (line 18), and Whitman's statement that "that object he became, / And that object became part of him" (lines 1–2). The two phrases of Whitman's statement refer to two related but different psychological processes, one we would call "identification" or "empathy," the other "memory"; the first, operating at the moment of perception, projects himself outward into objects; the second extends the perception and empathy forward in time, absorbing and collecting his experiences. Neither is a particularly intellectual process. The implication is that the more sensitively he projects himself, the more inclusive his memory. Furthermore, the poem implies that the growth of the individual child relies upon this combination of projection and collection, and only at one moment (lines 27–30) is there an overt reference to the powers of the child to reason or judge.

Each of the five verse-paragraphs consists of a single sentence (the question marks at lines 29–30 are parenthetical, the long fifth sentence ending only with the predication in line 39). After the introductory summary sentences, the finite verb forms occur at the beginnings of sentences 2 and 3, and at the ends of sentences 4 and 5. The rest of the poem consists of catalogues of noun-phrases listing the "objects" that "became part of him."

The four sentences following the introduction present stages of increasing complexity in the child's perception: first, a perception of details of the natural world, then of persons, then in a generalized way of his parents, and finally of his parents in detailed actions arousing emotional responses. In line 27, the child experiences his first doubts about what is real or unreal, and whether his trusting eyes have been reporting objective truth. These questions are followed by a review, in reverse order, of the objects of perception—back through the human world and its activities to the natural world of water and sky. The tone of the last lines, 31–39, emphasizes distance and the perception of variety and beauty.

The essential structure of the poem is thus a collection of objects perceived, moving from the natural to the human; a turning point at which the child raises intellectual questions about reality; and a generalizing recapitulation emphasizing beauty—as if the doubting questions had to be ignored in a willed act of perceiving the grandeur which individual "specks" yield when seen from a distance.

A final line which universalized this process to include the reader was dropped by Whitman in 1867: "And these become of him or her that peruses them now." Although the poem may seem more directly autobiographical without that conclusion, Whitman seems to have trusted that the process he presents will strike readers as being true of themselves even without the line. TRA

Walt Whitman **WHEN I HEARD THE LEARN'D ASTRONOMER** (page 314)

This poem expresses a conflict which may seem even more cogent today than when Whitman wrote it: precise scientific knowledge is an assault on the cherished mysteries of the universe. Feelings similar to Whitman's were voiced in the wake of man's first steps on the surface of the moon on July 20, 1969; as the cameras of rocket probes send back close-up photographs of the more distant planets in our solar system, the skies may seem to lose their appealing wonder.

Whitman's ironic contrasts are readily perceived because of their directness and abundance, and though it may be a violation of his attitude toward "charts" and "columns," they may be indicated as paired lists:

crowd in lecture room	individual man
much applause	silence
mathematical counting	"unaccountable" feeling
lighted room	dark night
indoors	outdoors
approving audience	tired and sick poet

sitting	rising and gliding, wandering
scientific precision	random looking, "from time to time"
scientific thought	poetic feeling

These ironic contrasts make the speaker's decision seem more natural, more attractive, more human. The initial repetition of "when" in the first four lines has a hypnotic sameness, imitating the poet's boredom with the regularity of scientific proofs; and the redundancy of "proofs, figures, columns, charts, diagrams" and "add, divide, measure" reinforces the sense of repetitiousness and—for the speaker—the meaninglessness of such data about the universe. The phrase "perfect silence" in the last line ironically comments on the supposed perfection of scientific knowledge: genuine perfection is not mathematical or measurable, but is the harmonious response of perfect feeling to perfect stars.

The poem presents Whitman's distaste for precise, rational knowledge and his love of emotional, instinctive wonder at the mysteries of nature. His choice of the word "mystical" rather than "mysterious" extends his preference into a claim that his experience surpasses the astronomer's knowledge in a religious sense as well. His insight into the wonders of heaven seems to him to penetrate the merely mysterious and to reach to supernatural wisdom. TRA

Richard Wilbur **THE MILL** (page 314)

The death of a friend must always move us to questions that we cannot answer, and leave us with a sense of emptiness and waste, especially if the friend's life did not end successfully, if life in some way defeated him. What has become, we may ask, of his memories, his appreciations, all his investment in living and experience? In the lost, abandoned mill with its wheel still turning and turning, Richard Wilbur has found the perfect symbol for those haunting, unanswered questions, that sense of emptiness and waste.

The organization of the poem emphasizes the passage of time. It begins with the "spoiling daylight," the late afternoon sun dying and for a moment coming in at such a slant that every mote of dust in the air is made visible and glistening. Then the friend recalls places in his past—"the names of streets, the exact look / Of lilacs" in Cincinnati in 1903, the turning mill wheel in an isolated valley in Brazil or Tennessee. The friend remembering is presented by the poet remembering. But the poet has already forgotten whether the mill wheel was in Brazil or Tennessee, and when he, too, dies, all of these memories will be gone. What will it matter, then, that these places ever existed? Time needs human life and human memory to give it significance. "Time all alone and talking to himself" has no more meaning than a mill wheel which continues to operate when it serves no human purpose.

Wilbur's choice of words for sound and meaning is uncannily precise. The "spoiling daylight" refers not only to fading daylight but to the passage of time that "spoils" all. The friend's voice that "rose from the shades" of the darkened barroom blends into the dead friend that rises from the shades of death in the poet's mind.

The word *sound* in "Your dead life's sound and sovereign anecdote" serves both as noun and adjective having two quite independent meanings, and *sovereign* not only means supreme but gathers in the meaning of a British gold coin from its association with "round sums" and "pocket change." The onomatopoetic verbs and repeated *k* sounds of the "crazy buckets / Creaking and lumbering out of the clogged race" reproduces the very sound and motion of the buckets; the word *rattle* is onomatopoetic and suggests a meaningless sound—talk that has no meaning. In the last line it is not only the mill wheel which "turns and turns," but the mind itself which turns this memory "over and over." Sound, position, and arrangement all serve the economy of meaning. LP

William Carlos Williams **THE RED WHEELBARROW** (page 315)

The simplicity of this free verse poem inevitably leads students to question "What *does* depend upon these things, and *how* much is so much?" The answer is "human life," both as physical existence and as esthetic experience.

Momentarily ignoring the visual details—"red," "glazed," and "white"—one might investigate the importance of the objects. A wheelbarrow is a basic farm implement associated with the most primitive stage of human toolmaking, only one step advanced beyond the use of sledges or unwheeled barrows for dragging heavy loads. Rain water is obviously an essential for farming as for all life, and chickens provide two common foodstuffs in their flesh and in their eggs. The objects, that is, can be seen as among the most basic in providing physical sustenance, and much therefore "depends upon" them.

By contrast, the visual imagery is nonutilitarian. Although paint does protect against rot and rust, the color red has no specific usefulness. The glazing of rain (and the potential rotting of wood that it implies) is more potentially harmful than beneficial, and a chicken is an egg-layer and a source of meat whatever its color. These visual references thus run counter to the utilitarian functions of the objects they adorn. But they provide contrasts and harmonies of color, shape, and texture, basic to esthetic enjoyment. White and red are clear contrasts, as are a shiny glaze contrasted to the downy softness of a chicken's feathers. While there is a contrast between the living and nonliving objects, one may also see a vague similarity in the triangular shapes of a wheelbarrow and a pecking chicken. (It helps students to see this if blackboard sketches are provided.)

The poem thus offers two distinct dependences: we depend upon farmers for our food (and they depend upon nature in producing it), and as sensitive observers we depend upon visual perceptions to feed us esthetically. TRA

The poem relates the awakening of the speaker's imaginative response to an experience of wordless expression, and the extended effect of the experience on him. Apparently on a walking tour in the Highlands of Scotland, the speaker sees and hears a girl gathering grain while she sings a native song. Moved by both her solitude and the sorrowful melody, the speaker tries to find correspondences between the unintelligible song and other human experiences, but finally acknowledges that whether he understands it or not, it has moved him deeply enough to live on in his memory.

In accordance with his theories about poetry as the "spontaneous overflow of powerful feelings," a power which he attributes to the singing girl, Wordsworth frequently strives to give his poems both immediacy and the sense of personal experience. In this case, however, his starting point was not at all personal: the poem is based on a passage from a friend's manuscript account of a Scottish tour. Thomas Wilkinson had written: "Passed by a female who was reaping alone, she sung in Erse as she bended over her sickle, the sweetest human voice I ever heard. Her strains were tenderly melancholy, and felt delicious long after they were heard no more." The poem reports this (with direct quotation and verbal echo) as if it had happened to the speaker, achieving immediacy in the first three stanzas by using the present tense.

The opening lines emphatically establish the solitariness of the girl, and awaken parallel feelings in the speaker: "single" (1), "solitary" (2), "by herself" (3), "alone" (5). He has, or imagines, companions whom he exhorts to "Behold" and "listen," demanding excited attention; yet this he balances against the injunction to remain quiet so as not to disturb the girl's song, and to preserve her sense of being alone. What strikes him most in the opening stanza are her solitude, and the "melancholy" nature of her song, which seems to overflow the deep valley in which she works (the Scottish Highlands are for the most part barren and sparsely inhabited, with arable land restricted to the valleys).

In the second and third stanzas, as he listens to the music in a foreign tongue, the speaker imaginatively searches for corresponding situations that will explain the emotions with which he responds. The second stanza offers two comparisons, both suggesting relief from the hardships of natural surroundings. The singer is like two very different kinds of birds in two contrasted geographical locales, implying the universality of the experience: the nightingale singing in an oasis in the parched Arabian desert, promising cool comfort to exhausted travelers; or the cuckoo signaling the coming of spring to the stark, rocky islands battered by the seas in the northernmost reaches of Scotland. Both scenes are isolated, forbidding and lonely; both are momentarily relieved; and both imply that the speaker feels himself isolated, wandering in a wholly uncongenial natural setting, momentarily restored by the beauty of the song he hears.

The third stanza moves from geographical extremes to contrasts of time and of social rank. The song might be a traditional lament expressing grief for ancient, heroic battlefield defeats, or it might refer to the "natural sorrow, loss, or pain" of ordinary daily life in the present. Just as loneliness and weariness were universalized in stanza 2, stanza 3 universalizes melancholy here and everywhere, now and in the past.

The third stanza has asked for intelligible fact: what is she singing about? In the final stanza, the poem suddenly shifts into the past tense, in its first line denying the possibility (or even the necessity) of understanding exactly what the girl was saying. As it turns out, the speaker's inability to understand the meaning of the song has been an advantage. He has found in the melody and in the singer's isolation the occasion for his own imagined creation of the universal themes of loneliness and melancholy. Looking back on this experience, he has discovered that his imagination was revitalized, and that his profound feelings have persisted even after he has mounted up from the scene of her singing.

A full, suggestive reading of this poem is in Geoffrey H. Hartman's *Wordsworth's Poetry, 1787–1814* (New Haven: Yale Univ. Press, 1964), pp. 3–18. TRA

William Wordsworth **THE WORLD IS TOO MUCH WITH US** (page 316)

This sonnet juxtaposes nineteenth-century Christian English faith in industrial development and mercantile values with a primitive faith in the pagan deities of nature. As one scholar puts it, it is in the traditional mode of the conflict between Christ and Pan, but the conflict is exacerbated by identifying Christianity with modern materialism and urban insensitivity to nature. Wordsworth places his speaker at a fulcrum: he is forlornly identified with the modern, and his own way of "glimpsing" natural vitality and harmony is by wishing he could be a pagan—though he knows intellectually that the beliefs of ancient Greece are "outworn."

The speaker stands in a grassy meadow on a calm moonlit night, in view of the sea. This placid and unspectacular situation makes him forlorn as he thinks of the worldliness that destroys emotional and imaginative responses to natural beauty. "We," including the speaker, have traded away the real power of imagination that we possessed; we "get" wealth, but we "spend" our hearts for it. Nature is no longer ours, nor we hers.

The opening quatrain abstractly generalizes, withholding the motive for the generalizations. It contrasts the presumed power of trade with the internal power of the imagination, and declares that the real cost of a materialistic value system is our hearts.

The second quatrain begins to set the scene, establishing the time and place: it is night, the sea is calm, the moon is bright, and the expected high winds of the seaside are subdued. The speaker poetically personifies sea and winds, an imaginative contrast to the philosophical generalizations of the first quatrain, representing the speaker's attempt to display his own sensitive image-making powers—but his images tend toward triteness, as lines 8–9 suggest by abruptly changing the tone to straightforward colloquialism. The phrase "for this, for everything" reveals a loss of imaginative concreteness, and the cliché "out of tune" emphasizes the speaker's failure either to feel or to create. As a transition from octave to sestet, these lines appear to give up the attempt to counter crass materialism with poetic originality.

Instead, beginning in line 9, the speaker swears (by his Christian God) his preference for a "Pagan creed" that would allow him to believe in such mythical nature deities as Proteus and Triton, as antidotes for his forlornness. But in fact he was not "suckled" in such a creed and can summon up only a glimpse of these nature gods, ironically created for him by great Christian English poets of the past. "Pleasant lea" is quoted from Spenser's "Colin Clouts Come Home Again," a description of Colin's first view of England (line 283); the reference to Proteus alludes to Milton's *Paradise Lost* (III.603–604); and line 14 refers again to "Colin Clout": "Triton blowing loud his wreathed horn" (line 245). Desiring to reach backward to a natural paganism, the speaker must rely on his Christian poetic heritage. Furthermore, he realizes that he cannot actually hold such beliefs, and is wistful about the "outworn" but imaginative mythological personifications of sea and wind, visible Proteus, audible Triton, representing a lost harmony between man and nature.

For further discussion of the mythical and literary allusions, see Douglas Bush, *Mythology and the Romantic Tradition in English Poetry* (Cambridge, Mass.: Harvard Univ. Press, 1937), pp. 58–59. TRA

William Butler Yeats **SAILING TO BYZANTIUM** (page 317)

In his book *A Vision* Yeats wrote that if he could be given a month of antiquity and leave to spend it where he chose, he would spend it in Byzantium about the year 525 A.D. Byzantium (later known as Constantinople and presently as Istanbul), the eastern capital of the Holy Roman Empire, was in that period notable for the flowering of its art: painting, architecture, mosaic-work, gold and silver metalcraft, book illumination, etc. For this reason it represented for Yeats a holy city of the imagination.

The title "Sailing to Byzantium" would seem to indicate that the poem is about a voyage; but line 1 ("*That* [not *This*] is no country for old men") together with lines 15–16 (". . . therefore have I sailed the seas and come / To the holy city of Byzantium") indicates that the voyage has already been completed. It is an imaginary voyage, of course, for it has been made not just across space, from Ireland to Byzantium, but backwards through time, from the twentieth century to the sixth. The important considerations, therefore, are not the voyage itself, but why the poet made it; and not Ireland and Byzantium, but what they represent.

The poem deals with the antitheses of the physical and sensual world versus the world of intellect and imagination, the mortal versus the eternal, nature versus art. Modern Ireland represents the first term in these oppositions, Byzantium the second. The poet, growing old (he was 63 when this poem was published) can no longer engage fully and unreflectively in the life of the senses, and longs for something beyond the life of the senses, for the life of the senses is mortal and dies. He finds what he is looking for in works of art ("monuments of unaging intellect"), which are eternal. The poem may be looked on as a kind of prayer: Let me leave this country of the young, the unreflective, the sensual, and the dying, and sail to the city of imagination and unaging intellect. There let my next incarnation be as an artificial gold-and-enamel singing bird that cannot decay as my body is decaying now but which will exist eternally. Let me be a work of art rather than a man!

Yeats thus seems to be elevating art above nature, the eternal above the mortal. But there is a catch here. What will this gold-enameled bird sing about? It will sing of "what is past, or passing, or to come"—a line that echoes line 6: "Whatever is begotten, born, and dies." Art celebrates the mortal world—the world of process, change, decay, and death. The poem thus has a circular movement in which the last line returns us to its beginning. The poet presents us, not with a preference but with a dilemma. He wishes to escape from life into art, but as a work of art he will celebrate life. Art is both superior and inferior to life. Though not subject to decay, it is an "artifice," without life. The dilemma is comparable to that presented by Keats in "Ode on a Grecian Urn" (page 289).   LP

William Butler Yeats   **THE SECOND COMING** (page 318)

In 1919, the year this poem was published, Ireland was in the midst of a bloody civil war; World War I had only recently ended (November 1918); and Russia was engaged in civil war following its Revolution of 1917. All these events portended for Yeats the approaching end of the Christian era, the historical cycle begun almost two thousand years earlier with the birth of Christ. In Yeats's historical theory the transition from one historical era to another was always marked by an epoch of violence and disorder.

The poem is divided into two sections. The first gives the poet's impression of the present. The second presents an apocalyptic vision of the future.

His description of the present is terrifying. The opening two lines present a symbol of a world out of control. In the ancient art of falconry the falcon was trained always to return upon a signal to the wrist of the falconer. But in Yeats's image the falcon has flown beyond the hearing of his master's signal. The adjective "Mere" (4) here retains its obsolete meaning of *absolute, entire, sheer.* "Ceremony" (6) had for Yeats particular value as connected with orderly and civilized living (see "A Prayer for My Daughter," which follows immediately after "The Second Coming" in Yeats's *Collected Poems*). The closing lines of this section describe a familiar crisis situation where good people, by nature moderate and tolerant, are uncertain what should be done, while the bigots, the masked riders, and the assassination squads are full of "passionate intensity"—all too certain in their ignorant minds that they know exactly what is needed.

The opening lines of the second section seem to sound a note of hope. "Surely," the poet declares, "some revelation is at hand"—the word "revelation" suggesting a divine manifestation; "Surely the Second Coming is at hand"—the words "Second

Coming" reminding us of the Second Coming of Christ prophesied in the Bible. Things can hardly get much worse; therefore these violent actions must be auspices of change, signs of the shifting from one historical era to another. No sooner has the poet uttered the words "Second Coming" than he has a vision. An image arises to consciousness in his mind (not just from his own unconscious but from the racial unconscious underlying it) of the stone sphinx in the Egyptian desert slowly coming to life and "moving its slow thighs." The vision is a vivid one. Yeats depicts not only its gaze "blank and pitiless as the sun" but the reactions of the desert birds to this amazing phenomenon. In indignant clamor they "reel" in circles above the slowly awakening sphinx; but Yeats with marvelous poetic economy depicts them only through their shadows (thus giving us in one picture the shadows, the birds that cast them, and the bright desert sun that causes them). The vision is brief, but now Yeats knows (or claims to know) that twenty centuries of "stony sleep" (the sphinx's) were "vexed to nightmare" by "a rocking cradle" (a metonymy for the infant Christ), and he also knows what "rough beast, its hour come round at last, / Slouches toward Bethlehem to be born." The vision is a vision of horror. The new era, its time come to replace the old one, is symbolized by a "rough beast." (The question asked in the last two lines is a rhetorical one, as shown by the ambiguous syntax of the sentence, in which "and" indicates the presence of parallelism but in which "what" can logically be linked only with "that" (19) ["I know that . . . and what . . . ."], making "what" not an interrogative but a relative pronoun calling logically for a period at the end of the sentence. But when was logic ever the most direct way to poetic power?)

Our expectation, set up by the title and by lines 9–10, that the poem would concern the Second Coming of Christ are shattered by the last two lines of the poem. It is the coming of Antichrist which is prophesied. Legends tell us that Antichrist will be born in Bethlehem, and Antichrist is referred to recurrently in the New Testament as the "beast." It is Yeats, however, whose genius has assimilated Antichrist with the desert sphinx and given him new dimensions of horror and evil by his use of the adjective "rough" and the verb "slouches."

Surely, this poem derives its greatness from the feeling of evil and horror it so powerfully evokes. Yet the most controversial critical question regarding the poem occurs just here. Scholars familiar with Yeats's historical theories (expressed most fully in his book *A Vision*) have pointed out that the era Yeats expected to follow the Christian one was more amenable to him than the Christian era, and that therefore the advent of the "rough beast" is to be welcomed. As Marjorie Perloff has pointed out, "The basic argument is whether the poem should be read as an independent text, in which case its language suggests that the 'rough beast' is bringing a new dispensation of nightmare and terror, or whether it should be read in the light of *A Vision*, in which case one may argue, as Helen Vendler does, that 'Yeats approves intellectually, if not emotionally of the Second Coming. . . . The Beast is a world-restorer.'" LP

Both his theory and his practice point to the need to read an individual poem by Yeats in the context of the rest of his poetry and of his life. A full understanding of this poem requires at least a reading of Donald A. Stauffer's analysis in *The Golden Nightingale* (New York: Macmillan, 1949, pp. 48–79). But even without the richness of the Yeatsian context, the poem has beauty and power that are available to the sensitive reader.

Both actually and superficially it is a meditation on nature and on the passage of time which alters the human observer but leaves nature essentially unchanged; it thus resembles Wordsworth's "Tintern Abbey" and Keats's "Ode to a Nightingale" (page 241), poems in which the response of the man is both intensely present and also intensely subjective and retrospective. External natural facts elicit feelings and memories and desires, and time present is contrasted with time past, human and natural. Nature undergoes cyclical changes but keeps returning to its same condition; the human being undergoes progressive changes which include decay and death, but also memories of earlier states. Nature is permanent and always in the present, man is transient but contains his own past, his sensitive present, and his predictions of the future.

The elegaic tone of this poem is established in the first stanza—autumn, dryness, twilight, stillness. But paradoxically the poem also contains terms that contrast with these: beauty, mirror-like clarity, brimming water, clamorous wings. Yeats maintains the tone, and also the contrasts, throughout the poem, summing up his inability to understand the swans in the simple declaration that they are "mysterious, beautiful" (26). Although he attributes much to them, they cannot be wholly captured in his language or his imagination, justifying the recurring Yeatsian strategy of the conclusion—a rhetorical question (for other examples, see "Leda and the Swan," page 122, "The Second Coming," page 318, and "Among School Children.") The questions in these poems are not really questions, for the poem has implied the answer, as it does here. The speaker does not really wonder where the swans will be (in fact, they will most probably be where they are now, in the streams and lake of Coole Park, and if not these particular swans then their indistinguishable offspring). Nor does the question really mean "what other men will be delighted by them," for any man who sees them will be delighted; nor does it mean "where will *I* be when 'I awake some day / To find they have flown away,'" for the answer to that is implicit too: since the swans represent to him the continuity and permanence of the natural world, any awakening that discovers them gone will be an awakening out of nature, into death.

The number "nine-and-fifty," phrased archaically and with an implied hint of magic, first introduces the "mystery" of the swans: although they seem paired "lover by lover," the number is odd. The mystery of this number is augmented by the other one, nineteen; both of them are prime numbers, both end in nine, and both sound so very precise that a reader inevitably asks their significance. Is there a meaningful link between 59 and 19? The speaker has carefully kept track of the number of years he has been returning to this spot, and has carefully counted the swans, year after year—and yet, as he reports, even on that first count he had not finished counting before they flew up off the water. How can he know their precise number? As they suddenly mounted into the air, perhaps disturbed by his presence, perhaps even reluctant to be numbred, they scattered (suggesting random motion) yet wheeled, they flew in rings but the rings were "broken." What this succession of images suggests is a precise but uncountable number, a patterned movement that remained incompleted: a contrast between the human desire to discover number and geometric shape, and nature's reluctance to be comprehended in such intellectual undertakings.

From this perspective, we can see that the qualities attributed to the swans in the remainder of the poem are human interpretations: their wings beat like bells (tolling the passage of time, to the observer?), they are lovers, the water is "companionable," they are "unwearied," their hearts do not grow old, and—a clear indication that the qualities are not inherent in the swans—"passion or conquest" *attend* them. They are therefore genuinely mysterious, for the poem has not penetrated their mysteries, but seen in them parallels and contrasts to the human condition, revealing the impossibility of understanding them for what they are.

The natural world, then, is impenetrable to the human observer. What remains in the poem is the situation that this places him in—seeing the swans in their continuity, recognizing in himself the changes that time brings, confessing the pain that these changes have caused, and projecting further loss in the future. As the final question indicates, there will be other men to fill his place (as in fact there have been other swans to replenish the flock), but there is no consolation for the man in that fact, nor does his verbal tactic of thinking of his future as an awakening lessen the sense of loss. TRA